The Best
AMERICAN
ESSAYS
2025

GUEST EDITORS OF THE BEST AMERICAN ESSAYS

1986   ELIZABETH HARDWICK
1987   GAY TALESE
1988   ANNIE DILLARD
1989   GEOFFREY WOLFF
1990   JUSTIN KAPLAN
1991   JOYCE CAROL OATES
1992   SUSAN SONTAG
1993   JOSEPH EPSTEIN
1994   TRACY KIDDER
1995   JAMAICA KINCAID
1996   GEOFFREY C. WARD
1997   IAN FRAZIER
1998   CYNTHIA OZICK
1999   EDWARD HOAGLAND
2000   ALAN LIGHTMAN
2001   KATHLEEN NORRIS
2002   STEPHEN JAY GOULD
2003   ANNE FADIMAN
2004   LOUIS MENAND
2005   SUSAN ORLEAN
2006   LAUREN SLATER
2007   DAVID FOSTER WALLACE
2008   ADAM GOPNIK
2009   MARY OLIVER
2010   CHRISTOPHER HITCHENS
2011   EDWIDGE DANTICAT
2012   DAVID BROOKS
2013   CHERYL STRAYED
2014   JOHN JEREMIAH SULLIVAN
2015   ARIEL LEVY
2016   JONATHAN FRANZEN
2017   LESLIE JAMISON
2018   HILTON ALS
2019   REBECCA SOLNIT
2020   ANDRÉ ACIMAN
2021   KATHRYN SCHULZ
2022   ALEXANDER CHEE
2023   VIVIAN GORNICK
2024   WESLEY MORRIS
2025   JIA TOLENTINO

The Best AMERICAN ESSAYS® 2025

Edited and with an Introduction by JIA TOLENTINO

KIM DANA KUPPERMAN, Series Editor

MARINER BOOKS
New York   Boston

Without limiting the exclusive rights of any author, contributor or the publisher of this publication, any unauthorized use of this publication to train generative artificial intelligence (AI) technologies is expressly prohibited. HarperCollins also exercise their rights under Article 4(3) of the Digital Single Market Directive 2019/790 and expressly reserve this publication from the text and data mining exception.

THE BEST AMERICAN ESSAYS 2025. Copyright © 2025 by HarperCollins Publishers LLC. Introduction copyright © 2025 by Jia Tolentino. Foreword copyright © 2025 by Kim Dana Kupperman. The Best American Series® and *The Best American Essays*® are registered trademarks of HarperCollins Publishers LLC. All rights reserved. No part of this book may be used or reproduced in any manner whatsoever without written permission except in the case of brief quotations embodied in critical articles and reviews. HarperCollins Publishers LLC is not authorized to grant permission for further uses of copyrighted selections reprinted in this book without the permission of their owners. Permission must be obtained from the individual copyright owners as identified herein. For information, address HarperCollins Publishers, 195 Broadway, New York, NY 10007. In Europe, HarperCollins Publishers, Macken House, 39/40 Mayor Street Upper, Dublin 1, D01 C9W8, Ireland.

HarperCollins books may be purchased for educational, business, or sales promotional use. For information, please email the Special Markets Department at SPsales@harpercollins.com.

The Mariner flag design is a registered trademark of HarperCollins Publishers LLC.

hc.com

FIRST EDITION

ISSN 0888-3742
ISBN 978-0-06-335159-2

PRINTED IN THE UNITED STATES OF AMERICA

25 26 27 28 29 LBC 7 6 5 4 3

"Zeppole (aka Awama)" by Khalil AbuSharekh. First published in *Your Impossible Voice*, Issue 30, Spring 2024. Copyright © 2024 by Khalil AbuSharekh. Reprinted by permission of the author.
 "The Pain of Travelling While Palestinian" by Mosab Abu Toha. First published in *The New Yorker*, September 21, 2024. Copyright © 2024 by Mosab Abu Toha. Reprinted by permission of the author.
 "Homeland Fictions" by Hannah Keziah Agustin. First published in *The North American Review*, 309.1, Spring 2024. Copyright © 2024 by Hannah Keziah Agustin. Reprinted by permission of the author.
 "On Boredom" by Nuar Alsadir. First published in *Granta*, 167, Spring 2024. Copyright © 2024 by Nuar Alsadir. Reprinted by permission of the author.
 "The Work of the Witness" by Sarah Aziza. First published in *Jewish Currents*, January 12, 2024. Copyright © 2024 by Sarah Aziza. Reprinted by permission of the author.

Solmaz Sharif, excerpt from "Dear Aleph," from *Customs: Poems*. Copyright © 2022 by Solmaz Sharif. Reprinted with the permission of the Permissions Company, LLC, on behalf of Graywolf Press, graywolfpress.org. Appears in "The Work of the Witness" by Sarah Aziza.

"Love and Murder in South Africa" by Eula Biss. First published in *The Believer*, Spring 2024. Copyright © 2024 by Eula Biss. Reprinted by permission of the author.

"How to Love Animals" by Matthew Denton-Edmundson. First published in *The Missouri Review*, 47.1, Spring 2024. Copyright © 2024 by Matthew Denton-Edmundson. Reprinted by permission of the author.

"Respect, or the Missing Relation" by William Deresiewicz. First published in *Liberties*, 5.1, Fall 2024. Copyright © 2024 by William Deresiewicz. Reprinted by permission of the author.

Louise Glück, excerpt from "Child Crying Out," from *Ararat: Poems* by Louise Glück. Copyright © 1990 by Louise Glück, used by permission of the Wylie Agency LLC. Appears in "Respect, or the Missing Relation" by William Deresiewicz.

"Sharing the Darkness" by Carolyn Forché. First published in *Irish Pages*, December 1, 2024. Copyright © 2024 by Carolyn Forché. Reprinted by permission of the author.

"Sea Grape Consciousness" by Alexis Pauline Gumbs. First published in *Orion*, 43.2, Summer 2024. Copyright © 2024 by Alexis Pauline Gumbs. Reprinted by permission of the author.

"A Little Slice of the Moon" by Summer Hammond. First published in *New Letters*, 90.1–2, Winter/Spring 2024. Copyright © 2024 by Summer Hammond. Reprinted by permission of the author.

"Within the Pretense of No Pretense" by Greg Jackson. First published in *The Point*, Issue 31, Winter 2024. Copyright © 2024 by Greg Jackson. Reprinted by permission of Georges Borchardt on behalf of the author.

"The Olive Branch of Oblivion" by Linda Kinstler. First published in *Liberties*, 4.3, Spring 2024. Copyright © 2024 by Linda Kinstler. Reprinted by permission of the author.

"Literature Without Literature" by Christian Lorentzen. First published in *Granta*, 168, Summer 2024. Copyright © 2024 by Christian Lorentzen. Reprinted by permission of the author.

"Man Crossing an Ice Field" by Laura Glen Louis. First published in *The Massachusetts Review*, 65.2, Summer 2024. Copyright © 2024 by Laura Glen Louis. Reprinted by permission of the author.

"An Age of Hyperabundance" by Laura Preston. First published in *n+1*, No. 47, Spring 2024. Copyright © 2024 by Laura Preston. Reprinted by permission of the author.

"Gone for a Spell" by Angie Romines. First published in *The Kenyon Review*, XLVI.4, Fall 2024. Copyright © 2024 by Angie Romines. Reprinted by permission of the author.

"Navel-Gazing" by Namwali Serpell. First published in *The Yale Review*, 112.2, Summer 2024. Copyright © 2024 by Namwali Serpell. Reprinted by permission of the author.

"The Shapes of Grief" by Christina Sharpe. First published in *The Yale Review*, 112.3, Fall 2024. Copyright © 2024 by Christina Sharpe. Reprinted by permission of the Wylie Agency, LLC.

"Nesting" by Jarek Steele. First published in *Colorado Review*, 51.1, Spring 2024. Copyright © 2024 by Jarek Steele. Reprinted by permission of the author.

"Corona" by John Jeremiah Sullivan. First published in *The Sewanee Review*, CXXXII.2, Spring 2024. Copyright © 2024 by John Jeremiah Sullivan. Reprinted by permission of the Wylie Agency, LLC.

Contents

Foreword ix

Introduction xvii

SARAH AZIZA. *The Work of the Witness* 1
 from *Jewish Currents*

CAROLYN FORCHÉ. *Sharing the Darkness* 9
 from *Irish Pages*

ALEXIS PAULINE GUMBS. *Sea Grape Consciousness* 17
 from *Orion*

CHRISTINA SHARPE. *The Shapes of Grief* 22
 from *The Yale Review*

ANGIE ROMINES. *Gone for a Spell* 34
 from *The Kenyon Review*

LAURA GLEN LOUIS. *Man Crossing an Ice Field* 51
 from *The Massachusetts Review*

HANNAH KEZIAH AGUSTIN. *Homeland Fictions* 73
 from *The North American Review*

EULA BISS. *Love and Murder in South Africa* 93
 from *The Believer*

MOSAB ABU TOHA. *The Pain of Travelling While Palestinian* 112
 from *The New Yorker*

KHALIL ABUSHAREKH. *Zeppole (aka Awama)* 124
from *Your Impossible Voice*

SUMMER HAMMOND. *A Little Slice of the Moon* 131
from *New Letters*

JOHN JEREMIAH SULLIVAN. *Corona* 156
from *The Sewanee Review*

NAMWALI SERPELL. *Navel-Gazing* 162
from *The Yale Review*

LINDA KINSTLER. *The Olive Branch of Oblivion* 171
from *Liberties*

JAREK STEELE. *Nesting* 190
from *Colorado Review*

NUAR ALSADIR. *On Boredom* 208
from *Granta*

GREG JACKSON. *Within the Pretense of No Pretense* 216
from *The Point*

LAURA PRESTON. *An Age of Hyperabundance* 239
from *n+1*

CHRISTIAN LORENTZEN. *Literature Without Literature* 262
from *Granta*

MATTHEW DENTON-EDMUNDSON. *How to Love Animals* 282
from *The Missouri Review*

WILLIAM DERESIEWICZ. *Respect, or the Missing Relation* 299
from *Liberties*

Contributors' Notes 309

Notable Essays and Literary Nonfiction of 2024 314

Foreword

What's Past Is Prologue

> The distinction between the past, present, and future is only a stubbornly persistent illusion.
> —Albert Einstein

I AM WRITING this foreword in March 2025, aware that these words will not reach readers until October. Predicting the future is an exercise best left to oracles; suffice to say that the history we are experiencing thrums with a disconcerting echo of the past and portends an abysmal path forward. Thanks to the internet and the innumerable science- and speculative-fiction offerings from Hollywood, we have many dystopias to contemplate: A nuclear exchange makes human life on Earth impossible. The wars may finally end, but the few survivors among the forcibly displaced are exiled, their dead buried under resorts and new flags. The lurking environmental collapse upends us as the seasons change; perhaps the seasons as we know them disappear (or are relieved of their names by executive order). A massive cyberattack or grid failure brings us to our knees. A pandemically inclined illness becomes the new plague. Books such as this one are burned or cost twenty times what they once cost. Our constitutionally guaranteed freedom of speech vanishes.

Regardless of the scenarios that may or may not come to pass between my writing these words and your reading them, this foreword is a missive from the past, that "cemetery of our illusions," as Émile Zola put it, where one stubs "one's toes on the gravestones." The essay is a particularly nimble form for collapsing and expanding our human perception of time, and allowing us to contemplate private and public histories. We look to the past to source our narratives—telling, recording, thinking them into being in the present, and sending them into the future, where they are listened to or read. Speculation, a chief characteristic of the essay, compresses past and future into a parallel dimension where the imagination of a here-and-now narrator wonders how the story may have turned out had something been said (or not) or done (or not).

Anthologies such as *The Best American Essays* are distinctive time capsules reflecting the idiosyncrasies of the writers and editors each book comprises. This volume, the fortieth in the series, preserves the history unfurling in the liminal zone between democracy and tyranny. In her introduction, guest editor Jia Tolentino describes our present moment as one in which "some infants ride on private jets swaddled in cashmere and others are bombed to death wearing diapers made of plastic bags." The cognitive dissonance of our quotidian lives reverberates almost everywhere, disturbingly becoming more and more normative, though if we pay attention to history, such dissonance *is* and has been the nature of human society since our species left its hunter-gatherer origins and organized into groups. There have always been those who have a lot and those who have almost nothing.

In a video from the ever-growing Disparate Realities genre, Jane Fonda accepts a Lifetime Achievement Award from the Screen Actors Guild. For her acceptance speech, Fonda—the quintessential American "icon" who contains multitudes of personable contradictions—is dressed in a sparkly pink confection and crowned with perfectly coiffed white hair. At eighty-seven, she looks remarkable. But I can't shake the sensation that how she *looks* contradicts the words she utters. After all, a month earlier, the Los Angeles fires burned over 40,000 acres, displaced tens of thousands of citizens, and destroyed the homes of many people, some of whom were attending the ceremony.

"Have any of you ever watched a documentary about one of the great social movements?" Fonda asks the audience about two-thirds of the way into her speech. "Like apartheid or our civil rights movement or Stonewall, and asked yourself [if you] would have been brave enough to walk the bridge? Would you have been able to take the hoses and the batons and the dogs?" She pauses before adding, "We don't have to wonder anymore, because we are in *our* documentary moment. This is it. And it's not a rehearsal."

A quiet moment passes before the audience members clap—I'm thinking they're unsure if applause is an appropriate response to the reality of an America whose democratic foundations are crumbling—and Fonda nurses the brief silence. Despite the wardrobe not matching the moment she is describing, I feel something like awe. Fonda has put her finger on the pulse of the history being made beyond the doors of the grand theater where American entertainment luminaries—dressed fashionably, each hair in place, bejeweled—are listening raptly to her words. For an instant, I wonder if she might quote Richard Wright's observation about history, that "few are the people who know the meaning of what they are living through, who even have an inkling of what is happening to them."

The phrase *documentary moment* makes me think we are looking at our present as if it were already curated as history, captured forever on film for future generations to watch. And Fonda is not conjuring even the merest hint of Richard Wright when she continues, urging us to be brave and find in our midst another "Norma Rae, or Karen Silkwood, or Tom Joad." She tells us that the word *woke* simply means people who care. She calls for love "on the other side of the conflagration," for community and attending to the vulnerable, for not isolating, and for imagining a more beckoning, welcoming future.

What she does not say is that the This Is It in which we are living has been on its way since humans started unsettling the land instead of living, heaven forbid, *with* and *in* it. She does not mention the *real* cost of eggs, the "price of the ticket," James

Baldwin called it. The price being paid by chickens who suffer a suffocating nonlife in factory farms, by the land and waters poisoned by runoff from these farms, by the immigrants and working poor who harvest the eggs, and by anyone who eats those eggs and the concoction of psychic and tangible poisons they contain.

A speech such as Fonda's is a kind of essay, one that follows the introduction-body-conclusion structure we all learned in high school and which ends, in this case, with closure, whose purpose is to tidy up the messiness of life, allow reconciliation with disaster, abuse, death, injustice. The speech is intended to instill hope and attempts to motivate listeners to action. You don't have to untangle any big concepts or do anything much but take in what's being said, react with a nod, smile, frown, or applause. Afterward, you do something else. Maybe you lie in bed imagining if you could have been as brave as your forebears. Despite the immortality afforded it by the internet, such a speech is an ephemeral artifact, becoming a viral meme today that will be replaced with something else tomorrow.

Still . . . the speech intrigues me because of Fonda's skill with pause and concision to deliver a message and inscribe it in memory. Truly resonant essays rely on the rhythmic pulse and urgency derived from *speaking*, which is where "voice," that difficult-to-explain quality of transcendent writing, originates. Think Montaigne dictating to his amanuensis, Virginia Woolf delivering the talks that became "A Room of One's Own," oratory by Sojourner Truth on enfranchisement and by Frederick Douglass on slavery, the cadences of the Harlem church and jazz in James Baldwin's prose, N. Scott Momaday's insistence on the silences that offer sanctuary to words.

The essay as we think of it was born in the minds of the ancients, influenced by Montaigne's sixteenth-century examination of the self, and further shaped by eighteenth- and nineteenth-century British authors, but the form seems peculiarly suited to American writers. The essay and this country came of age together. America was founded—its constitution and laws amended—

according to a strange (and sometimes contradictory) mix of essays, some of which began as oration, others published in periodicals or as stand-alone pamphlets. I'm thinking here of ten in particular: Cotton Mather's *The Wonders of the Invisible World* (1693); Samuel Sewall's *The Selling of Joseph* (1700); Thomas Paine's *Common Sense* (1776); Ralph Waldo Emerson's *Nature* (1836); Margaret Fuller's "The Wrongs of American Women. The Duty of American Women" (1845); Frederick Douglass's "What to the Slave Is the Fourth of July?" (1852); Frances Ellen Watkins Harper's "Our Greatest Want" (1859); Ida B. Wells's *Southern Horrors: Lynch Law in All Its Phases* (1892); Emma Goldman's *The Psychology of Political Violence* (1911); Zitkála Šá's *Oklahoma's Poor Rich Indians* (1924).

The essay preserves and is freighted with the past, but, like the voices it broadcasts in first-person singular and like memory, it is also a miscellaneous artifact composed of ephemeral thought tempered with emotion. As taught in school, American history omits much of its ephemera—including many of the aforementioned essays and the ideas they articulated—which may be the reason our memory of what happened before us is so inadequate to the task of understanding what is happening to us now. Ephemera's fleeting quality is part of the essay's charm (and that of performance art) and perhaps explains the essay's current appeal, given our distracted minds in this attention-economy era. Also, what one thinks in one's own present time—and writes in an essay—may well change and be refined. Or be forgotten. On a geological scale, humanity is but an ephemeral blip, essaying to remain by leaving behind books, structures, paintings, films, recordings—proof that we lived and died, thought and were thoughtless, loved and hated, hurt and were hurt, made things that delighted and destroyed.

I read many hundreds of essays in 2024 whose primary preoccupation is with the terrible wounds humans have sustained because of what James Baldwin called the histories that have trapped us and are trapped within us. Topics that dominate today's literature of personal history include illness, sexual and physical abuse, systemic oppressions and identity, gender nonconformity, loss and grief, relationships gone bad, parenting challenges and being the child of a person who didn't know how to parent. Here the essay is particularly American in its ability to undress and confess, reveal, and be cathartic to the writer while also suspending and preserving injury, as if in amber, for readers to behold. When an essay is successful, the genesis and progression of the wound (the particulars of its "situation," as Vivian Gornick calls it) is the scaffolding for story, or the meaning made of what happened.

A good number of narratives come across my transom that focus on humanity's relationship to the natural world, and in 2024, an abundance of these essays focused on our relationship to water. American history, it should be said, is dwarfed by the natural history contained in the waterways, shores, forests, mountains, and plains of this continent, whose small and threatened percentage of conserved wildness exceeds (for now) that of the island empire whose disaffected colonist offspring voyaged here and wrought so much destruction. Also prevalent in 2024 were astonishing works of reportage scrutinizing the many ways in which the world and the country are falling apart, from environmental collapse to drug addiction, technology gone awry, gun violence, sex trafficking, and genocide and the war zones in which crimes against humanity are committed.

"Of hard-fought engagements or sieges tremendous what deepest remains?" asks Walt Whitman in a poem about the American Civil War. In this anthology, what deepest remains is offered through accounting, probing, contemplating, witnessing, telling, setting down, wrestling with. Here you will discover testimonies and personal narratives about genocide and survival; exile and community; oblivion and legacy; love and faith; disease, grief, and boredom; nonhuman animals and plants; poverty and hyperabundance; consciousness and solipsism; the loss of literature and the work of art; pretense and respect. Here you will find the work of twenty-one writers, all clinging to their own loves and quests to make meaning of their inner and outer worlds, all of whom are connected in this one volume. There are no solid conclusions reached, but each essay earns the right to be inconclusive, to *not* know anything but the questions it asks.

Nomination Guidelines

The Best American Essays features a selection of essays published in North American periodicals (or by North American writers in foreign English-language publications) each calendar year.

These essays are works of literary achievement that show a keen awareness of craft and originality and forcefulness of thought.

Qualifications for essays nominated to the series are: original publication as an unabridged stand-alone essay in a nationally distributed North American periodical or by a North American writer in a foreign English-language publication *and* publication in English (originally written in English or translated into English by the essay's author) *and* publication during the calendar year for the volume.

For the most up-to-date and detailed nomination guidelines, please visit https://bestamericanessays.substack.com/p/nomination-guidelines.

Acknowledgments

This year's guest editor, Jia Tolentino, curated with grace and diligence an anthology that captures the complexities of our world and then wrote a brilliant, insightful, and forthright essay to introduce the volume. Nicole Angeloro at HarperCollins/Mariner has been an ongoing and dependable source of support, assistance, and humor in perfect measure. Without her, this book—and many others—would not be in your hands. The Essayist's Calendar and Interviews, two features of the *Best American Essays* newsletter on Substack, would not be possible without the hard work of two editorial assistants from Emerson College's Masters in Publishing and Writing program, Bayani Young in 2025 and Cheyenne Paterson in 2024. I am grateful for these two talented writers, for their efforts and for their teacher, Jerald Walker, who steered them my way and whose own fierce love of the essay has been evident in this series since 2007.

I am blessed with people and nonhuman animals near and far who keep my spirits aloft, and for the many acquaintances and former or current colleagues who support the essay. I remain humbled and awed by the energy and grace of the many tireless editors who celebrate and conserve contemporary literature by meeting deadlines, polishing manuscripts, thinking about design matters, and managing the business of the hundreds of periodicals that publish the work of today's writers.

Dedication

This volume is dedicated to Janet and Baron Wormser, whose love, counsel, art, and encouragement have sustained me in these dark times.

KIM DANA KUPPERMAN

Introduction

TO ME every essay is personal. It's the writing form that most closely corresponds to what I'd argue is the central project of being alive—trying to understand that strange fact itself and then act on its implications. I mean: we exist on the only planet in the universe that is known to sustain life, at a time when this planet, over four billion years into its existence, is within centuries from tipping into human uninhabitability. We were born without our consent into profound opportunity, our material agency located somewhere on the spectrum between the daily three dollars and change that a quarter of the globe subsists on and the fifty-four million dollars that Elon Musk makes each day off other people's backs. In this world, we have everything we need and are surrounded by suffering; some infants ride on private jets swaddled in cashmere and others are bombed to death wearing diapers made of plastic bags. We want to be human and we want to take care of (at least some of) each other, and yet we live in the grip of systems that incentivize nothing but dehumanization, and we are also personally terrible plenty of the time. Within all this we are idiosyncratic and wildly particular, with individual loves and secrets and families and specific relationships to sex and work and longing and meaning and talent and trouble. We have only one life in which to negotiate this in real time.

The essay asks the writer to show the work of this negotiation. And it asks the reader to come along for the process, to walk with the writer in the searching, self-doubting, redoubling, agonizing liberatory act of working through. That's the form's gift. As a reader, the essay has taught me how to think. As a writer, the essay—and its adjacent scrap forms in my life: the journal entry, the blog post, the piece of TextEdit detritus—has taught me how to live.

Shortly after Donald Trump's first presidency, I decided to spend a couple of years writing essays to be collected in a book. I was curious what the form would look like when fully inhabited by my brain's hungers and limitations and also untethered from the conventions that come from publishing in any specific outlet. I found, then, that for me an essay was usually privately motivated by a question: What happened during the decade when the internet went from seeming good to revealing itself as terrible? Why did I stop believing in God and start doing drugs and feel that nothing was gained or lost? And my essays, which doubled in size like dough under my fingertips, had I any skill at baking, always suggested to me that the answers were more complicated than I wanted them to be. They also suggested that the answers were not the point, exactly. The point was figuring out *how* one could go about answering a question honestly.

The essay for me serves as a crucial reminder that, while life frequently feels unfathomable, you can commit to a type of work that will force you to begin to fathom it. This work requires you to have a clear and mostly unforgiving understanding of who you are: I could not pretend, on the page, to have a different kind of brain, cool rather than warm, cerebral rather than instinctive, conclusive rather than discursive. This work also asks me to move toward a better version of myself: someone clearer and more honest and more present than the woman who's otherwise zoning out on the bus and buying milk with Tap to Pay, living thoughtlessly through the parts of each day that never make it to permanent storage.

At my best, I have found, I am generally unable to arrive at any answers. But I think—I really do—that that's okay. I believe that both life and writing ask us to aspire toward, rather than reach, and I suspect we get a lot farther if we don't operate under the idea that there's a stopping point that might satisfy us. Clear solutions exist in plenty of arenas in this world—public policy being the most consequential and constantly abjured of these—but in my life, and in my writing, I think of my project as mainly one of finding my direction. I am grateful for the essay: a container for that project, in which we can identify a direction and follow it as far as we can.

All of these essays were originally published in 2024, a year that fractured and confounded, maybe permanently, my understanding of the world and how to act within and upon it. What happened in 2024 is that the genocide in Gaza didn't stop. The bombing continued from its third to its fifteenth month. Sixty-seven children died every day on average. By October, after a year of the war, three-quarters of buildings and nearly the same percentage of crop fields were destroyed; upward of 90 percent of the population faced acute hunger. What was there to do about this atrocity, funded by billions of American tax dollars while 20 percent of our own children go hungry? The most visible mass protest movement in the United States, the college encampments that appeared in the spring, were repressed viciously—professors and students were beaten and arrested; the NYPD flooded Columbia in riot gear. I wrote my representatives and I took my little kids to protests and I sent money to GoFundMes and it didn't matter. My state rep wrote back to me saying that he would never support a ceasefire. My senator wrote back saying that he wanted a ceasefire, but it was obvious that he did not.

This was different from what happened in 2023, because, back then, much of what was to come seemed impossible. To those who believed in the project of Israel and the right of the country to displace and dispossess Palestinians, the message following Hamas's terrorist attack and hostage-taking on October 7 was that the Middle East's only democracy—the only moral country, the one that supports gay rights, the citadel singlehandedly preserving the security of a uniquely and profoundly persecuted people—had a right to defend itself by any means necessary. Cell phone footage emerged immediately of what this actually meant: premature infants left to die in their incubators. "At first—when we in the West were not yet accustomed to the bombing and siege of hospitals, still unfamiliar with the ashy pall of dead children's cheeks—this footage pulsed with moral urgency," Sarah Aziza writes in "The Work of the Witness." She goes on:

> Back then—in the recent, unreachable past—it was possible to think that acts so egregious would condemn themselves. Even Israel initially nodded to the idea of red lines, sprinkling flimsy denials over still-smoldering debris—*we didn't strike a hospital, we only kill terrorists, we aren't using white phosphorus* . . . But soon even the thinnest pretense was dropped. *Let them watch*, the regime seems to say, disseminating its own footage of razed neighborhoods, Palestinians blindfolded and stripped. It has proved to itself that the red line does not exist.

In 2024, the spineless center went mostly silent on Gaza, even though the majority of Americans wanted the US to stop funding this war—61 percent of all voters, including 77 percent of Democrats and 40 percent of Republicans. The leaders in both parties did not care. Many people seemed to be stuck on the correct premise that both Israel and Hamas were immoral actors, eliding the fact that the US had sent thirty-eight billion dollars in a decade to only one of them. Aziza asks in her essay: What was it for? All these photos and videos, the newborns in shrouds, the parents wailing over body bags, the orphaned children carrying dirty water to their siblings, the men being tortured by Israeli soldiers—what did it mean to look at this, to amplify and re-amplify it, to try to find the words to put to our convictions about it? "We know that war destroys language, as it destroys everything within its zone of prosecution," writes Carolyn Forché, in an essay that begins with the bunkers in Ukraine and ends with the destruction in Gaza. She quotes Czesław

Miłosz: "The poetic act changes with the amount of background reality embraced by the poet's consciousness." For us, now, she writes, what is required is the vigilance to understand that the background reality of our words—all of them, not just by writers—is war. That we ought not slough it off to function but allow ourselves to react to it instinctively, the way "horses run back and forth . . . before a storm."

In 2024, I stopped trusting or taking seriously people for whom Gaza was not in the background reality embraced by their consciousness. But Gaza was a test that so few of us were passing. That animating question—how do we understand the world, and what do we do about it?—can be put in more specific terms: How can we conceive of our entanglement with systems that consign people to misery, even if they benefit us, and how do we dissent from and sabotage these systems? People tried, in 2024, getting themselves arrested on highways, in government buildings. Three US citizens publicly burned themselves to death in protest. Greta Thunberg spoke about Gaza and lost all the simpering corporate-fleece-vest support she'd had when she was merely speaking about the soon-to-be-uninhabitable Earth (not that the people with their hands on the levers had done anything meaningful about that either). Elected officials did not take up their constituents' cries for a ceasefire. The year 2024 did something to break my faith in representative democracy, and certainly in the party I've always voted for, which in the presidential election made it clear they would continue to support the genocide but differentiate themselves from the Republicans by performing sadness about it.

I have tried not to be so stupid as to believe that the years prior to this represent a calm worth returning to. What passes as normal is a slow-burning emergency. "It's the thirty-year mortgage," Alexis Pauline Gumbs writes, in her essay about global warming. "The extractive corporation. The colonial, anti-Indigenous insistence that our relationship to land should be the same through changing seasons and wider ecological changes. It's the fear of change itself. The denial that we will ever die. That's the disaster." But inevitably, as I read through the treasure trove of finalist essays for this collection, I looked for writers who were seeking a way to live through this without ducking, denying, retreating. "What I am experiencing now, what I think many of us are experiencing, is a kind of distributed mourning," writes Christina Sharpe, in an essay that starts with the race massacre at a Tops Friendly Market in Buffalo in 2022.

In her piece about the Frontier Nursing Service and midwives in Appalachia, Angie Romines meditates on her distance from the evangelical religion of her young life, and from that community's reflexive practices of care for each other—of going to where a person needed help and helping. "My hands and my mind don't know what to do with themselves these days," she writes. "If I have a soul, I don't know what it's for if not for saving." Of course, there are issues of capacity. Laura Glen Louis, on her numbness after years of caring for a spouse with severe Alzheimer's: "You tamp your responses, and over time that tamping spills over into your response to the trials of the global unfortunate, to the plight of friends." (And of course I have tamped for far worse reasons—inertia, cowardice, selfishness.) In her essay about capital and displacement in the slums of metro Manila, Hannah Keziah Agustin writes, "And I think about the curse coming upon all who have lived on earth in luxury and self-indulgence, who have fattened themselves on the day of slaughter." Eula Biss, whose work is often about the complicated relationship between individual and collective interests, writes about a trip to South Africa, meeting people who have suffered under slaughter and those who have sailed on. "A white woman came along the path with a child on a tricycle, trailing glittering red steamers from the handles, spangled by sunlight," Biss writes. "I looked through the woman's smile into her skull, and thought, *How do you live with yourself?* The answer to this question came to me instantaneously. She lives with herself, my mind told me, in exactly the same way you do."

There are two pieces in this collection by Gazan writers. Many readers of this anthology will likely have read Mosab Abu Toha's essay "The Pain of Travelling While Palestinian," published in *The New Yorker*. Rereading it, what I admired was its control, its aperture. Abu Toha focuses narrowly on the experience of being bureaucratically humiliated, of fighting back tears in airports, of attempting to cross borders with impossibly won documents citing his citizenship in a place that many don't believe exists. The essay is set in corporate space, under fluorescence; the backdrop—mostly veiled, though winds of blood and death blow through the curtain—is hell. "I've lost hope that we will return to our previous life," a friend tells him.

The other Gazan writer, Khalil AbuSharekh, grew up in a refugee camp and now lives in Houston. The narrative takes place in the instant after a server at an Italian restaurant brings him zeppole with his coffee; the sweet dough brings on a fugue of recollections of his childhood—his burning desire for new shoes, which he acquires as if through a miracle and then destroys, accidentally, in a bike accident a mere few days later. "I concluded that day that mankind was involved in a conspiracy," AbuSharekh writes. At that line, something in me ran back and forth. We were in fact conspiring against him. The shoes that AbuSharekh craved as a child are linked by that conspiracy to the shoes I buy new for my daughter, buoyed by the US tax code that was built to shelter me only as long as I didn't need shelter, one that takes money from the people in my community who themselves can't buy sneakers for their children but have to send part of their minimum-wage salary to buy bombs that kill other kids.

And yet, the reminder in AbuSharekh's essay is that, to a child, the shoes are tragedy enough. We aspire toward beauty, comfort, personal thrill, no matter the frame. Summer Hammond's essay "A Little Slice of the Moon" features an abusive mother who forbade her daughter, a teenage Jehovah's Witness, from going out on a date with a dreamboat she worked with at McDonald's—and yet Hammond, gracefully, affords her mother longings of her own: "She tried to decorate the trailer as though it were the big, old farmhouse she'd dreamed of in her childhood, lace curtains dancing in the windows, whimsical chicken and rooster plates, wildflower murals on the walls she painted by hand." All we want—new shoes, sunlight through the curtains, that person to text us, the child to sleep peacefully. To get back to zero, a zero that can seem like infinity, as John Jeremiah Sullivan writes in his essay "Corona" about routinely becoming grievously ill in foreign places. He got COVID in the fjords, hallucinated and sweated. It went away. "And it turns out this was all you had wanted, or what you had wanted most," he writes. "That never lasts."

In 2019, I accepted an invitation to speak at a conference in Melbourne, almost on a lark: friends of mine would be there, and perhaps I could see some exciting animals, and, crucially, the conference organizers had offered to fly me first class. I also knew I might get pregnant at some point around or after the conference—in fact I did get pregnant about a week after I returned to the States—and so I had the instinct to make the most of the last stretch of my unadulterated freedom. I went to the bookstore and treated myself to a stack of paperbacks. Later, as I passed through the liminal spaces of antipodean travel, the dinners alone, the unoriented wandering, the stolen afternoons in gardens full of plants I'd never seen before while everyone else I knew in the world was sleeping—always with my reading material—I realized I'd chosen a series of books that had, almost exclusively, to do with safety, emergency, the surreal, the social contract, the natural world. Something deeper than my attention was focused on those concerns. I must have felt on the brink of something, wanting to know what would survive a rearrangement. I guessed then that I was anticipating the possibility of a baby. Now I wonder—I don't even believe in this, but still—if I was somehow perceiving 2020, the rearrangements that that year would bring.

I always find myself doing this: devouring first, realizing later. Just last week I noticed I'd read Alan Hollinghurst, then Gary Indiana, then Lucy Sante all in a row, and then that I had been thinking, obviously, about love, concealment, transcendence, and frustration within troubled desire. Reading through the nominated essays for this anthology, I first set aside the ones that struck me hardest and then looked to them to understand what had been happening on that unbiddable level of the mind. Quickly it became clear I'd been looking for work that aligned with Namwali Serpell's definition of art, in her essay on criticism, "Navel-Gazing": the "exposure of incommensurable values." I was looking for vigor rendered from the depths of exhaustion, for lightness where you would expect the dark and heavy, for safety in uncertainty, for trouble in calm. I was looking, as most of us are, for a way to both remember and to start anew. Linda Kinstler's "The Olive Branch of Oblivion" is about this very pursuit, as codified in ancient political theory. "The Roman adoption of the Greek practice," she writes, "suggests that oblivion was not understood as a blanket amnesty, nor as an absolute commandment to forget, but rather something in between, a somewhat ambiguous legal, moral, and material commitment that enabled political communities to come back together while at the same time preserving—memorializing by means of a mandate to forget—the memory of what tore them apart."

And speaking of holding together what some might call incommensurate, the opening of the essay "Nesting" by Jarek Steele is as memorable as anything:

> The summer I was pregnant, I watched with growing detachment as my breasts asserted themselves and my spreading hips echoed my mother's. I had the urge to nest—procuring diapers and wet wipes, obsessively dusting, developing a sudden, unexpected interest in scrapbooking—and became, for a short while, someone I was not. That's not true. I was that person just as surely as I am this person, bald and bearded, typing at a dining room table. Unless that's not true either. If you asked me then, when I was nineteen, if I ever thought I'd be a man, I would have said it was impossible, but the truth shifts, and I suppose the space you're in shapes the person you are as much as you shape it.

I realized that I was also looking for a broader sort of reframing, a reminder of our negative capability, that quality that is constantly eroded by the never-ending parade of the given on our screens. I wanted to read words that were angled toward this problem. When a person is bored—boredom meaning restlessness, dissatisfaction, unconscious avoidance; all the things that bring me to my phone—as we so often are, Nuar Alsadir writes,

"You're unable to fantasize. You can't even think." Greg Jackson writes in "Within the Pretense of No Pretense": "Power, as it had long been understood, pertained to what you could do to alter reality. First you imagined how reality could be different, then you endeavored to make it so." But now, the "new power did not arise from imagining what could be done. What could be done arose from the choice laid out before you."

That choice currently consists of selecting between various degrees of capture. Laura Preston, in her essay "An Age of Hyperabundance," about being the dissenting speaker at an AI conference, describes a future—planned for, highly capitalized, positioned in different words as thrilling progress—of:

> . . . screens in every establishment and no way to get help, a future in which extractive algorithms yielded relentless advertising, a future of a crapified internet, too diluted with sponcon and hallucinated facts to be of any use. In this future, if you wanted to use a product you would have to download an app and pay a monthly fee. It was a future of ultra-sophisticated scams and government surveillance, a future where anyone's face could be spliced into porn. Our arrival in this future would be a gradual surrender, achieved through a slow creep of terms and conditions, and the capitulations had already begun.

How do we imagine a future that looks otherwise? Through the instincts that emerge in raw, unmediated, ungovernable human experience. Through organizing our labor rather than allowing others to fracture it. Through art, through writing. Christian Lorentzen, in "Literature Without Literature," says on fiction: "Not restricted to the empirical, it is free to invent, it has recourse to fantasies that are truer than real life. It is less enamored with disclosing the obvious." Would that we could be more the same way.

But how amazing that writing allows us to practice. That writing provides a playground upon which to attempt the kind of motion that applies, with more consequence, in the larger and infinitely less controllable world. Some days this seems to simply come down to the wrangling of our self-assertion: how to magnify it when the world is opposed to it, and how to tame it when the incentives run otherwise. It feels like so many of us are looking in the direction of humility. Toward righteousness without self-righteousness, toward the friction and confusion that we are encouraged to try to swipe away, toward a kind of newness and remaking that will actually require us to give up something. We owe this to each other. Every writer in this anthology is describing the same world. Matthew Denton-Edmundson writes in "How to Love Animals" about seeking a relationship with animals "in which we allow them to alter us almost as much as we alter them"—the thought applies more broadly. We all share everything. In these words, we plead with each other to remember that fact. In his essay "Respect, or the Missing Relation," William Deresiewicz writes, "I think of the concept of *tzimtzum*—the act, in Kabbalah, whereby an infinite God creates the world by contracting himself to make room for it. The ego also tends to fill immensity. Self-contraction is a decent rule of conduct, and a useful prayer would be *Lord, help me to make myself small.*"

JIA TOLENTINO

SARAH AZIZA

The Work of the Witness

FROM *Jewish Currents*

IN THE mornings, as others stumble toward their coffee, I wake and gather news of the dead. First, I check WhatsApp, where, on the best days, I will receive a picture of bread—my family has eaten today. On the worst days, I learn of relatives starving, sick, or killed. Next, I turn with loathing to social media. Too weary, anymore, to brace myself, I compel my thumbs to scroll (could there be a more banal verb for this, the perusing of atrocities?). Horror follows abomination follows tragedy, a gliding series of symmetrical tiles, each one smaller than my hand.

Watch, I tell myself. I see what must have been a building, though all that remains is a smoking hill of sharp debris. *Watch*, I tell myself, as thin men in sandaled feet rush into the frame. They begin pawing at the slabs of cement, rebar, brick. Shouts ricochet. The camera moves closer. My ears begin to ring. I long to click away. *Watch. These are your people.* I force my eyes to stay.

Bear witness. This, an admonition often repeated through these killing weeks. *Bear witness,* a cry against the fierce, orchestrated attempts to deny the devastation wrought in Gaza and the West Bank. *Bear witness,* we tell ourselves as helplessness threatens to engulf us on our far end of the telescope. *Bear witness,* we say, yet three months into a livestreamed genocide, we must ask—what does all this looking do?

Gazans have indeed sought our eyes and attention amid these days of peril. Defying Israel's targeting of journalists and their families—which has made this the most dangerous conflict for journalists on record—Palestinians have risked everything to document and share. From the first hours of the carnage, they have rushed toward bombed-out buildings, swinging cameras to capture arriving doom. An immediate, reflexive instinct: to record, expose. As if the scale of violence had shocked even siege-worn Gazans into thinking, *This time, surely, Israel has gone too far. Surely this cannot stand* . . .

And so, mere meters from strike sites, their hands still shaking from terror, these survivor-creators have broadcast the unmaking of their world. Their dispatches are an act of resistance, transmitting truths systematically excised from legacy media. From the start, Israel has forbidden all outside journalists from entering Gaza, save for the few reporters they escort on orchestrated tours. These journalists are prohibited from speaking to Palestinians while on the ground, and are required to submit their reports to the Israeli military for approval before publishing.

Chillingly, many of the young, now-famous faces of this living archive—people we presume to call by their first names, Bisan, Plestia, Motaz—have focused on creating content in English. In this, they have made clear that these images are not simply intended to capture their intimate experience, but to move the unseen audiences of the West.

And at first—when we in the West were not yet accustomed to the bombing and siege of hospitals, still unfamiliar with the ashy pall of dead children's cheeks—this footage pulsed with moral urgency. Back then—in the recent, unreachable past—it was possible to think that acts so egregious would condemn themselves. Even Israel initially nodded to the idea of red lines, sprinkling flimsy denials over still-smoldering debris—*we didn't strike a hospital, we only kill terrorists, we aren't using white phosphorus* . . . But soon even the thinnest pretense was dropped. *Let them watch*, the regime seems to say, disseminating its own footage of razed neighborhoods, Palestinians blindfolded and stripped. It has proved to itself that the red line does not exist.

It is gutting to watch this realization dawn on Gazans' faces, too. Across grinding weeks of slaughter—throughout which the US has denied Palestinian casualties while vetoing international ceasefire resolutions—Western-facing reporters have grown more anguished, and angry. They confront a world in which their genocide garners millions of witnesses, and yet continues apace. "I shared enough and God knows it was for him and my country," wrote Motaz Azaiza on social media in early December. "Our situation is tragic far further than you can imagine!" His words were both indictment and lament: "Remember that we are not content to be shared, we are a nation that is getting killed . . . how alone we are!"

Bisan Owda's daily dispatches are a time lapse of a young woman pushed from shock and sorrow toward a shattered rage. For weeks, her posts have been a testament to her past life as a *hakawati*, storyteller—eloquent and moving reports, often edited with text. But by December 28, she appears on screen with a thinned face, her brown eyes smoldering. "Now I'm really questioning, until when? I mean we've recorded all kinds of massacres, against hospitals, schools, civilians, in the streets, in the shelters, everywhere . . . and nothing has changed . . . I mean we've recorded everything, we've shown you things you've never seen in Hollywood. We've recorded them. And nothing has changed."

The dilemma of the diasporic Palestinian: In exile, we are forced to witness Palestine from a distance, and yet remain intimately bound to the events unfolding there. We straddle multiple vectors of power and oppression, and struggle with how best to respond to the murder of our kin. I feel the sting of Owda's words, the moral implications of my position as a tax-paying US citizen. Yet, as a Palestinian with roots in Gaza, I have wrestled with my own questions of disclosure. I, too, know the impulse to publicize my family's tragedy, to demand witness of others.

In the first week, I considered posting a picture of my father as a six-year-old refugee in Gaza. This, my small contribution to a discourse which seeks to make our humanity legible, and thus worthy of mercy. But I hesitated, unwilling to instrumentalize my father's innocence. All my life, I have watched our beauty and worth precluded as a matter of course. What did I hope to gain, by exposing his sweet, young face to the world?

In an organizing meeting I attended shortly after, we debated the merits of sharing the worst images of violence, the most horrific videos. The broad consensus in the room was that the visuals of dismembered and crushed children would be what moved the Western world to act. I raised my voice in doubt, groping for language to articulate what gives me pause. No, I do not believe this genocide should be sanitized. In fact, I want to shatter Western innocence. I want to detonate their delusions of morality, incriminate their alibis of *self-defense*. It is responsible and right to engage and amplify these images; there is no sensitivity worth protecting at the expense of the murderous truth.

And yet, and yet. Our bodies are so precious. They grow more precious every murderous day. I feel protective, wary of the mass dissemination of our grief. A growing conviction that such images should be in some sense earned, reciprocated with gestures of committed action—or what is this looking for? A common poster slogan at protests: YOU CAN'T SAY YOU DIDN'T KNOW. We are saturated with this knowing now. If we never saw another photograph, our purpose would still be clear. This week's photographed corpses should have been saved by last week's ceasefire; the same will be said every week until this evil ends.

Ultimately, I posted the photo of my father, his face redacted. Not an appeal to, but an interrogation of, would-be witnesses, an attempt to turn the gaze back onto the spectator. What does it feel like to encounter even this small disruption in access to us? If it triggers surprise or frustration, what does that say of the viewer's expectation, their intent? Is compassion for this boy conditioned on the legibility of his face?

Sometimes, it is an act of power to withhold, to refuse to show. "They can't see us," I have often said, speaking of the masters of the West. What I mean is, "If they could see us, the current world order would collapse." This is true of so many bodies upon whom oppressive, extractive power rests. Their unhumaning is inherent, a prerequisite to these systems' continuance. Our invisibility is not a matter of lacking images, but of a social-political vision in which true witness is precluded.

This is why legibility fails.

Witness, in the English, usually carries connotations of criminal court. A witness is one who speaks to the veracity of an alleged event. Perhaps the motivations of Gazan reporters, at this later point in the genocide, might be read more through this frame. Despite their professed feelings of futility, Owda and Azaiza, along with others like Wael Dahdouh, continue to document Gaza's deepening catastrophe. At great risk to themselves, they provide us with the evidence of criminal cruelty, bankrolled by the West. One hopes the day will come when this proof is used in trial.

Yet I have been pondering not the English, prosecutorial *witness*, but the Arabic. In this, our language, the verb *to witness* comes from the root شهد. This is also the source of the much-maligned word شهيد, *shaheed*, which means, literally, *witnesser*, but is often translated as *martyr*. It is a word with many folds of meaning and history. It carries connotations not only of seeing, but of presence and proximity. To be a witness is to make contact, to be touched, and to bear the marks of this touch.

Shaheed is the word Palestinians use to describe those lost to Israeli violence, a word which has drawn condemnation from American universities and press, who once again presume to know the meaning of Arabic-rooted terms, without bothering to investigate. They allege the word *martyr* glorifies death for death's sake. But in this context, it should be read as honoring the truth these brutalized bodies speak. Their flesh, marked by colonial violence, makes visible the wild injustice they endured. Which is to say, their martyrdom tells us the truth about our world.

In the strange, pseudo-intimacy of social media, the most revelatory moments are the least scripted. And they are certainly not expressed in English, however impeccable. In an Instagram Live on December 5, I watched Owda weep as she spoke candidly, in Arabic, of her exhaustion and fear. Some bilingual viewers translated her words into English in the chat. Other viewers, responding to the English, flooded the comments with praise for her heroic strength. But when Palestinian journalist Faten

Elwan joined her stream, she offered not encouragement, but comfort. *Don't be brave*, she urged, also in Arabic, her voice trembling with emotion of her own. *Don't be strong. Bisan, don't be anything. Just be yourself.*

Herself. What of that self do we, her distant followers, know? And how much of it will survive? Owda's tears bear witness to the world behind her weeping. Only she knows, exactly, what she mourns. But her sorrow, like every Palestinian's, points to the deep violation that is war. Contrary to the myopic depictions in Western media, grief is not our natural state. We must recognize that Gaza is a vastness of which this slaughter, and our glimpses of it, are only the barest piece.

تعبنا, تعبنا!, I hear over and over again, when watching Gaza in Arabic. It could be rendered in English as simply *we are tired, we are tired*, but a more accurate translation would be *we have come to the limits of ourselves, we are empty, exhaustion consumes us.* تعبنا, تعبنا, Gazans repeat, speaking in plural even when interviewed alone. As miraculous as Palestinian *sumud* may be, it is not limitless. Our endurance should be a means, not an end. What Gaza longs for—deserves—is justice, liberation, and life.

My relatives, like Owda, have expressed both sumud and lament. Like Refaat al-Areer's prescient poem, in which he foresaw and reclaimed his likely coming death, my own relatives have sent missives of how, should they die (God forbid), they want their stories told. From my twenty-five-year-old cousin Nabil: "We are still here. We are in the evacuation zones. We do not know where to go. All the places are crowded and epidemics are spreading . . . If we don't meet, write about me. I loved life, I loved the field of pharmacy, and writing, and I was a peaceful, dreamy person."

Standing with one foot inside the horror, witness is never abstract. For all my misgivings about legibility, I honor the wishes of those living on the land, beneath the bombs. I am asked to hold eulogies on standby. I am asked to tell their stories. And whether or not I pick up my phone, I can never truly look away. Every Palestinian can attest: Each day of continued genocide is an irrevocable mark on the soul. Each dropped bomb takes part of us, even when our flesh is spared.

As long as Palestinians are alive to record and share their suffering, the duty and dilemma of witness will remain. As we look, we must be aware that our outpouring of emotion has its limits, and its own dynamics of power. Grief and anger are appropriate, but we must take care not to veer into solipsism, erasing the primary pain by supplanting it with our own. As the Mojave poet Natalie Diaz has observed, empathy is "seeing or hearing about something that's happened to someone and . . . imagin[ing] how I would feel if it happened to me. It has nothing to do with them." Or, put more succinctly by Solmaz Sharif: "Empathy means / laying yourself down / in someone else's chalk lines / and snapping a photo."

Rather, we—those outside of Palestine, watching events through a screen—ought to think of ourselves in relation to the legacy of the shaheed. Our work as witnesses is to be marked; we should not leave it unscathed. We must make an effort to stay with what we see, allowing ourselves to be cut. This wound is essential. Into this wound, imagination may pour—not to invade the other's subjectivity, but to awaken awe at the depth, privacy, and singularity of each life. There, we might glimpse, if sidelong, how much of Gaza's suffering we will never know. This is where real witness must begin: in mystery.

Perhaps the fundamental work of witness is the act of faith—an ethical and imaginative leap beyond what we can see. It is a sober reverence of, and a commitment to fight for, the always-unknowable other. This commitment does not require constant stoking by grisly, tragic reports. Rather than a feeling, witness is a position. It insists on embodiment, on sacrifice, mourning and resisting what is seen. The world after genocide must not, cannot, be the same. The witness is the one who holds the line of reality, identifying and refusing the lie of normalcy. Broken by what we see, we become rupture incarnate.

Or, much better expressed in the words of my cousin, the pharmacist,

ما زلت مصرا نحن لم نعتد القصف ونخاف من كل حدث ولم نعتد مشاهد المعاناة ، ان القلب دائما ما ينفطر ولم نعتد المجازر الذي يرتكبها الاحتلال فلكل شهيد حياة

I continue to insist, we have not gotten used to bombing and we are afraid of everything happening to us. We have not gotten used to the sight of suffering. No, it always breaks our hearts. We have not gotten used to the massacres perpetrated by the occupation. No. For every martyr, there was a life.

CAROLYN FORCHÉ

Sharing the Darkness

FROM *Irish Pages*

—*For Dr. Baha Alashqar, of Odesa and Gaza*

Scrims of memory.

FEBRUARY 24, 2022. I wake with a start at midnight. A nightbird striking the window? A bat in the eaves? Maybe someone in the theater of my sleep gave me a nudge—someone I don't know in waking life. It is cloudy and warm this night, so the waning moon isn't visible through the window beside me, nor the bright star Antares to the right of it. There is no wind. There have been no sharp knocks on the door as I seem to hear sometimes in my sleep, and no imaginary bell. A stillness has descended on everything: the pile of books on the bedside table, the water glass lit from within, and across the room, a gallery of people looking out from their photographs as if through windows in the past. Nothing moves. *Something has happened*, is what the darkness says. It had to do with the maps I had been studying in recent days, with the drawings of tanks and the arrows pointing at Ukraine. At one time, such as in Beirut years earlier, I would have reached for the Grundig shortwave radio and spun the dial through frequencies of music, language, and white noise. Now I reach for my cell phone and begin to scroll, tenting the light with a bedsheet so as not to disturb my husband's sleep. At first the world seems quiet. Kyrgyzstan's president has signed a decree banning the slaughter of cattle during funerals. Anti-war protesters have gathered outside the Russian embassy in Berlin. Singapore reports a record number of COVID cases. I solve the Wordle puzzle and the Mini Crossword, and then I play the game of guessing how many words can be made from the same seven letters, using the same single letter in each of them. I learn that it will rain tomorrow. I hear the water heater turn on then off again. Car lights from the road pass over the walls. Maybe in the distance a racoon is opening a garbage can. It is all very normal, but something bothers the mind. *This has to do with the war that is coming*, is what the darkness is saying, and it is right. The country on the map is now ringed by battalions and tanks, convoys with their missiles pointing at the clouds. The Russian military forces are arrayed along the borders of Russia, Belarus, and occupied Crimea.

The air raid sirens sound just after dawn in Kyiv, and some minutes later in Lviv. Blasts are heard in the cities of Dnipro, Mariupol, Kramatorsk, and Odesa. This has to do with a city near the sea, *city of wheat and light, city of limestone soft enough to cut with a hatchet*, as I had written in a poem about Odesa. Poems sometimes whisper in the dark like this. They appear in the dark like lights when the eyes are closed. Within hours, I would know what woke me up. In Kyiv it was already morning, and it was clear that a full-scale war against the people of Ukraine had begun, a war to destroy kindergartens and libraries, theaters, farmer's markets, hospitals, filling stations; a war on universities and maternity wards, factories and shopping malls, apartment blocks and playgrounds; a war on a language spoken for centuries, on the history of a people, on folk songs and dances, fairy tales, literature, and food; a war, as I saw it, upon *an opera house, a madhouse, a ghost church with wind for its choir / where two things were esteemed: literature and ships, poetry and the sea*. These lines are from a poem I wrote for the Ukrainian-born poet Ilya Kaminsky after we traveled to Odesa two decades ago, when it seemed possible and even restorative for him to go back, to see once again the city of his childhood, the city he left with his mother and father in the years just after the collapse of the former Soviet Union.

This was not my first trip to that part of the world. A decade earlier, I had driven through Belarus toward Ukraine to document the conditions of people living in the exclusion zones surrounding the damaged reactor at Chernobyl: the elderly people who refused to leave, and refugees from the war in Chechnya, who found safety in the peace and quiet of the place. In memory, the giant blue cabbages growing in their radiated gardens are visible through a scrim of acacia trees lining the streets of Odesa. The passage of time has caused these journeys to happen all at once, the images flickering like photographs in a chaotic slide show. Ilya and I are walking in the cold wind toward the Potemkin steps when he interrupts this reverie by playfully inviting me to dance, as suggested by the title of his first volume of poems, *Dancing in Odessa*. And so we waltz down Prymorskyi Boulevard, and later, over a samovar of black tea in the Hotel Londonskya, he confides that emigration is death. "You must die when you board the plane and walk into your resurrection as you disembark in the new land. If you are unable to do this, you remain a corpse. I'm not sure I can say now that emigration is a good thing."

That trip was the first of many for him. He even went back during the war, in part to visit his ailing uncle, to bring whatever aid and comfort he could to his relatives and friends, the poets he had come to know in the decades since that first journey, poets he had been translating and publishing, and now was trying somehow to rescue, in whatever way he could. Most Ukrainian poets had chosen to stay behind when millions of women, children, and elderly men boarded the trains, piled into cars, or walked to the country's borders. Like everyone else in the West, I was confined in my knowledge of this exodus to photographs and video footage: arms reaching through train windows, crowded platforms, children in snowsuits, house cats and small dogs tucked into winter jackets, roller boards, rucksacks, wheelchairs. Some had packed believing they would only be away a short time. I wondered what they had chosen to bring with them and tried not to think about all they had left behind. I did, however, understand that the images before me did not transmit how cold it was, how raw the air, how painful the boots and shoes, did not convey the desperate hope for a toilet, a sip of water, a place to dry out the mittens and socks. In the photographs, the black smoke pouring from burning apartment blocks doesn't sting the eyes or burn the throat; there is no stench of cordite and no overpowering petroleum odor of war.

Soon after the invasion began, the writer Askold Melnyczuk asked me to join a Zoom gathering of Ukrainian poets, sponsored by the PEN American Center. Despite our far-flung locations, on the computer screen, it was as if we were all in the same apartment house, looking out from our different windows. In Ukraine, it was already dark. The mood in our dimly lit poetry building was solemn. Vasyl Makhno was in New York; Ostap Slyvynsky and Halyna Kruk were in Lviv; Oksana Lutsyshyna was in Austin, Texas; Iryna Shuvalova in Beijing; and Oksana Zabuzhko tried to join us from Warsaw, but was unable to get the technology on her borrowed computer to work. Askold welcomed us. There were greetings and sad smiles, shrugs and knowing looks. I knew that I would share a poem I wrote for Ilya, titled "Exile," but in the hours leading up to our meeting, I also composed a message in the form of a poem, an urgent message written quickly and read in its raw state. In the days that followed, the message was published, translated into Ukrainian, and letter-pressed as a broadside in both languages against a field of sunflowers.

IF THERE IS INK

If there is ink for this hour if there is
something to say to write that would
send the tanks the convoys and transports
into reverse on the roads they have rutted
send them back to the borders they crossed
send them back, and the hours too that have passed
since dawn on the twenty-fourth day of the second month
send those hours with them, and the enemy
soldiers dragging with them their crematorium
and the corpses of their fellow soldiers they have left
behind and their own wounded send them back if there is ink
if there is something to write that would raise the cities
from the ruins the apartment blocks hospitals schools
that would put the cities back as they were
I would give everything to fill my pen with it

This was before Mariupol was razed to the ground, before its theater was bombed, killing six hundred people who had taken refuge within it; before the discovery of the torture chambers and the corpses of Bucha; the aerial bombing of Vinnytsia, Chernihiv, Kyiv, and Izium, a litany of cities and towns; the siege of the steelworks; a child photographed lying dead beside a baby carriage; a mother in labor carried on a litter from a burning maternity ward. It was possible in those first weeks and months to imagine myself to be following "the news," especially by reading *The Kyiv Independent*, just as it was possible to hope that the sanctions would work, that the courage of a besieged people could prevail against despotic aggression, that the largest land war in Europe in almost seventy years would not end in thermonuclear war; that Ukraine would somehow survive this onslaught against significant odds. After all, hadn't the Russian warship been sunk off the coast of Snake Island? Hadn't the farmer's tractor towed the broken tank out of a field? Didn't they put these images on postage stamps? The warship and the tractor-towed tank?

I lie in the dark most nights, aware that at that very moment, on the other side of the world, a rocket had struck a power plant and the lights had gone out. And then I was lying again on a basement floor in Beirut many years ago, listening to the thunderous shelling of Ras Beirut from the Maronite east. Almost every journalist posted to Beirut was in that hotel basement, along with a handful of people from neighboring apartments. There were thirty or so of us. Beside me was a young Lebanese girl lying under her coat, whispering to me about her life, and wondering if there would be anything left in the morning. "Of course, there will be," I reassured her, "they can't destroy everything." However, the truth was that yes, they could. I feared that our building would be hit and we would be crushed beneath it. "We have to sleep," I said to the girl. In the morning, we will wake up, and it would be over. I said things like that until she fell asleep, and then I lay there, staying awake to keep the world intact. That is how one thinks in a makeshift shelter under bombardment.

As I scroll through photographs taken in Kherson or Nikopol, I remember not only the stench, but the deafening sounds of detonated ordnance, acrid dust and debris, the screeching of metal on metal, the coughing of the mortars and shattering of glass. In the morning, the streets of Ras Beirut were covered with broken windows, green, jagged scraps that made it look as though the streets were iced. It was hard to walk. And there is so much else one can forget: how for hours or even days nothing happens, and it seems safe to come out because after all it is necessary to find food and water, to prepare meals and wash up, to think about where to go next. I remember the young boy who every day ran from doorway to doorway with a tall stack of pita bread he balanced like plates in a circus act. He sometimes had to dodge rifle-fire, but he never dropped the bread, and people watching from a slight distance cheered him on as if he might not die at any moment, as if this were an extreme sport.

Sometimes in the early hours, I discover my friend Edward awake in Odesa. He is on Facebook's Messenger. I ask him if he is somewhere safe, in a shelter or basement. "No," he replies. Then: "Around 20:00 hours, two heavy shots sounded right next door to our house. It was our defense firing. I now live not far from the restaurant where you and I dined. My wife and three animals. I do not lose heart. We are not afraid." Then: "A few hours ago there were ten shots, very loud, so my head ached but we are not discouraged. We think it will be over soon." Later: "In Odesa there were several volleys from the sea and the air. In the city for a long time a siren and a distant bombardment were heard. My wife and I and our three pets—Santa, Puma, and Charlie—are calm and confident in our victory. We are waiting for the end of the war. Thank you for being with us."

October 2023. I begin texting, sometimes through the night, with a doctor who had taken shelter, first in the hospitals where he worked, and later in a white tent pitched in a city of tents in Gaza. He texts me about his work, tending to the wounded and maimed. He texts about sickness and disease, lack of food, lack of water, lack of medicine and medical supplies. He sends photographs and videos taken on his phone, and he tells me about his bombed house, his uprooted olive groves, his family, and the beautiful life they once lived in Gaza. His Ukrainian wife, whom he met while studying medicine in Odesa, had already been evacuated by the Ukrainian government, together with their five children. But without Ukrainian citizenship himself, the doctor had been unable to join them. When aerial bombardment of Odesa intensified, his wife and children fled again, taking refuge in Germany. I had begun working with a small group of friends in the United States and Egypt, who were helping people to cross the border at Rafah, and that is how the doctor was able to reach Cairo, where he is now enduring the very long wait for an appointment at the German embassy to plead for a visa to visit his family. He texts photos his wife sends him from Germany: his children in snowsuits, the littlest in a carriage. He sends a video someone took of him as he extracted a coin from the esophagus of a starving child.

April 11, 2024. The genocidal wars against the people of Ukraine and Gaza continue through the sleep of all who still live in safety. Lying awake at night I insist to myself that yes, this is happening again now, in the heart of Europe and in Palestine. What the Polish poet Czesław Miłosz wrote is true: "If a thing exists in one place, it will exist everywhere." There is nothing that cannot happen, nothing impossible where humanity is concerned. War is an old story. As for human survival and so-called civilization, there are no guarantees. In our times, everything senses that an end might come, that annihilation is possible.

We know that war destroys language, as it destroys everything within its zone of prosecution. Under conditions of such extremity, language is wounded, fragmented, cratered. It is put to military use in the creation of euphemisms that have become all the more sinister with the advance of technology. What is happening before our eyes is not "warfare" but a "military operation." Mass murder is "ethnic cleansing." In Ukraine and Gaza, there are no "shortages" of food, water, and medicine. These are deliberately withheld as a weapon of war. We say the "fighting began" as if on its own, and not in response to an order. We "come under" attack as if positioning ourselves by our own volition. While firing rockets at apartment houses, we speak of the civilian dead as "collateral damage" so as not to admit that we are intentionally killing noncombatants. War does not begin as a sudden occurrence, like an automobile accident. Preparations are made and can be seen from a long way off, like a storm on a horizon. Yet against this destruction, poetry is written in the midst of war and in its aftermath. As might be imagined, many of these poems do not survive. They disappear into the pockets of corpses and the drawers of demolished desks. The poems that do survive often have a strange tone: ominous and pleading, as urgent as an SOS or *m'aidez* sent into the night from a damaged ship. These poems are often addressed to the future, like messages in a bottle (Paul Celan) or to those who live in safety beyond the war zone. In reading poems as witness, we read all that the poet endured, all that she saw, felt, tasted, and smelled. These are reports from the human soul, from the depths of being—not factual dispatches such as would appear in newspapers, but "facts of art," attesting to the truth of the human experience. The poet writes as if making an incision in consciousness. At the site of this wound, language breaks, becomes tentative, interrogational, kaleidoscopic. But it endures. In the words of Paul Celan at Bremen: "One thing remained attainable, close and unlost amidst all the losses: language. Language was not lost, in spite of all that happened. But it had to go through its own responselessness, go through horrible silences, go through the thousand darknesses of death-bringing speech."

According to Miłosz, "The poetic act changes with the amount of background reality embraced by the poet's consciousness." Awareness of that background reality demands vigilance, this very wakefulness in the dark, and is sustained through the faculty of the empathetic imagination, by our ability to respond to hidden forces, to disturbances in the cosmos, the way horses run back and forth across a pasture before a storm, or migratory birds sense an early winter. The background reality for those who live far from the war zone is the war itself. It shares the darkness with us, the moment of night.

ALEXIS PAULINE GUMBS

Sea Grape Consciousness
FROM *Orion*

After the flood she consulted with her taproot, who said, Not yet, we will continue to hold the land. And she sent thinner roots out shallow. Spread wider so she wouldn't fall. She gave the fungus their message to carry. Reddened her veins to accept the salt. After the flood. Between floods.

Between floods her hands became sunshades and fans, green and cool. Better than flags, they beckoned thirstful pilgrims.

She knew what every tree knows from staying still and studying the sun. The refuge of her shade was of the moment, ever changing. And so she welcomed every erstwhile refugee with what she had. Her arms grew variably wider or narrower through the days. But she always kept them open. No one could mistake them for guns.

And maybe this was how she taught the people patience while everything was changing. Maybe this was how she trained her stressed-out symbionts to just let her ideas hover within reach until the end of summer when each idea achieved its fertility and fell.

And then the bird people and the lizard people and the lost people (that's us) put her grape ideas in their mouths. And just like that, her vitamin-rich wisdom flooded our immune systems. We were able to digest the whole situation better. Which was that another flood was coming. More wind.

Some people wouldn't be surprised that my best friend in Anguilla is a sea grape tree. *Coccoloba uvifera*. We grew up together. We grew wide together. We love the same ridiculous thing, which is a small strip of land between a bay and a salt pond that we know will one day get back together and just be one sea again. And yet we hold on. Awaiting the same failure. In the meantime, we ask each other how best to be as beautiful as we are. How to offer refuge at the end of the world, in the middle of a wet convergence. How to nourish passersby with whatever we have to give. We have become brown. Relatively thick-skinned. Tolerant of salt.

Immediately after surviving a hurricane that flooded her home, Audre Lorde wrote, "We have created [structures] as if they will last one thousand years. But wind is our teacher." During a hurricane, my relatives will line their cars up against the shoreline, knowing salt will rot the engines, a desperate collaboration with the sea grape roots to keep the land from washing away.

And so I listen to the wind as Cocco shapes it in her green and reddening hands, trying to learn something about the flood. I'm assuming that, even if you don't live at the shoreline (which I don't, most of the year), you know that the flood is coming. Flood as a context. The general increase in erosion-based floods caused by human overbuilding, the failure of dams against the older power of rivers, the massive rising of the ocean. Even if you don't live at the shoreline, you might soon.

I would recommend befriending a sea grape tree, or whichever of her cousins holds the world together where you live now. Or wherever you're about to go.

I'm sure I heard the word *flood* plenty of times in graduate school. But I only remember one time. I was starting a job at the writing center. I love supporting writers. I was at the training retreat along with the other new fellows from different departments. I was already imagining myself sitting in one of my favorite places, the library, listening eagerly to someone's project idea and supporting them to fulfill their creative and intellectual impulse. But there was a problem. The supervisor of the program casually mentioned that we would be required to guess—not to ask, but to guess—whether any of the people coming to us for writing help were international students, and to note that "information" (our baseless guess) in a special data file. As a member of an immigrant family, I was suspicious of the dubious requirement to surveil and guess citizenship status. Who looks "international"? Who sounds "international"? Is there a smell? Should I ask what each student ate for lunch?

I didn't articulate those exact questions that day. I simply asked, "Why?" The director of the program explained that it was just something they wanted to keep track of, so that the writing center would not be overwhelmed with international students, preventing domestic students from accessing the services. I remember the specific words she used then: *If you open the floodgates . . .*

And I had to get a different job.

This supervisor, so trained in US norms of expression that she ran a writing center at a prestigious university, used what she understood to be the perfect word to describe the fragility of xenophobic barriers to access: "floodgates." She was not being original or poetic; she was repeating an excuse for discrimination against immigrants heard routinely on the news and on talk radio. We should treat immigration as a possible flood. A threat of property damage. A reason for insurance.

Flood is not exactly the wrong metaphor for mass migration. Migration is natural. It is not a disaster. And a flood doesn't have to be a disaster either. As Toni Morrison reminds us, a flood is simply water remembering where it once was. But the human-caused rising of the oceans and battering of shorelines are becoming major drives for migration around the world. Even then, migration itself is not necessarily a disaster. It's the levee form of the scarce nation with a scarce amount of resources for a scared amount of people that creates a false blockage in the flow of life on land. It's the mistake of imagining that sand will stay still when it too migrates with the currents of the sea. It's developers building luxury homes with a beautiful view of the edge of the world on land that's about to fall into the sea. It's the thirty-year mortgage. The extractive corporation.

The colonial, anti-Indigenous insistence that our relationship to land should be the same through changing seasons and wider ecological changes. It's the fear of change itself. The denial that we will ever die. That's the disaster.

If I die first, will you bring what remains of me to the roots of *Coccoloba?* If she's gone, just throw my memory in the sea. Because I too am attached to particular places. I too want to stay and build community where I am. As of yesterday, I am even paying a mortgage. But what my sea grape sister is teaching me is that we have had the wrong teachers for too long. I have been learning how to be alive from dead structures, brittle and stingy institutions who lie to me every day about longevity. I need different teachers if I am ever going to learn the difference between surrendering and giving up.

Coccoloba uvifera wants me to remind you that her leaves are not flags. They are solar panels. Though she stands on the shoreline, she is not enforcing a border. Though she does not walk, she is as alive as any current. She does what trees do: turn the sun into sugar, creating the sweetest future they can so their seeds will travel somewhere, land well. She is practicing nutrition as migration. If we listened to the wind between her branches, the fungal symbionts at her roots, I think we could learn another way to be.

My Shinnecock ancestors and relatives write with oyster shells. They tell the future with the purple lining of the shells on the shoreline waiting to become sand. The name Shinnecock means "shoreline people," for their relationship with the shoreline that goes back many centuries at the very least. It is my belief that the Shinnecock and other Indigenous shoreline practitioners on every continent are best positioned to lead collective flood adaptation because Indigenous groups have remained in relationship to what a multispecies existence teaches us about change. Right now, Shinnecock water scholar Kelsey Leonard is advocating for the rights of water because, from a Shinnecock perspective, water is a relative, an ancestor, a source of life. Not a problem. Is the flood our family reunion?

*

Water is also a mirror. And if we truly reflect upon water, listen to water like the elder she is, she will tell us what we don't want to know about ourselves. That our species in its dominant mode of pretending to be separate from all other life is the destructive force, the threat, the encroachment, the disaster. But we don't have to be. The water in us has perfect memory. It remembers who our relatives are, it remembers how change feels, it remembers what makes life possible; it even remembers other life-forms and configurations of elements in the cosmos. And this is why I am not giving up. Instead, I surrender to the water within me, the flood coming through me, transforming my hands and my veins. I can learn to love this planet at the end of the world. And the edge.

CHRISTINA SHARPE

The Shapes of Grief

FROM *The Yale Review*

> ... but how, what would the world be with us fully in it ...
> —Dionne Brand, *The Blue Clerk*

1.

On May 14, 2022, Roberta A. Drury, Margus D. Morrison, Andre Mackneil, Aaron Salter Jr., Geraldine Talley, Celestine Chaney, Heyward Patterson, Katherine "Kat" Massey, Pearl Young, and Ruth Whitfield were murdered at a Tops Friendly Market in the East Side of Buffalo, New York.

Before and After Again, an exhibition currently on view at the Buffalo AKG Art Museum, presents those women, men, mothers, fathers, grandmothers, friends, children, aunts, cousins, uncles, daughters, sons, a deacon, a community activist, gardeners, people working, meeting, out buying groceries, and those who survive them, as people in their lives. *Before and After Again* shows people in relation and in community. Living. People loved and mourned. The artists and writers who curated the exhibition—Julia Bottoms, Tiffany Gaines, and Jillian Hanesworth—say that part of their challenge in presenting it was to "celebrate the vibrancy of extraordinary lives in the presence of a wound that will never heal." The curators are clear that this exhibition is meant to function as a gathering place and not as a memorial.

2.

At the annual literary festival NGC Bocas Lit Fest in April 2024 in Port of Spain, Trinidad, the writer Edwidge Danticat is in conversation with Elizabeth Walcott-Hackshaw. Someone in the audience asks a question about grief, which is really a question about life and more specifically a question about a writing life during grief.

In Danticat's memoir, *Brother, I'm Dying* (2007), which is about the deaths and lives of her father and her uncle while she was pregnant with her first child, she reflects,

> I write these things now, some as I witnessed them and today remember them, others from official documents as well as the borrowed recollections of family members. But the gist of them was told to me over the years, in part by my uncle Joseph, in part by my father. Some were told offhand, quickly. Others, in greater detail. What I learned from my father and uncle, I learned out of sequence and in fragments. This is an attempt at cohesiveness, and at re-creating a few wondrous and terrible months when their lives and mine intersected in startling ways, forcing me to look forward and back at the same time.

"I am writing this," she continues, "only because they can't."
Danticat writes with such precision and clarity about death and grief. The work is moving, and it is scrubbed of the sentimental and the maudlin.

3.

I am always rereading *Brother, I'm Dying* when I'm on an airplane.

There is something about the plane, its untethering space, between times and places, that allows me to meet so readily the many gifts of the book—among them language and memory.

4.

In the exhibition materials for *Before and After Again,* Jillian Hanesworth says, "Once we stop thinking about art as something that we're infusing into the situation to help us and instead we think about art as a living, breathing part of us, we understand that we're just being given this water, this air."

Danticat writes in her *New Yorker* essay "The Haiti That Still Dreams," "Art is how we dream."

5.

It is my sighs that give it away to myself. When I catch myself sighing, I remember that after my mother died, I sighed for years—it was a part of mourning that I had not known to anticipate. What I am experiencing now, what I think many of us are experiencing, is a kind of distributed mourning. R. calls it "ambient genocide."

I know that some call this feeling around climate catastrophe "climate grief." Kate Zambreno writes about grief as ecological, as "concerning both the individual and the collective, the human and the nonhuman."

When the climate is everything and the catastrophe everywhere and also somewhere(s) very specific, there is also climate rage.

6.

At Bocas, Danticat tells us that when she was writing *Brother, I'm Dying*, she looked forward to returning to it each day because in the pages of that book she got to visit with her father and her uncle. To spend time with them.

I know that grief is a vessel, a conduit for relation, but I am nevertheless startled into a new understanding when I hear that. Danticat expands what I understand grief to be and to make. She enlarges its shapes. Names it as connective tissue.

I feel, now, that I know differently the pain but also the possible joys of staying in the company of a loved and missed one through the work of remembering on the page, in the mind, in the world.

Language is one way we make and sustain relation. Words are one way we begin the work of unmaking and changing the shape of the world.

"Words are to be taken seriously," Toni Cade Bambara insists. "Words set things in motion."

That is the power of the iterative.

7.

In December, *Protean* published "Notes on Craft: Writing in the Hour of Genocide" by the Palestinian American writer Fargo Nissim Tbakhi. Tbakhi names "Craft" as "the network of sanitizing influences exerted on writing in the English language" by the professional contexts through which it circulates and acquires prestige, including universities and publishing houses: "the influences of neoliberalism, of complicit institutions, and of the linguistic priorities of the state and of empire." He continues:

> Above all, Craft is the result of market forces; it is therefore the result of imperial forces, as the two are so inextricably bound up together as to be one and the same. The Craft which is taught in Western institutions, taken up and reproduced by Western publishers, literary institutions, and awards bodies, is a set of regulatory ideas which curtail forms of speech that might enact real danger to the constellation of economic and social values which are, as I write this, facilitating genocide in Palestine and elsewhere across the globe. If, as Audre Lorde taught us, the master's tools cannot dismantle the master's house, then Craft is the process by which our own real liberatory tools are dulled, confiscated, and replaced.

Craft tells us that the market matters. Craft tells us to modulate our words. Craft tells us that if "we" do it well enough, "they" will listen. Craft tells us to be silent about genocide. To be silent about genocides, about antiblackness and white supremacy. "Craft," Tbakhi continues, "is a machine for regulation, estrangement, sanitization."

But Tbakhi also notes, "Anticolonial writers in the US and across the globe have long modeled alternative crafts which reject these priorities and continue to do so in this present moment." Instead of Craft, I think about work. The work that we, writers, are doing now as we try to attend to the violent world and also to what might be in excess of it.

What are the words and the forms with which to do and say and make what we need to live in now? Not only in some future time but now. *What is our work to be?* isn't a grand question. It is a simple question. The question at the base of our writing.

8.

Writers who try to do this work are told that our words don't matter. When we demand a ceasefire and an end to occupation, we are told that those words are meaningless, that they do not prompt action, and that they cause tremendous injury (as in, to demand a ceasefire or to demand that the genocide in Gaza end is to cause injury and not to demand the cessation of injury). To name a person, institution, state, or a set of acts as racist or anti-Palestinian or antiblack is to cause injury. It is not the racism that injures, it is not the bullets and bombs that injure, it is the words that seek to name the injury—that name a murderous structure like apartheid or settler colonialism—that cause injury.

Meaning is in crisis. And we are embroiled, everywhere, in contests over meaning—which are also contests of power, contests over living. And dying.

When Anne Boyer resigned as poetry editor of *The New York Times Magazine* in November 2023, she wrote on her Substack,

> Because our status quo is self-expression, sometimes the most effective mode of protest for artists is to refuse.

I can't write about poetry amidst the "reasonable" tones of those who aim to acclimatize us to this unreasonable suffering. No more ghoulish euphemisms. No more verbally sanitized hellscapes. No more warmongering lies.

If this resignation leaves a hole in the news the size of poetry, then that is the true shape of the present.

9.

This past academic year, as I prepared for class, I kept wondering how we were supposed to do our work and what that work should be. I wondered how the students in the class were supposed to do their work, even when the work that we were doing was relevant to what we are living through and trying to witness and to interrupt. We adjusted. We talked. We held space. We read. They were present. They showed up, and together we did our work.

In a three-hour seminar that I led at another university, I asked a group of students and faculty to read Steffani Jemison's "On the Stroke, the Glyph, and the Mark." It's a piece of writing that I both like and admire—her objects of inquiry, her sense making, and how she builds the essay through thinking and wondering.

Jemison's first sentence is: "I have made a mark, and I do not know whether I am drawing or writing."

Jemison is not talking about Craft.

She is talking about work. She is writing about writing/drawing/thinking/escape.

What is the work of composition, of mark making? What should our marks mark? Hold? Move toward?

The artist Joumana Medlej likewise moves between writing and drawing, perhaps also thinking of escape. She is making a mark in lieu of a name, in lieu of many proper names. She is making a mark for every murdered Palestinian. On March 17, 2024, she posted on X: "With 31,500 killed you-know-where so far, I was struggling with number blindness. When numbers become so large they lose all meaning, how do you remain awake to the scale of the slaughter & the personhood of the victims?"

From the artist Torkwase Dyson, I have learned (again and again) that the practice of mark making is a practice of navigation.

10.

We should rid our writing of the domestication of atrocity, rid our writing of the tense that insists on the innocence of its perpetrators, the exonerative tense of phrases like "lives were lost" and "a stray bullet found its way into the van" and "children died." We should rid our writing of this dreadful innocence. We should refuse the logic that produces a phrase like "human animals" and a "four-year-old young lady."

11.

Driving through the neighborhood where we are staying in Salvador in the state of Bahia in Brazil, we keep encountering a particularly long and steep hill. Our friend tells us that it is called Ladeira da Preguiça—the Steep Hill of Laziness.

Slave owners, those who claimed to own other people, named it that. This hill that they did not walk and that they made enslaved people walk up and down carrying heavy goods that they themselves would not carry.

The slaveowners in Brazil, like everywhere black (and blackened) people were enslaved (in Brazil that was until 1888), maintained that the people they literally worked to death were lazy.

And that steep hill that they were forced to ascend and descend, hour after hour and day after day, was named Lazy Hill. They were named lazy. This is devastating language, brutal language.

This is language that undoes.

12.

The descriptions of a prison in El Salvador. The description of a small boat that drifted across the Atlantic to Tobago. The plans to recolonize Haiti. The warnings that twenty-five million people in Sudan are at imminent risk of famine. The descriptions of massacres that Israel has carried out against Palestinians. The wide-open, shocked eyes of the Palestinian man abducted by the IDF. The descriptions of the Greek coast guard throwing people into the sea.

13.

What must we, as writers, animate and set into motion in place of such language?

In "The Sentence as a Space for Living: Prose Architecture," Renee Gladman writes,

> For all my writing life I have been fascinated with notions of origin and passage, though rarely in terms of ancestry—since I don't know where I'm from. I don't know the languages or landscapes that preceded the incursion of English and what is now the United States into my lineage. Yet, the violence of that erasure—all the inheritances interrupted—is as foundational to my relationship to language and subjectivity as is grammar. . . . I open my mouth in my own life and I want to distort, rearrange, mispronounce the available vocabulary.

Mispronouncing can rearrange language and open it up; distortion might be a way-making tool that undoes available vocabularies.

And a sentence can also be a space for living through an occupation or preoccupation with the line, with grammars and imagination.

14.

"Encampments are not only zones of demands & refusals, but also processes of communing, making decisions together, enacting solidarity as a verb, embodying autonomous & collective liberation. They are themselves zones of imagination, of connection, of pre-figuring life & new worlds."

This is Harsha Walia writing about the student encampments on campuses in the United States and Canada and France and the United Kingdom and elsewhere.

This is a vocabulary and a practice of our possible living.

15.

As I write this, the university where I teach has sent in riot police to disband an encampment that has been established for less than twenty-four hours. All the universities calling in riot police think that they know the future. They don't really know what they are making. They know what they want, but they do not know what they are incubating.

16.

Alexis Pauline Gumbs's "In the Middle of Fighting for Freedom We Found Ourselves Free" is a preface to June Jordan's remembrance of Audre Lorde, her sister in struggle. Gumbs is channeling Jordan's clarity about her and our perilous times. She writes, "The students are teaching us that, though we cannot undo the incalculable loss of genocidal violence, it is not too late. It is exactly the time to be braver together in service of a livable future. It is time for what June Jordan calls . . . 'words that death cannot spell or delete.'"

17.

After the Israeli bombing of Rafah on May 26, 2024, the hundredth or thousandth massacre in Palestine in seventy-six years, Jennine K writes on X, "The flour massacre, the tents massacre, the hospital massacre, the refugee camp massacre, the 'safe corridor' massacre, the endless massacres, in homes, on the streets, in tents, on foot—eight months of massacre after massacre after massacre." The poet Ladan Osman writes, "Who or what will cool the eyes of those who witnessed and recorded this carnage, saying: People of the world, look at this?"

Terrible acts. Unbearable. Who is called on to be a continual witness to the unbearable, to survive and carry it?

Each time I write that the genocide being carried out by Israel against Palestinians is unbearable, I name a position or positions. I name distance, because the Palestinians who are living this, those who are somehow surviving this, are bearing the unbearable, are being made to bear the unbearable over and over and over again. Their witnessing is a refusal to be silent in the face of genocide. More than that—they are necessary utterances in the midst of devastation.

In April 2024, I read that since October 2023, Israel has dropped over seventy thousand tons of bombs on Gaza.

Who can survive this? What survives of those who survive this, eight months and counting of constant terror? Those who move to what they are told is a "safe zone," only for that zone to be bombed?

Thousands of people, likely tens of thousands of people buried, alive and dead, under the rubble. I read in *The Guardian* that people report walking though the destroyed streets and having to bear hearing people calling for help and being unable to help them.

Selma Dabbagh writes in the *London Review of Books*, "According to the UN, it could take up to three years to remove the bodies from the 37 million tonnes of rubble in Gaza, which is also contaminated by unexploded ordnance, up to ten per cent of which, they estimate, 'doesn't function as designed.'"

Unbearable.

Unbearable, and entire populations are being forced to bear it anyway.

18.

At the end of May 2024, as we are on our way to the airport in Salvador, L. tells us that there are more than three million people living in the favelas of Salvador. He says that a majority of the black people in Salvador live in one of the many favelas and that it is less expensive to live there than in other neighborhoods or in social housing.

L. also tells us that 260,000 people disappeared during the most intense period of COVID. L. does not know where they went.

How do more than a quarter of a million people go missing?

These are economies of scale. Economies of value.

During the same trip to Salvador and on our drive from Salvador to Cachoeira, another friend, G., an architect and professor, tells us that the government moved many people to social housing, but they did so with little thought to how people were assigned to a place. They gave little consideration to the distances that people were being moved or to the infrastructure or lack of it. G. tells us that these moves broke up communities and families. She also tells us that, except for the people on the ground floor, no one in social housing had access to back gardens.

No possibility of extending space horizontally or vertically. That possibility to move up or out is one of the infrastructures of life in Brazil.

G. tells us about the *laje*, "a flat concrete roof." These kinds of roofs are considered by some to be incomplete. In the vocabulary of city officials, these structures are unfinished, an eyesore. But in another vocabulary, of those who live in them, the laje is the space of the possible.

They are not incomplete; they are a future promise. It is an architecture that reaches upward, that gestures toward plans. It is an architecture against the foreclosure of possibility.

19.

On June 5, 2024, Omar Hamad, a pharmacist, writer, and film critic from Gaza, writes the following on X: "Describing last night as a harsh night is inaccurate. Out of sheer fear, our hearts reached our throats, as if we wanted to vomit them out. The bombing didn't cease for a single moment. I don't know how the sun rose upon us again."

Not harsh. Something else. Some other word. Some other force of terror.

Each day I come to know even more clearly and urgently that we must commit to the fight for meaning. Not to concede the words, concepts, terms that we need to think and imagine and make livable lives.

This is some of what is required of our writing, some of what our writing can do, some of what our writing is for, in the face of all of this.

ANGIE ROMINES

Gone for a Spell

FROM *The Kenyon Review*

> Nobody really wants to keep secrets, not even the dead. People leave clues everywhere, and if you pay attention, you can piece them together.
> —Deborah Harkness, *A Discovery of Witches*

THEY SAY the Appalachian Mountains predate the dinosaurs, Saturn's rings, the oceans even. While the range itself is nearly 500 million years old, the rocks that form the Blue Ridge Mountains, on its eastern edge, are 1.2 billion years old. Although the snowcapped crags of the Rocky Mountains might strike some people as more impressive, the Appalachian Mountains rose up before a single living creature containing blood and bones walked on dry land. The rolling hills are not as sharp or as high as younger ranges because of their sheer age, millennia of erosion having smoothed their edges and ground down their peaks.

Appalachian Kentucky was my family's home for a long while—nearly two centuries—but the mountains have outlasted our time in those hills, as they have outlasted so many things. My father's side was there the longer, having left Virginia in the mid-1700s to settle in Southeastern Kentucky, fewer than one hundred miles from the Cumberland Gap. The last ones out were my paternal grandparents, aunts, and uncles, heading north to Indiana sometime after World War II, in search of factory work they never really found. My family's two-hundred-year stint inhabiting the various hills and hollers of the Cumberland Plateau in Eastern Kentucky was a blip, a sneeze in the lifespan of those weathered-down, tree-covered mountains. And yet, we were there. For a spell. And now we're gone.

My great-great-great-grandmother became a midwife by accident. In 1974, twenty-five years after her death, an article written by Kathleen Brown Lawson appeared in the *Menifee County Journal* about her unofficial midwifery practice. The twenty-year-old Mary Etta Sorrell Brown had gone to visit a neighbor in the mountainous, heavily forested backcountry of Eastern Kentucky, just north of the now popular rock-climbing mecca of Red River Gorge. Her neighbor went into labor during the visit, and a doctor was sent for. No one knows why the doctor never came, but Mary Etta was there to catch her first baby in 1885, and she didn't stop catching them (or dressing the babies, as the colloquialism went) until close to the end of World War II. My great-great-great-grandmother offered her layperson midwifery services for free, often accepting a piece of smoked meat or a bag of ground meal as a thank-you. When asked why she chose to take her little black satchel deep into the woods to deliver those babies, she simply said, "I've got girls of my own, and it crosses my mind that if it was them, I'd want somebody [there]."

For the birth of my second son, we had only a twenty-minute drive through the city of Columbus to the Ohio State University's hospital. By the time we hit the hospital exit, I was convinced that I was about to have a car baby. My husband pulled right in front of the building and left the car there instead of parking. He grabbed me a wheelchair, and I melted out of the passenger seat. Based on what the intake staff could observe of my gray face, drenched in sweat, they decided I looked miserable enough to be taken straight back to the room where they would check to see how many centimeters I had dilated, my body writhing as the contractions rippled over me with hardly any breathing room in between. I was a pile of person in that wheelchair being rolled down the hallway to the triage room.

Time to check under the hood. "Eight centimeters," the nurse said quietly. I knew I needed to be seven or fewer to get an epidural. I knew I was beyond any help or salvation. And still I asked, begged. As they put me back in the wheelchair and pushed me across the hall to a delivery room, I began chirping as loudly as I could, "Epidural, epidural, epidural," my voice watery and weak.

"Oh my god, is there a bird in here?" asked the young nurse pushing my wheelchair. She looked up at the high ceiling, craning her neck to peer at the exposed steel beams.

"No, it's her," answered my husband, pointing at my curled form in the chair. "She's asking for an epidural."

We all laughed a little until the next contraction hit me like a two-by-four cracking across my backbone. *This is my body, broken for you.*

> The great mass of evidence, from whatever quarter, declares a profound connection between witchcraft and womanhood.
> —John Demos, *Entertaining Satan: Witchcraft and the Culture of Early New England*

As a layperson midwife, Mary Etta Sorrell Brown delivered nine hundred infants. The article in the *Menifee County Journal* states that just one single baby did not survive, because it was born with a split spine, a condition we now call spina bifida. The March of Dimes statistics show that the current newborn mortality rate in Kentucky is around six infants for every thousand live births. Mary Etta Sorrell Brown's rate was significantly less than that without any of the tools of modern medicine and, in most cases, without access to running water. While the article didn't specify what exactly she carried with her in the small black satchel she brought to each delivery, the supplies couldn't have been more than some alcohol for sanitizing, some clean rags, and perhaps a knife or some shears for the umbilical cord. I imagine her greatest tool was simply her presence, her willingness to come when called and stay until it was over.

Mary Etta's infant mortality rate—the loss of just one single infant over a fifty-nine-year midwifery career—is not only a statistical anomaly, it's virtually unheard of. And yet, I don't believe that Mary Etta Sorrell Brown, a deeply religious woman married to Green Berry Brown, a Church of God minister, would have lied about such a thing. My sister, who tends to be more open to the mystical, thinks the unfathomable live-birth rate of Mary Etta could mean that our great-great-great-grandmother was a hill witch, that even staunchly Christian people can fold ancestral rites and practices into their faith to create some sort of amalgamation of a belief system.

A hill witch or a granny witch is a well-known figure in Appalachia. She is typically an older woman in the community who uses herbs and homeopathic remedies to help heal families and neighbors in the holler. In the past, some women, for all intents and purposes, were practicing granny witches but as good Christian women would never have called themselves such. Many of them used (and still do use) a blend of traditional herbal remedies and faith healing, a Christian practice found predominantly in charismatic denominations. The Church of God, which Mary Etta and her minister husband, Green Berry, belonged to, is a Holiness-Pentecostal denomination that leans heavily on the power of faith healing, calling parishioners up to the altar and asking them to drop their crutches and walk. The lines between mysticism and the Christian faith are especially blurred in charismatic churches. The handling of snakes, the drinking of poison, the speaking in tongues, traditions sanctioned by a good number of Appalachian Pentecostal churches, are not terribly different from spiritualist practices of communicating with spirits or moving objects with the mind.

When I was growing up in evangelical schools in the Y2K era, spiritualist objects like the Ouija board and tarot cards were seen as "of the devil." Yet spiritualism, as it was practiced in its heyday at the end of the nineteenth century, was often interwoven with Christianity. Rather than seeing spiritualism and its gifts as antithetical to Christianity, around the time Mary Etta Sorrell Brown was catching babies down in Kentucky, it could be seen as an enhancement, a booster to the traditional Christian faith—when practiced in the spirit of light, not the spirit of darkness.

> Thou shalt not suffer a witch to live.
> —Exodus 22:18

While many granny witches offered healing and divination aid to those in need and were considered valued members of their small communities, some could also have a sinister side. As in *The Wizard of Oz*, there are good witches, and there are bad witches. The Latin term *maleficium* refers to a particular type of sorcery or witchcraft that brings harm to others. The power of the devil is said to be used in this type of magical practice, where witches are reported to transfigure themselves into animals, bring blight to crops, maim livestock, and cause torturous pain or even death to those who cross them. Nearly fifteen years after Mary Etta caught her first baby, two counties north of her home, another possible hill witch with a reputation for maleficium was burned alive in Rolph Holler, Fleming County, Kentucky. According to a collection of oral narratives gathered by Daniel Rolph about his family in the eponymous "holler" around the turn of the last century, there were three sisters—Hulda, Mariah, and Sal Collins—who were known throughout Rolph Holler as witches. Rather than denying or downplaying the community's accusations of witchcraft, the Collins sisters seemed to enjoy the power that came from the label. They used the superstition of their neighbors to influence those neighbors to do their bidding and stay on their good side if they didn't want their livestock cursed or their bodies hurt.

Oddly enough, the witch hunt seems to have been spearheaded by Hulda's own son, Wash Lamar, who claimed that his mother had turned him into a cat and that he had "come to" on the roof of their house after climbing up the chimney when he was in cat form. He also said his "old maid aunts" often were transfigured into cats after taking hold of a broom. He was said to have taken to paddling his aunts as punishment for "collecting herbs for [the] diabolical." Some residents of the holler claimed that Hulda and her sisters were practitioners of "image magic," saying they had a chair they would stick sharp pins into whenever they wanted to cause pain to someone who had crossed them, until the offending party would come crawling and screaming to the witches, begging them to remove the pins and end their torment. Mariah and Sal Collins died seemingly natural deaths in the 1880s, with one local doctor noting that Mariah's "legs and arms were drawn up like [those of] a cat in its death grip," a supposed posture assumed by a witch in death.

And then, for unclear reasons, just before the turn of the last century, the remaining Collins sister, Hulda, was burned to death in a remote Kentucky holler on a wooden platform that her son, Wash Lamar, most likely helped build. One of the writer's relatives, a midwife and granny witch named Sarah Smithers Rolph, was particularly disturbed by the burning of Hulda Collins Lamar, since she also was called a witch by the people of Rolph Holler because she used herbs in healing. As Sarah walked home with her daughter Rose after delivering a child, they witnessed "the smell of burning flesh and the screams of the woman" and rushed on their way before they could be burned alongside their neighbor. What it must've been like to go out to their next delivery, knowing that the aid they were offering a laboring woman could mean their end, with their own lingering ashes carried away on the wind.

> But all the magic I have known, I've had to make myself.
> —Shel Silverstein, "Magic"

The four of us, back when we were girls, had been raised by evangelical parents who feared witchcraft and who had sent us all to the same Baptist school, Blackhawk Christian, in Fort Wayne, Indiana, where we had clung together as friends. Emily and I found each other first, in kindergarten. Aubrey was folded in just after eighth grade, when her Quiverfull parents (fundamentalists, like the Duggars) finally allowed her to leave their strict homeschool setting and attend our small Christian school. Kimmy was the last girl to join. Just before our junior year, her parents pulled her from the only other evangelical school in our Indiana town to come to Blackhawk, since our school was more academically rigorous, and Kimmy was the smartest person any of us had ever met. Still is.

When the four of us were together, we were safe, whole, untouchable. This was life-giving at Blackhawk, which was not kind to girls in the late nineties and early aughts. We were all there as we sat through assembly after assembly, teachers and administrators telling us that the bodies God had given us to inhabit were stumbling blocks to the boys and men in our life. One administrator, while dictating how wide the straps of our tops needed to be, told us: "You girls are making it hard to be a male teacher around here." The girl who had gotten pregnant out of wedlock her senior year had been tasked with apologizing to the entire student body at chapel before being expelled. The boy who had gotten her pregnant graduated with the rest of his class as if nothing had ever happened. We were there as girls together, listening to chapel speakers tell us that we would need to submit to our husbands one day, before heading off to algebra. No one can understand us the way we understand one another. Perhaps this feeling of the familiar, in the sense of a creature that is soul-linked to a witch, is why we were not frightened as we dipped into the occult, holding on to each other as we had all along.

In the San Jacinto Mountains of California last June, I was at Aubrey's head, gripping her shoulders, while Kimmy was at her feet, gripping her ankles, the two of us grounding her according to the directions we had found by googling which chakras we were supposed to hold a pendulum over. Emily, my friend of more than three decades, hovered above Aubrey's splayed-out body, allowing her pendulum she had just purchased at a witchy shop in Idyllwild to whirl around Audrey's core area, making wide, frantic circles.

"Emily, I can see your wrist twitching. You're moving the pendulum," I said with an eye roll. "You're supposed to let it dangle and let *her* energy move it." In spiritualist circles, this is a very common argument in with the ideomotor effect—meaning that a subject might move their body reflexively, without any direct intention or consciousness.

"I swear, I'm not," said Emily, but I released Aubrey's shoulders and clutched Emily's wrist to make sure. Aubrey was trying to decide if she wanted a second child, five years after the birth of her first. The rest of us were done having children, so this question felt very important. The last baby.

"Just hold it out over her womb," said Kimmy, giggling as she had been doing all day. We tended to revert to the younger versions of ourselves when we gathered.

"I swear, I'm not doing this," Emily said as I still gripped her wrist. I wasn't convinced that her pinched fingers holding the fulcrum point of the pendulum weren't facilitating the whirling rhythm, but I had to admit, the pendulum seemed to dance around Aubrey's flat, empty stomach.

While Emily's was the most active, each one of the pendulums we bought in town gave a *yes* over Aubrey's womb when we asked if she should have another child. Not that we took any of it seriously. To do so might be inviting the evil spirits in to play, something we had been warned against for as long as we could remember. Looking back, I still don't know if Emily was making the pendulum circle Aubrey's womb when we had our harmless, silly foray into witchcraft in California last year. But I do know that a few weeks after we returned to the different states in which we live, Aubrey sent us all a video message telling us our little game had worked. The last baby was coming.

> Seven generations of my family are buried in Kentucky soil, and among these are the bodies of my own two children. In America, much had been done for city children, whereas remotely rural children had been neglected. My work would be for them.
> —Mary Breckinridge, founder of Frontier Nursing Service

From the time I was just a toddler, my mother, who was a nurse, trained me to go into the medical profession just like her. At night as she lay down with me for a bit, she would tap different body parts—my knee, my jaw, my finger—and I would tell her the correct terminology—patella, mandible, carpals and metacarpals. Unfortunately, even though I have an inherent drive to be of service to others, the mere thought of veins makes me pass out, so I became a teacher instead of a doctor. My mother became a teacher too: in addition to practicing medicine, she is a professor of nursing, and she was the one who gave me the crudely photocopied article from the *Menifee County Journal* about our baby-catching ancestor. When I asked her if she knew any more about Mary Etta Sorrell Brown and her lay practice than what was in the article, she told me she didn't but to look up Frontier Nursing Service, a midwifery school that was founded in rural Kentucky and one that my mother, in the past, looked into attending to become a midwife herself.

Southwest of Menifee County, less than an hour from the Tennessee border, lies Hyden, Kentucky, the county seat of Leslie County and the birthplace of the Frontier Nursing Service, or FNS, which was founded by Mary Breckinridge in 1925. Though the first midwifery school in America was established in the mid-1700s, Frontier was the first to deploy nurse-midwives— medically trained professionals who specialized in childbirth. For this field to have originated in rural Eastern Kentucky and not in an East Coast city is something of a miracle. Women in the FNS program were put to work in the field, riding on horseback through inclement mountain weather to reach their laboring patients.

Mary Breckinridge was from an "Old South" family: her grandfather served as the final secretary of war to Confederate president Jefferson Davis. Her legacy is complicated by this heritage and by her support of eugenics (as is the legacy of Margaret Sanger, founder of Planned Parenthood). Even though she came from a political dynasty and a family of means, she chose to train as a nurse in New York City before returning to the South to marry and raise a family. By all accounts, Mary Breckinridge was wholly devoted to the concept of motherhood, even writing articles for *Southern Women's Magazine* on the subject, but her own time as a mother was destined to be short-lived. Her daughter, born prematurely, lived just six hours. Her lone remaining child, a son, succumbed to a fatal illness soon after his fourth birthday.

Twelve days after the death of her son, Mary Breckinridge volunteered for and was accepted into the nursing service of World War I. While stationed overseas, she divorced the father of her deceased children, became a certified midwife at the British Hospital for Mothers and Babies, and observed how midwives in the Highlands were able to provide care to women in remote areas of Scotland—a model she would reproduce in Eastern Kentucky. When the midwifery model crossed an ocean with Breckinridge after the war, there was a very sound geographical reason why the Highland practices could be mirrored in Appalachia: they are the same terrain—the same mountains. Fifty million years ago, when tectonic plates crashed into each other one time too many, the Scottish Highlands were cleaved from the Appalachian Mountains, creating two sister ranges, thousands of miles apart.

It's doubtful that Mary Breckinridge had any knowledge of this link, considering the concept of Pangea had only very recently been theorized when she formed her midwifery school. Using her family's old-money connections paired with the desire to support mothers and babies, possibly in response to the motherhood she had lost, Breckinridge created the Frontier Nursing Service. Because there was no official school of nurse-midwifery in the United States at the time, many of the midwives traveling by horseback in Eastern Kentucky to deliver babies were imported from England, Ireland, New Zealand, and elsewhere. These women, dressed in dusty-blue military-style uniforms, were a civilian cavalry of sorts, following nervous fathers through streams, forests, and hollers to reach laboring mothers. Their unofficial motto was "If he can get to me, I can get to her." The midwives became so closely associated with childbirth that Kentucky children were told that babies came not from the stork but from the saddlebag of an FNS midwife.

Frontier Nursing Service midwives' care of rural mothers and their babies led to Kentucky having some of the lowest infant and maternal mortality rates in the nation. Part of their success lay in their holistic approach of treating the entire family and environment that the child was being born into. Inoculations, snakebite treatments, and more were the purview of these rural medical professionals. The level of postpartum care mothers in the Frontier Nursing Service's territory received was jaw-dropping even by modern standards. A laboring woman could count on a midwife to stay in her bedroom with her for the duration of her delivery, whether that was hours or days. New mothers and their newborns were visited in-home by FNS midwives once a day for ten consecutive days after the birth.

I felt fortunate that my insurance offered one postpartum in-home visit from a nurse a few weeks after I gave birth to my second son. I knew I was not okay, but I didn't know how to explain what was wrong with me, how to name it. The pain of that precipitous labor had been so great that my brain did me the courtesy of blocking out large swaths of that memory. My body, however, remembered it all. In the months after giving birth for the last time, I experienced debilitating migraines (the postpartum nurse could not recommend any medication beyond ibuprofen since I was breastfeeding), panic attacks, and the inability to choke down solid food. When I told my primary care physician about my panic attacks and that I was losing huge handfuls of hair every time I showered, she laughed at me, saying I was nine whole months postpartum—after all, she was six months postpartum and doing absolutely fine. On paper, I should've been fine. My "natural" delivery of my son was quick and without complications. I had a supportive, domestic workhorse of a husband, and my nurse mother, who drove over to Ohio from Indiana to check on me often. I had paid leave to rest and recuperate. And yet, my mind turned on itself. I felt as if my body had been carved away from my soul and was then hastily pasted back together without care or thought. I remember walking to the bathroom a few weeks postpartum and thinking to myself, *I wonder where I am right now.*

I can't help but imagine what that time of motherhood would have looked like if a midwife had stayed with me by my bedside. If I had had a knowledgeable witness to my state of unwellness who could actually have helped me or at least made me feel less alone. I might have had more than two children, or at least been able to take a full, deep breath after delivering the two I did have. My suffering could've been made smaller, my load less heavy, if someone, anyone, who knew what she was doing, had been there to see me through to the other side. How is it possible to have felt more isolated and beyond the reach of aid as a city mother in the twenty-first century than those Leslie County, Kentucky, mothers felt a hundred years ago, knowing a midwife on her horse was thundering through the woods to get to her in time?

> In th[e] matter of witchcraft . . . public opinion is supreme. . . . Witch-hunting never flourishes unless the common people are eager for it.
> —George Lyman Kittredge, *Witchcraft in Old and New England*

On June 15, 1648, Massachusetts Bay Colony midwife Margaret Jones was executed by hanging from an old elm tree. According to the journal of Governor Winthrop, at the "same Day and Hour she was executed, there was a very great Tempest at Connecticut, which blew down many Trees." In neighboring Connecticut Colony, the first settler-recorded tornado occurred at the exact same moment as the first execution of a midwife in the American colonies.

> We went outside and there was just nothing left. West Liberty was gone. It was just gone. We felt like we didn't have a chance. We had just paid our rent early that morning. I want to go home so bad.
> —Teresa Eldridge, quoted in "West Liberty, Kentucky, Virtually Destroyed by Storm," Hiram Lee and Ryan Rahilly, *World Socialist Web Site*, March 5, 2012

Mary Etta's daughter, my great-great-grandmother Lizzie Brown, was born in West Liberty, Kentucky, 129 years before a spring tornado outbreak would tear that small Appalachian town to shreds. Just after that deadly storm in March 2012, I drove through Menifee County to get to neighboring Morgan County, but at the time I hadn't known the county's name or that I had familial links to the land. People from those rural areas in Eastern Kentucky often refer to their county rather than their hometown, since the high schools are organized by county. As outsiders going by the news reports, we knew the area we were headed to—laden with pallets of water bottles, chain saws, and canned goods—just as West Liberty, the mountain town obliterated by an EF3 tornado that cut an eighty-six-mile path from Eastern Kentucky all the way into West Virginia, killing twenty-two Kentuckians.

Back then, I was still attending an evangelical church and Bible study regularly with my husband, working mental overtime to hush my doubts about the faith I was born into. My intent at the time was to focus on the good—the sense of community, the emotion I felt during worship, the opportunities to give of our time and energy in service to those who most needed it. As reports of the tornado's devastation spread throughout the country, we all watched the scenes of wreckage on our screens, wishing we could help. When one of the pastors organized a team of volunteers to go down from Columbus to help with cleanup, my husband and I both signed on. West Liberty was close to my husband's childhood home in Lee County, so the disaster relief felt a bit more personal.

We left Ohio early in the morning, and by that afternoon, our fifteen-passenger van was driving around West Liberty, looking for someone to assist. I'm not sure how we ended up on a wooded hillside, helping a woman in her sixties retrieve her personal belongings that had been ripped from her mobile home and scattered throughout the oddly unscathed forest. She had walked to her daughter's brick house next door before the storm hit, so she had survived. If she hadn't left her mobile home, she could've been one of the fatalities. I remember how heavy her clothes were as I picked them from shrubs and tree branches. They were leaden with rainwater and smeared with mud. We collected as much as we could, and the men took everything to a laundromat in town that had survived the storm. The women in the group were tasked with folding the warm, clean clothes before driving back up the hill to deliver the laundry to her.

During our time cleaning up in West Liberty, we heard a lot of stories that sounded like tall tales. Someone said that an elderly man was found dead, still sitting in his recliner. Someone else said that they had heard a man in downtown West Liberty was hunkered in the basement with his family and thought the power had come back on, since a bright light shone above him.

But when he looked up, he understood that it was the sky he saw, the sun piercing through the winds swirling and roaring above him. We heard that one of those wooden signs people have on their porch, saying things like THE RIVINGTONS, EST. 1987, was lost from a home in West Liberty and found deposited in the mud in West Virginia.

At the time, I was confused by how a tornado could even happen in the Appalachian Mountains. As someone who had grown up in the Midwest section of Tornado Alley, I knew a flat expanse of ground is what a tornado needs to take and maintain shape along with speed. To protect yourself from a tornado is to go down, below the flat plane where the tornado thrives. Hunker underground in your basement. If you don't have a basement, as our childhood home did not, your mother can plop you into an empty bathtub with your sister and put a twin mattress over the top of you, hoping the plumbing anchored in the ground will help hold you in place. If you're caught in a car during a tornado (one of the most dangerous scenarios), you're supposed to find a ditch, some sort of recess in the earth, to tuck yourself into while the storm passes over you. The landscape of West Liberty, located in the foothills of the Cumberland Mountains, should not have supported a mile-wide tornado for eighty-six miles. And yet, it had.

The town of West Liberty was too quiet when we drove through. FEMA had spray-painted numbers on the houses to denote how many survivors were accounted for. The capriciousness of the storm could be seen in a perfectly intact home left standing next door to its neighbor's pile of rubble. We slept on the floor of a church in a neighboring town, in a room where children are taught about the Flood and Daniel and the Lion's Den on Sunday mornings just as I had been taught decades before. At another church, on top of a hill in West Liberty, we were fed by a group of parishioners as we took a break from our tornado cleanup. Two middle-aged women in FEMA jackets sat down at the table with us, smiling politely before tucking into their lunches.

But while many churches in the area stood tall after the storm, with their pastors, I'm sure, crediting God's sovereignty in sparing the house of the Lord, West Liberty United Methodist church was absolutely leveled by the gale-force winds that struck the town. The white brick church with its modest steeple was just one year away from its one-hundredth anniversary when the tornado ripped its bricks from their mortar. A new church was built in its place three years later, using stained glass, a handful of chairs, and the old bell salvaged from the destroyed historic building. And so, God is praised for sparing so many churches and homes. He is praised for allowing the rebuild of West Liberty United Methodist. Either way, God wins. Those who died are in heaven with Jesus, and those who were spared still bear Him witness on this temporal earth.

I don't go to church these days for a lot of reasons, but the easiest to explain is that I don't believe in God. The concept of a being that wants your family to find the perfect Siesta Key condo for spring break but who lets your neighbor's toddler die of a brain tumor is just not one I'm willing to entertain anymore. I don't think tornados are punishment or God's will or anything more than wind without purpose or reason. I don't think hill witches were supernatural beings so much as they were women like Mary Etta, who remembered the women who came before her and pulled from that generational knowledge to guide new mothers along their way.

But there are things about the believer's life, about belief in big and unnameable things, that I miss. I miss how easy it was to help people. How you could just fold yourself into a group of parishioners and paint a safe house for victims of human trafficking or collect a shaken woman's magenta terry cloth robe and jean shorts and fold them extra carefully for her because she's been through enough. It's disorienting. My hands and my mind don't know what to do with themselves these days. If I have a soul, I don't know what it's for if not for saving.

> The illusion, however, was perfect while it lasted.
> —H. Wedgewood, in Reuben Briggs Davenport, *The Death-Blow to Spiritualism*

At the end of her article about Mary Etta Sorrell Brown in the *Menifee County Journal*, Lawson takes too sentimental a turn for my taste, particularly for a journalist. Lawson writes, "Mary Etta Sorrell Brown left us to go be with her Savior, whom she had served so faithfully for so many years. But in the hearts of those who loved her and in the many lives she helped along rough ways, she will always live. Her unselfish devotion to others has left footprints that can never vanish from our lives." While my first reaction to this passage was to roll my eyes at the saccharine, I do wonder what it would be like to have someone write, a quarter of a century after my death, that I had helped others along rough ways. That my life had been one of service and faith. That there would be an echo of me and the work I did for others, after I was gone.

There is an ease, a comfort in the idea of being guided down the right path by an outside, benevolent force. But when I start to think like that, I have to also wonder that if the faithful, the blessed, are guided along by a sovereign hand, then who guided that funnel cloud from my great-great-great-grandmother's home in Menifee County through Morgan County, until it stopped in Lincoln County, West Virginia? Who knit together that single infant Mary Etta lost during delivery, its spine split in two for no good reason? Who watched, doing nothing, while hundreds of women, so-called witches, were burned alive in His name, for His vengeance? Rather than believe in a God capable of such indifference, such evil, I think I believe there is just us, here, together.

My younger son, my last baby, was born on my thirty-second birthday. He loves hearing his birth story. His sweet little cheeks bunch up in a grin when he asks, "Remember the first birthday gift I ever gave you? It was me being born! Remember how you said I came out? Like a cannonball shooting right out of you."

Unfortunately, the birth descriptor isn't really hyperbole. A cannonball, or perhaps its larger cousin, a bowling ball, launching itself from my body in one horrific, screaming surge was exactly what it felt like. The nurses were yelling at me to *Stop! Stop! Stop pushing!* as if I had a choice. As if the Appalachian Mountains and the Scottish Highlands could've clung to each other all those millions of years ago, not allowing the Atlantic to come between them. The nurses hollering at me were trying to buy the on-call resident some time, but there was no time to be had for her. With one jagged motion, I rolled from my side to my back, and my son burst into this world, right into the doctor's hands. Only one of her hands was gloved. There was no time. No time at all. But her hands were there, ready and unready in the same moment.

When I was a child attending evangelical schools, the image of Christ's nail-pierced hands was offered up by my teachers as a symbol of eternal love and sacrifice. It's a wonder to me that a man was placed at the center of the faith—a symbol of giving it all, until everything he had ever been was gone, to be made new again. In real life, in all the stories passed down by our mothers and grandmothers from the times before, those who gave everything were nearly always the women.

A lot of comfort and respite comes from being a person who believes in a higher, benevolent power, a peace that I can no longer access even if I wanted to. There are no giant invisible hands nudging me this way and that. No hands but my own, here, lying in my lap, palms facing up toward the heaven I no longer believe in. Hands that painted flowers on a gift for Aubrey's last baby, whom we like to pretend we conjured up in the San Jacinto Mountains that bright June day. Hands that tuck my sons into their bunk bed at night, knowing they won't lie awake imagining hell as I did when I was half their age, because I've made sure that no one has taught them what hell is. Hands that are mine to move with, to reach with, to grasp with, to let go with. And isn't there more than a little bit of magic in that?

LAURA GLEN LOUIS

Man Crossing an Ice Field

FROM *The Massachusetts Review*

HE HAD just come back from hut-to-hut hiking in Austria, and I was dragged out by a coworker who thought I had mourned enough for a man she had dismissed with a shrug. The Greek Taverna was in full Saturday-night swing, with the clarinet snake-charming the Kalamatianós, that sexy, quick-slow-slow handkerchief dance. Lines sinuated around the dance floor. Sweat flew. Two men cut across from the far side. I turned to leave. My friend blocked my exit. He got there first, was better dressed, had moves, and stood straight enough for me to forgive both the nylon of his tight shirt and the blue flamingos preening on it. He pulled me into the chain. I had enough folk dance to fake it. Perhaps sensing my reserve, he proposed not dinner but the less loaded lunch. It turned out we lived only eight blocks apart, though one of those blocks was half a mile long. I was barely formed, vacillating between medical school and film studies. He not only had a job; he had a career, a purpose, a passion. One date led to another, decades passed. In between we rafted rivers, hiked deserts, skied mountains, argued about foreign films and the duty that comes with the privilege of citizenship (he then still a tax-paying alien). We threw parties, poled under the Bridge of Sighs, sailed on Lake Zürich, read in the Luxembourg Gardens, burnt our first Christmas ham, married, had a son, three rats, four cats, one dog, and got some sand between our toes.

He was fond of saying, "Life begins at forty," which was about the time he and his first wife divorced. I thought him younger and he thought me older, which is to say we both perceived the gap in our ages to be about the same and much less than it was. Once I realized how old he was, it was too late. He was the most protean man I'd ever met. And he loved my father. His mother died of cancer at sixty-three, his father of a heart attack at seventy-one, and I wondered if I could handle being widowed in my fifties. I *was* widowed in my fifties, but not in a way I could have imagined.

If I mentioned butternut squash soup, he'd place it on the table, having first tempered the sweetness with cauliflower. He knew that to feed me well was to win my short attention span. He taught himself plumbing, carpentry, electrical, serigraphy, drove a blue MGB GT. He skated backward, encouraging his kids onto the ice, he skied, he cycled. Can you fall in love with someone for how he leans into a corner or how he dismounts while still in motion, throwing a leg over the crossbar? A man in motion is a thing of beauty.

Maybe the rift started with the arrival of our child sixteen years later and my need as a nursing mother to eat dinner before midnight, which necessitated my taking over the kitchen. He was an inventive cook, but he no longer cooked for me, ergo he no longer loved me. Were it so simple. While I struggled on five or six hours of sleep shepherding our son, he took a mistress with whom I could not compete: his research. A friend ten years ahead of me in motherhood told me that children were divisive, leaving me to count the ways. They didn't have to be, but I was later sorry to find myself in her camp. This same friend later said of herself and her ex-husband, "I mourn the people we once were."

While I was out walking the dog, the disease crept up and eased its fangs into my husband. Like fissures, trace and silent, the incremental changes in reasoning escaped me. We all misplace keys. Not normal were the assumptions and accusations that our son or I took them. Cluelessness would be a cliché—brilliant scientist = absent-minded. The mind is absent. The mind is traveling at the speed of light, rounding Jupiter. It's swan-diving into black holes and pulsars and galaxies of ginormous dimension so far away we squash that vastness into compact, staggering powers of ten. He read, he wrote. Mostly he sat. The theorist, piqued by the unknown, by the luring riddles of the universe, seeks to explicate, to mortar answers with mathematical clarity, with equations, proofs. QED. The mind does not shut down because the host is reading Galileo or Gorky, crisping sweetbreads, or nailing drywall. From the subatomic—quarks, those tiniest bits of matter in the universe—to the *cosmos* (a six-letter word burdened with containing the uncontainable): here is where his mind ranged. And as he said more than once, "The universe is ever-expanding." Not just ever-expanding but expanding in *acceleration*. As we blink. Then he hopped off the ski lift and carved down KT-22, linking one turn to the next with dance-like elegance.

Some of us thrive because we are nurtured and encouraged, others because we are stymied, denied. His high school counselor told him to go to trade school because he wasn't smart enough to get into college. He went to college, on scholarship. Got his PhD, full ride. By the time I met him, he lamented that the significant research in particle physics was nearly exhausted, yet he had decades of productivity still to give. What to do? The man read astrophysics. Taught himself astrophysics. Who does that? The birth, fate, and order of the universe became his constant occupation. In time, he began publishing papers in this new field, prompting at an astrophysics conference the snide *What are* you *doing here?* and a defender's passing rejoinder *He just kicked in his afterburners.*

Yet this man—who had roamed in his imagination all over the cosmos, through whom I observed the beauty of the life of the mind, who shared my love of reading, wandering, art, music, and who taught me by example to embrace solitude, this man who never failed to impress with his unerring sense of north—this same man, when I asked him one day to pick up our teen son at his friend's house, said, *Yes, of course*, then returned a moment later, because he could not recall the classmate, his address, or where that street might be. This man, who had negotiated effortlessly in countries whose languages he did not read or speak, whose alphabets were, you know, *Greek*, now could not remember how to get across a town he had lived in for over forty years. No recognition. Cognition. Ignition.

Half a mile west of Steve's. A flicker. *You go down Claremont Avenue from Steve's garage.*

I watched with alarm as he struggled to gather into a coherent image our friend and his service station in the shadow of the Claremont Hotel and knew that something was horribly askew. The separation we had been in that was inching toward a divorce was instantly derailed. His internist ordered a cognitive assessment, and I was crushed to see my husband's hesitation when asked to count backward from one hundred by sevens, when physics rests imperatively on a bedrock of a higher mathematics for which most of us have no vocabulary or any hope of comprehension. Mild Cognitive Impairment. While not all MCI leads to Alzheimer's, all Alzheimer's brains begin their downward spiral with Mild Cognitive Impairment. I seized on the word *mild*, clung to it, while beneath this crackling surface lay a sinkhole large enough to swallow our entire family.

His neurologist prescribed a statin (as atherosclerotic plaque clogs the arteries, amyloid plaque clogs the brain) and medications to improve neurotransmitter function (memory, awareness, performing the tasks of daily living). Our ability to locate ourselves in the world depends on a spatial recall. Lost gradually, along with words and ideas, is the ability to envision. We can no longer see as far as before, can no longer form a picture of a vast distance. As our ability to visualize shrinks, our physical world also shrinks, along with our ability to find our way home. It was as if his imaginative exploration of the universe had bungeed past its elasticity and snapped. Hyperbole reared in inverse proportion to the atrophy of language, nuance, and the complex gray scale: *Best. Worst. Always. Never.*

There was the public him that he now strove to present: measured, reasoning, calm, gracious, articulate, *former*. The private him—the one he let only our son and me see, the one we lived with and protected, here at home where he felt safe to be his emerging, diminishing self—that person was evolving into someone we didn't recognize. Even after many years of slow decline, he would talk to his doctors about his research, about

ISIS, about Syria, about the 2013 Merkel reelection in Germany. He'd sit tall, alert, cross his legs, achieve such a complete semblance of his former self that I was questioning why we were at the doctor's office. The minute we left, he slumped and shuffled. The air went right out of him. That this deflation could occur over the few seconds it took to walk down a flight of stairs unveiled the mighty effort he exerted to present any picture of his former self for the few minutes he was in the presence of someone he considered an intellectual peer. Maddening that he didn't try that hard with us. But maybe he did. Maybe he was even more vacant when alone.

The doctor prescribed medications to moderate his inflammatory temper—the elephant in the room. We'd coast. Then the meds lost their efficacy, and we would be again broadsided by uncharacteristic outbursts from the Mr. Hyde that Alzheimer's engenders. The most challenging task was one I was profoundly unable to learn: redirect. Redirecting meant letting untruths stand unchallenged. Crazy-making also was that our son and I were the only witnesses to these aggressive behaviors. Even my stepdaughter, twenty-one years my son's senior, had never been subjected to her father's outbursts. But there was grace, at least for him: of the things he couldn't remember was his own aberrant, explosive fury.

When our son was still young, my husband began working longer hours, coming home for dinner in a rush, disappearing afterward back to his office. I thought it a phase and supported that ability to focus on his work. Yet maybe the flurry of productivity (three books in ten years) came from a glimpse that his days to do meaningful research were numbered, in ways that he, and we, couldn't begin to imagine. One day there was no ignoring the cumulative, escalating accusations ("Who threw out my papers?"), the vehement denial of truths ("What stop sign?"), the abrupt flare-ups, the bursts of rank profanity I had never heard from his lips, delivered with a hostility that made my head snap. (Fuck. Bitch.) One day I woke up and realized this was not the man I married.

For more than ten years we lived with a steady decline that we could no more arrest than we could rope a glacier. Author of a couple hundred scientific papers and five books (only two of which are accessible to readers like you or me), he could no longer follow his own brilliant train of thought. It was heartbreaking. To not recognize your own words is to not recognize your self. After one particularly harrowing exchange (triggered by a remark so innocuous I could not recall it moments later), I took my son aside, desperately trying to recall the man I fell in love with, wishing him to know his gentle, brilliant, dispassionate father as I did. "This is not your dad." My son snapped. "This *is* my dad."

He was right. The man I married was history. The plaque that chewed up his memory also ate away at his personality, as if he, and we along with him, were in an alien body-snatching movie. The man he was becoming was the one my emerging adult son knew: mercurial, repetitive, argumentative, adamantly insistent, quick to profane, and—equally hard to take—quick to tear up when he calmed down and reran in his mind what he had just so fiercely accused us of. Sadder than our loss of this man was his loss of himself.

For nine or ten months the antipsychotic drugs would work their leavening magic. Then the flare-ups resurfaced. Back to the neurologist to tweak his medication. After a few years, we finally got a cocktail that consistently stabilized his mood. Even at the ten-year mark, his decline was slow compared to others, due perhaps to early detection, or to his lifelong intellectual engagement, or to his continuing to read and read and read, everything from Amado to Mahfouz. Literature nourished and grounded him after the abstraction of physics. But perhaps his slow decline was due mostly to his continuing research, his writing. *I write, therefore I still am.*

Summer, at a dinner party years before our son was born, he and his Bombay colleague, both having spent their formative years as British subjects, cast a spell over our rapt table with their easy volley of Shakespeare: lines from *Julius Caesar, Hamlet, Macbeth, Henry V.* Not having taken notes, I'll evoke instead that evening's French movie aura with quotes from the movie *Quiz Show.*

Man Crossing an Ice Field

DAD (THE POET MARK VAN DOREN): "Some rise by sin, and some by virtue fall."
SON (THE WRITER CHARLES VAN DOREN): "*Measure for Measure.* Do a great right but do a little wrong."
DAD: "*Merchant of Venice.* Oh, what men dare do, what men may do, what men daily do, not knowing what they do."
SON: "*Much Ado About Nothing.* Things without remedy should be without regard. What's done is done."
DAD: "Things without *all* remedy. *Macbeth.*"

Things without all remedy. That was the trajectory he was on. Yet his illness was not something he visited on himself. He had not lied, cheated, plotted, lusted, murdered, smoked, drunk, or snorted himself to Alzheimer's. And while there is not guilt, there is shame: shame from diminishment, from the normal indignities of aging exacerbated by the new baseline that you cannot be trusted to be alone. Your capacity for analysis, for imaginative inquisition, for reasoning, is compromised, falling away faster than the coastline of the Maldives. *Capacity.* It's a legal definition. I was cautioned to not get mired in conservatorship and grateful he trusted me, conferring on me without hesitation the power of attorney. In exchange for that trust came even more responsibility. Like belaying.

Down the road of diminishment is not being able to perform the euphemistic "activities of daily living." It's a wasting. The surgeon with the shakes, the theorist whose mind is being eaten away, the ballet dancer who can no longer land a grand jeté (cf. New York City Ballet's Tanaquil LeClercq, sidelined at twenty-seven by polio). It's a wicked joke. We lose the very muscles and skills we relied on most to articulate and hone our passions.

Early on, when all our energy and patience were funneled into calming down his dad, our teenage son would say in fear and frustration, "Why do I have to be the grown-up?" A writer friend, herself having nursed a mother-in-law with Alzheimer's, asked, "Are you writing about it?" Tears threatened. "No! We're still in it." Her son, full of empathy, offered, one grunt to another, "It's aggressive. And regressive."

In their series on Alzheimer's, *The New York Times* announced one sunny morning that caretakers often do not outlive their charges. That was stark. My son was at risk. I was at risk. (It explained his anxiety every time I got a cold. *I can't do this alone*, he would say. *Of course not.* And I doubled my efforts to eat well, work out, sleep more, manage my stress.) While my girlfriends begged me to get help (we weren't that desperate), they didn't offer to spell me or spring me for a break. They were also tired of hearing about it. I don't blame them. The story changes only in that it gets worse. You want to look away, because this could be you. In either role. One girlfriend moaned about having to take care of her husband during his post-glaucoma recovery. "He can't drive. It's daily errands and doctors' appointments. I have to do everything. It's been weeks." Oh. *You mean like when he took care of you for months after your shoulder surgery? And again, after your second shoulder surgery? How long have you been married? Suck it up, girl.* Another *Times* article talked of the loneliness and isolation. Listen, people: Alzheimer's is not contagious.

My girlfriends also called me a saint. I'm no saint. This disease, like most, teaches you not to splat into hyperbole, in part because the patient's own language appropriates extremes. If I were having a particularly trying day, I'd retreat. Think of something much worse than the situation I found myself in. No bombs dropping on my town.

When our son was young, my husband suggested I quit my job, that writing was what I was meant to do, that we could tighten our belts, manage on his salary. My own personal Medici, he made possible the writing life. What cruel irony then that he not only encouraged, but supported, the writer who is now splaying him out as a victim of a disease she would not wish on her worst enemy.

In silence lives beauty and solace. In silence we can hear ourselves think, can work toward a solution, resolution, possibility, imagination. In silence we find the way to our best selves. But to *keep silent* is to suppress, to dwell in pretense. The not-speaking and the silence itself become what in *A Primer for Forgetting* Lewis Hyde says is an "unfinished task," those things that clutter our minds and subconscious with their unfinishedness and unresolvedness. They fester. Being declarative strikes the first blow in taming our demons. There is no shelter in denial.

During the witching hour, he would barrage me with questions as I was ever trying to get dinner on the table. One night he made a statement so irrefutably false I had to speak up. Big mistake. It triggered an iterative rant so complete that after a few minutes I stopped, vegetables burning, and began to doubt my own memory. Over his shoulder, I could see our son shaking his head, *No, Mom, you're right.* I took a breath, dropped the argument. I didn't need to win. I just needed not to feel like I was losing my mind.

When our son left for his final semester in college, I took a writing studio as sanctuary, as ballast. Every night I'd work a Sudoku puzzle, and when that failed to distract, I switched to KenKen. I needed to end the day with a solvable problem that tested not the polymath knowledge of crosswords but logic: a problem that demanded patience, looking ahead, weighing options, and holding them until the only possible unique pattern of numbers fell into place, like the coded rain in *The Matrix*. A problem that when solved restored momentary order so I could sleep.

With a humbling empathy, our son returned home after graduation to help me with his dad. Neither of us predicted that such generosity would keep him from forging ahead with his own life. The following years were a trial, years about which we later developed a symbiotic amnesia. Still I resisted moving his dad to assisted living. Was I waiting for some medical miracle? Or some medical catastrophe to relieve me of having to make that decision? What if catastrophe fell instead on me?

Whole Byronic verses still rolled off his tongue with the mention of any word from these opening lines: "My hair is grey, but not with years, / Nor grew it white / in a single night." The poem spirited us to dank dungeons, salt in our nostrils, rising tides, chains, starvation, lucky rats. The Prisoner of Chillon watches, helpless, as his brother wastes to death. Muscles atrophy, the body consumes its own fat to stay warm, skin slackens. You fall asleep from hunger and thirst, then wake to a skeletal structure that was once your brother; not unlike what my son and I were witnessing, but instead of the body, it was the mind. The word *three* tripped this: "They chain'd us each to a column stone, / And we were three—yet, each alone; / We could not move a single pace, / We could not see each other's face." His parting line to the front-desk staff whenever we went on an outing: "So, long. It's been nice knowing you." Once outside, "Freedom!" We laughed as I fought my guilt—for him feeling locked up, in a beautiful place with caring staff, but locked up.

Eight, nine years into it, he asks in all innocence, "Do I have Alzheimer's?" Like that, we shifted from denial to the beginning of acceptance. In the past, because he didn't own the disease, because he didn't want people to know, out of respect, I didn't talk about it. I was complicit. I knew silence. Silence is a cancer. If we didn't talk about *it*, it didn't exist (rape / the Japanese occupation / Alzheimer's). Out there, in the universe—*that's* silence. Once again, Rilke comes to mind. Or Les McCann and Eddie Harris singing: "Tryin' to make it real, compared to what?"

A friend asked, "How cognizant is he?" My husband asked me every time he saw me, whether out of genuine interest or because he didn't remember he had asked the day before, the hour before, "What are you working on?" a question whose curiosity and inquiry always moved me. One day I said, "I feel overwhelmed. I can't concentrate, can't decide what to work on; stories and essays demand my attention, poems need finishing." He said, "Laura, work only on what you love." Heartbreaking? Such clarity still?

I was twenty, and the young men three, fit, and full of cock. They came into the fabric store where I was working, alone. They locked the door, fanned out. Had me surrounded. More frightening than that was my husband throwing his shoe across the room, dark with rage, barely able to summon even a gram of self-control. Then there was the day when he cornered our adult son when I wasn't home, accusing him, again, of throwing away boxes sent home from the office, boxes of books, pre-prints, letters. He could not hear or remember that we had labeled all the cartons, attached an inventory to each, shown him where in storage those boxes were. He was convinced that we had thrown out something valuable, though he could not name what that something was.

Our son is six feet tall, young, agile, muscular, but of lighter build than his father, and his father was physically blocking his exit, his energy enlarging him in the doorway into not so much a physical threat but an emotional one. Son phoned. *You have to come home. Right now.* That should have been the last straw. I failed to protect my son while working overtime to take care of a man who could no longer care for himself. With me home as a buffer, my son regained his equilibrium. It was our fortune (or misfortune) that when one of us was losing it, the other was more tempered.

"Has he ever hit you?" A telling question from a fellow chorister whose mother had Alzheimer's. It would have been clearer if he had. Even more stark had he hit our son. The solution to move him to a home would have been inarguable. Still, we kept putting his needs before ours. On the most beautiful of days, the accusations would rear up from some innocent comment. But perhaps they weren't innocent. Attempts to "correct" his version of things sent him into a rage. (They would me, were I the one afflicted.) He yelled. I was the only other person in the room, ergo, he yelled at *me*. That cartoon where the poor slob has his clothes blown right off his body by another's rage? Like that. I felt increasingly on edge. Flayed.

You tamp your responses, and over time that tamping spills over into your response to the trials of the global unfortunate, to the plight of friends. I'm shamed in replaying these incidents, the most glaring being told by a dear friend that over the weekend her husband had a heart attack and was in hospital, ten years younger than I and much too young to have a heart attack, yet the news barely moved my needle. Nor did hearing of a swim buddy whose damaged mitral valve revealed her breast cancer. My empathy bank was depleted.

There was no big blowout, no pivotal event. We were buried

by accretion. Perhaps it was the talk I had with the husband of a friend, a man I had just met and with whom I had such engaged conversation that everyone else at the table got up and left. (In *The Names*, Don DeLillo said, "Conversation is life, language is the deepest being." This is the same big talk long missing in our marriage, stranded by Alzheimer's mind-numbing repetition.) I don't know how this man at the party got me going. He wasn't talking to his wife (who seemed barely able to keep from leaving him if he didn't stop drinking soon), but about me and our situation he had absolute clarity. "Laura, you have to set a deadline."

Perhaps it was my three concussions in three years. December 2012, I was following my son in his car back from the dealership, foolishly trying to keep up with him on the freeway, no problem on a good day but I was 103 degrees with flu and hallucinating. I missed a truck in my left blind spot, overcorrected, no, no, a big Mack on the right, overcorrected again, rocked the car back and forth as I struggled to stay in my lane and not flip, making life and death decisions at 70 mph, my brain ping-ponging in my skull. I shot a glance at my son ahead in the fast lane heading into an unbanked curve and prayed he was not looking in the rear view. My car finally righted. The trucks dropped back. I eased off the gas, coasted on mercy. Took the first exit.

My son pulled right up behind me. *Are you all right??*

Concussion. Whiplash. Did you see any of that?

I saw all of it. Then: *Thanks for being such a good driver.*

Was I such a good driver? I had gotten myself into that vise between the trucks. But the squeeze that is Alzheimer's is one you cannot correct for. There's no avoidance reflex, no pill, no exercise, no excising, no psychotherapy. Nulles. Na. Da.

A year later, I backstroked full-bore into the end of the pool (how even lifeguards drown), then couldn't remember the combination to the lock that I had opened before showering just minutes earlier. Swimmers found staff with a bolt cutter so I could retrieve my clothes. When my son picked me up, the ladies cautioned him to keep an eye out as I had been slurring my words. Eight months later, at the same party where Mr. Big Talk told me to set a deadline, I stood up too early while walking under a deck to a stairway under construction and compressed my neck. Traction, I needed traction—a week later I was driving toward the freeway and just knew. I bit the bullet (there's no anesthetic for this kind of pain). I pulled over, called my son.

"Mom, I was just thinking the same thing."

The marriage had ended long ago; still I felt tremendous loss. I felt like I was abandoning my husband. I was. A couple of years back, I told him there would come a day when I'd have to make the hard choice and make our son my priority. He nodded. Moving him to a facility was a decision the three of us would work on together. Years prior I made site visits with my sister-in-law, asking myself, *Would I want to live here?* The choices were dismal. Now the search took on real urgency. Our son surprised me by offering to help. He insisted. He saw things I missed. We dismissed places despite their proximity as too depressing, lacking in activities, too urban, all hardscape, one despite the lavish white napkin, gourmet leg of lamb lunch with which we were courted. Finally, a convivial facility, no locked gates (which would turn out to present its own downside), gardens, flowers, lots of windows and natural light, views, a warm and knowledgeable staff. The deciding point? Son: "The staff doesn't turn over. They have been there for years." Even Mr. Leg of Lamb was surprised. He owned that their turnover rate was about nine months. Still, not ideal, not home. But the home staff had occupational fatigue. The home staff is ideal until it is not.

I sat down with my husband and recalled all his many gifts to the family, our many travels together, his financial planning, his forethought to get long-term care insurance. I recounted his favorite stories, one told so often any of us could recite it verbatim: A fishing hole in a Wyoming campground. He approaches an old geezer nursing his line. A moose comes thrashing down the bank. Moose are impressively large mammals with equally impressive towering racks. The old geezer didn't flinch. "Mighty brave, young feller." My husband, "I don't see you running." "Well that's because y'er between him and me." He loves this story where he's the straight man. We laughed, we cried.

When I told him he needed around-the-clock care and we could no longer provide it, that our son was stuck and needed to move on with his life, which he could not do if our lives continued to be centered on his care, he nodded. We talked so long, our son knocked on the door to see if we were okay. We three cried some more. We drove him over to see the outside of the complex, which he found inviting, even serene. We took him to one of his favorite restaurants, an Italian unpretension run by Iranian sisters and their aunt, who always hugged him and plied him with their signature molten chocolate mousse, whether we ordered it or not. "On the house," as if they knew we were a family in desperate need of chocolate's curative powers.

The next day he had a tour of the facility, was shown the available units, chose the very one we thought he might like best (reassurance in corroboration), met the staff, all smiles and welcome. Our son insisted on doing the move and enlisted the help of his best friends. My stepdaughter arrived at dawn, took her dad to buy shower curtains, a potted plant, made him lunch while we set up his new apartment so that he wouldn't have to watch the dismantling of his home. By sunset all books, CDs, his tonsu, yellow leather couch, my little secretary that he loved, his father's desk chair, his reading chair and lamp, his badger bristle shaving brush, all in place, his flannel pajamas and slippers bedside. The sun was setting red and orange as my stepdaughter brought her dad to his new home and a begonia for his window.

He was brave and stoic. He smiled. Everything familiar. Books, his CDs, old family photos. The staff arrived with balloons. The four of us went out to dinner. We laughed. He told the moose story. The day I signed the papers turning over my husband's care, I broke down and cried.

Listlessness set in, though we were unaware of any new risk. I had trouble concentrating. Many starts, rambling, illegible notes, nothing to completion. Most days I stared out the window or shopped online, pajamas, slouchy sweater, tea. More tea. Sure signs of depression, had I seen them in someone else. We indulged our separate addictions. I was out singing three nights a week. My son smoked too much pot, spent hours playing video games, a pastime I thought he had long outgrown. He stayed up late, got up at noon, lacked direction. He was more listless than before and didn't know how to spark his life. I woke one day and realized we were grieving.

I talked to other parents of adult sons. One feared putting his much older son out would land him on the street. Another said, *Be patient, he'll come around. If you push too hard, he might enlist.* In desperation, I suggested we work the *Times* crossword together. We fell for the Spelling Bee, making as many words as possible from the honeycomb of letters where every word had to contain the troublesome one in the center, trying to be the one to find the pangram that used all seven letters. In desperation to get him out of the house, I tossed him the keys to my MX-5 (which he had picked out given my parameters: stick shift, reliable, responsive, corners well, a car with which I could have a real dialogue). The only caveats: we stay on back roads and explore new territory. We'd buzzed out the freeway-like loop of Briones, a thirty-five-mile cyclist's mecca on which you could ride almost without seeing another car. "Open it up!" The intimate childhood ritual of bedtime reading and quiet reflection before surrendering to the night was now supplanted by talking while we cooked or while he drove, the rhythm of the road loosening much of what we had clung to just to keep our equilibrium. As we buzzed grass-chewing cows and drying reservoirs he'd tell me about tire compounds, limited-slip differentials, torque curves, and how horizontally opposed engines lower the center of gravity. It was all about nailing the apex.

What was so horrible, the instances that set us so on edge, that filled us with so much despair, since now we couldn't remember anything more injurious than his dad accusing us of moving his keys? It took nearly a year after we moved him to assisted living before I was finally able—compelled—to write about it. (Joan Didion: "Writers are always selling somebody out.") We were working the crossword one day when out of the silence, he said, "I have a hard time remembering all the awful things."

A year after we moved my husband to assisted living, I passed in the hallway a new member. With him was his daughter, much younger than I, in whom I could see the thousand-item checklist etched on her brow, and hoped my words of welcome were warm and encouraging. She returned a tight smile. "I've aged so much this year."

What was so bad that we finally had to step aside, let the professionals take over? In order to carry on another hour, we put difficulty out of mind. Buried it. I made a list. Added to it over the next weeks as each memory returned to either of us. For months afterward, I'd find lists slipped into books, in journals, on bank receipts, on backs of envelopes, on paper towels from the pool, lists made during this year of recovery, and each time I would have forgotten I'd already made a list of things not to forget. And they all said the same thing. I was stuck in my own Möbius Memento hell.

We were headed down the hill one afternoon. A cyclist fell as we rounded the corner. My husband slowed but ran over his backpack in the road, and kept going even after I yelled at him to stop, the crunch of eyeglasses a sickening echo. Confusion and shame masked a refusal to admit he'd done anything wrong. He ran many stop signs, then slowed and stopped for green lights. Another time he and our son arrived to pick me up at the studio. Son was furious. His dad had hit a parked truck while parking, and uncharacteristic for him, didn't check to see if he had done any damage, didn't leave a note, and minutes later denied that he had even touched the car. I summoned my most reasoned, dispassionate self. We returned, made sure the truck was fine.

In the two-year war of getting him to stop driving, we did not enjoy the support of his daughter, his neurologist, or the DMV. They were not witness. Doctors address the welfare only of their patient (not that of the family or the innocent, unknowing public). They tout driving as a hallmark of independence, and the emotional decline that can come with the loss of it. The emotional toll on the family was not their concern, we were not their patients. I did not want my husband to confuse the gas for the brake and leave behind a trail of the maimed and dead. Our son refused to ride with him and offered to drive him everywhere. But autonomy was life to the man. I would want no less. He failed his driving test twice, and still the DMV allowed him to retest. I called the DMV. What the heck? *We don't have the authority to limit a person's rights.*

It took two years of begging his neurologist before he finally wrote the letter to the DMV informing them that his patient had Alzheimer's and shouldn't have his license renewed. What changed? During a routine check-up, the doctor said something so innocent neither of us could reconstruct it, and my husband snapped. Blood. Fangs. Did the doctor flinch? Yes, he did.

Not on the list of things not to forget, along with my three concussions, was our son's ski accident where he broke his humerus, unverified until months of physical therapy failed to help while silently wrecking its own contraindicative damage. He could not lift his arm past his shoulder height. He could not continue as a barista. Could not lift anything. Could not drive a stick shift. Couldn't *shoulder* anything.

Also not on the list of things not to forget was the rash whose first itchy spots appeared in Tanzania. The trip of a lifetime was made possible by my dear brother and sister-in-law hosting my husband while we were gone, while their daughters joined us. The rash appeared in May 2015, after the first two concussions and before the third one in the fall, when it returned in a rage. Surely I'd been bitten by an obscure arachnid. Ground zero was a spot on my left hand. The rash migrated along the left side of my neck, up the left side of my face. It would subside, then flare up along my right arm. The itch was unbearable. I checked into urgent care, threatening to tear off my skin. The doctor sent me to a dermatologist who put me on weekly UV treatments for a few months, gave me a topical cortisone and a two-week cycle of methotrexate, a drug once used for cancer patients. To short-circuit the virus. The rash lessened only to pop up elsewhere. After five years it finally went dormant. PLEVA, he said, a rare autoimmune skin disorder. Then he asked me with the benevolence of a priest, what was happening in my life. I said my husband has Alzheimer's. He nodded. (Jury duty, same thing. Instant deferral.) Months later I was lamenting to a friend that I was unfocused, couldn't concentrate, couldn't finish anything. She reminded me I'd been on methotrexate, and I probably had chemo brain.

In Alzheimer's, abnormal proteins, beta-amyloid plaque, and tau tangles gang up and chomp at brain cells with Pac-Man relentlessness. First to fall is the hippocampus, where new memory is formed, ergo, the short-term memory loss. The patient experiences pleasure but often has no memory of it, which truncates memory's regifting pleasures. Memory keeps emotions alive. Life then exists in the moment, which is not the same as living in the moment. The plaque marches on to the front of the brain, the region that controls language, reasoning, logic, problem solving, and planning; the patient loses impulse control, control over his emotions. In time, he loses the ability to sort out sensory perceptions, smell, hearing, taste. The holy versatile chicken by which he swore and on which he based many of his own fine recipes? "I don't like chicken. Never have. Never will." In time, even the pathways to old memories singe and shrivel. I was crushed when he recently did not recognize himself in a photograph as a young man of forty ("Here's my daughter, but who is this man with her?"), or recognize his own voice and hand in his letters home ("This is literature. But who wrote it?"). Eventually the plaque deals the final blow to the control center regulating the heart and lungs. A cross section of the Alzheimer's brain looks like a termite infestation of your home. Your wood is dust. What was healthy pink matter is now a pitted, skeletal wasteland. Ironic, cruel, and wrenching that a man who has made of his life one of the mind—of logic, of observation, of reason, of measured lateral inquiry, of an elastic imagination—that this man would have as his crippling disability the strafing of his mind.

Lewis Hyde says that what is resolved is forgotten. It's the uncompleted tasks that weigh on us, that are ricocheting in our memories. The brain jettisons detritus. In Alzheimer's what is jettisoned—and in an advanced state, jettisoned almost immediately—is what was just said, what was just lived. The mind is no longer on fire.

Imagination allows us to roam. Memory allows us to relish, to recall, return, enjoy, to evoke—to call again. Without imagination, possibility atrophies. Without memory, the day, the hour, the moment is lost, as if with each step the earth under our soles falls into the dispassionate abyss. Imagination allows us to fly to the back of the nebula and see that it looks nothing like a crab, nothing like what we thought we knew of the universe. Memory, my son said, developed so *Homo erectus* would learn where was the best game in town, and not to drink twice from the same black water. Memory developed for survival. Memory enables us to hold a sense and accumulation of self. This is how we arrived at where we are today, the sum of what we have lived. Memory allows for self-reflection.

People die without warning, disappear without warning. We are naive in thinking we have time, that time is infinite. It might be, but not for *us*. Air crashes, earthquakes, tsunamis, nuclear meltdowns, sudden death—all catch our breath. But the prolonged death is an insidious haunt. Torture. Starvation. Immolation. Kitty Genovese. The eighteen-year waste and wither.

A five-year-old and his father chase and dodge each other up and down the lane, laughing with water bazookas as big as the son is tall, soaking each other to the skin. The father pivots, catches his son mid-run and lifts him right off his feet. The boy throws his head back, laughs, and, just as suddenly, having hit some limit, collapses into his father's arms—this man who once leaned across the dinner table and explained the Big Bang (a clap of a word for that one brilliant, singular, *silent* moment) and riffed on the mystery of what might have existed before, on the explosion that created outwardly expanding, floating baryonic matter, and a universe that today is still accelerating at the reach (providing silent cosmic counterpoint to our greed, our murderous, puny international squabbles), from which, after a scant three hundred eighty thousand years, finally came a very, very, very low hum one-trillionth of a hertz, the hearing of which the ear was not yet even an idea. In time, hydrogen, helium, the earliest featherweight elements. My man leaned across the table. *The birth of the universe is a mystery and a marvel. We are not alone. We are made of the stuff of stars.*

This Alzheimer's is not *my* Alzheimer's. I'm a caretaker, collateral damage. I have no right to tell you this part of his story. Yet I'm doing it. Our stories intersect; we're both in it. (*Rashomon*.) Newsman Jim Lehrer: "Cover, write, and present every story with the care I would want if the story were about me." Would I want to present myself as out of control, as unaware of being out of control? During menopause, I was also out of control and unaware until my little boy stuck his neck out. "Mom, why are you angry all the time?" I stepped way back, kept watch. He was right. I would fly off the handle at the littlest thing, something I neither wanted nor could control. I was a horror to myself. I read. I researched. Having been spared from the debilitating cramping and mood swings that infect most women with PMS, my cosmic payback was to have had all that hormonal chaos banked with interest, unleashed in middle age and without warning. I stood sentry over my flares. I still couldn't control them, but I could take my Ms. Hyde for a hike until I passed through that hormonal debris.

How do I dare talk about my husband's story? How dare Richard Avedon photograph his father's last days? Better to ask how I dare stay silent. Losing our minds is frightening. If someone so brilliant could be felled, through no neglect or action of his own, then that axe could fall on any of us, a stunning blow with a long, dispassionate bleed. Yet Alzheimer's in no way diminished who he once was, or the all of what he achieved.

Perhaps shame or denial had nothing to do with not being able to own his condition. Anosognosia affects up to 80 percent of Alzheimer's patients. From the ancient Greek: *a-*, "without," *nosos*, "disease," and *gnōsis*, "knowledge." A person with anosognosia is unaware that he is afflicted. A bipolar's or schizophrenic's refusal to take her medication might be directly related to her anosognosia. She doesn't realize she is bipolar; why should she take meds? One summer, we found his Risperdal in the garbage, the most crucial of his medications. Risperdal is a second-generation antipsychotic drug, one that rebalances the levels of dopamine and serotonin in the brain and is used to mitigate mood and the most aggressive behavior of Alzheimer's. If he wasn't aware he had Alzheimer's, he would deny any need for medication. Yet he was cognizant enough to read the fine print:

Risperdal could lead to an increase in deaths, and he reasoned that the pills were dangerous. Death is a possible side effect, but he was on .25 mg, the lowest efficacious dose without which Mr. Hyde dominates. Some take as much as 4 to 8 mg. Years later, his mood was so stable I asked the neurologist about lowering his dosage. He agreed it was worth a try. The pills were cut in half. Fine for about a month, then the aggressive behavior returned. The staff noticed. We noticed. Back to his quarter of a milligram. I try to imagine the mental and psychic conditions of those who need sixteen or thirty-two times that amount. It was only recently that my husband gently asked, "Do I have Alzheimer's?" and "Perhaps I already said that? My memory isn't so good anymore." We laugh. It's that or cry.

During the pandemic lockdown we were rescued by the nightly video call. To enliven the conversation stalled by repetition, we took turns reading aloud and discussing Andrea Wulf's "The Invention of Nature." It was remarkable what he could still parse and crushing that he could then not recall. I recounted his life story, including stories I know only from his having told me. *You were six and sat behind a girl whose pigtails you dipped in the inkwell. She turned and slapped you.* "Gloria Poulton." He blushed in the recollection, reliving the startle and joy of being slapped by the pretty girl on whom he had a crush. *Our son turned six in Venice. You two played chess on the patio. The glass blower in Murano made a green horse, which he turned and handed our son. The brakes on our rented Alfa failed on Mt. Bondone.* I summoned details, hoping for something as vivid as Gloria Poulton's slap to awaken memory. But while I journeyed down memory lane, my husband was visiting virgin territory. "What's wrong with me?"

Does my husband want me to tell this part of his story? If I were to ask him whether writing about this phase of his life was all right with him, would either answer, yes or no, be an informed, uncompromised, capacitated answer? Would he want to write this story himself?

He was a robust and dapper forty-three when I met him, armed with an unassuming intellect and a topographical map. He had just returned from two weeks hiking hut-to-hut in Austria, starting near Schladming, where in August there can still be snow on the ground. At one hut he met three men, one in a sling, one with bandaged ribs, the third with a bandaged head (as if they were characters in a parable), injuries sustained from their descent on an ice field that lay in his direct path the next day. The summer had melted the top layer of ice, exposing a litter of head stones just over a pace apart, rocks that broke their falls as each of these men slipped. The men glanced at his cleatless boots and wished him good luck. The next day he found the ice field, surrounded by a thick forest and sufficiently steep as to not question its measure, with the trail tantalizing on the far side. Too late in the day to turn back, there was nothing to do but cross. He skirted the edge as far as he could before finally stepping on to the field, goating from rock to rock, taking the icy two-step as needed. Before starting across, he confessed to the ice field his deep admiration and his considerable fear. He bowed. He said, "Pardon me. I mean no disrespect." Then he pissed on it.

HANNAH KEZIAH AGUSTIN

Homeland Fictions

FROM *The North American Review*

THE HOUSE is gone, and so is home. What remains is wreckage—tattered plywood, electric lines hanging from bared ceilings, pools of motor oil, dust, and detritus. Everything we own sits outside of our house in Mandaluyong, previous lives tucked away neatly in cardboard boxes, loaded into a moving truck. Our house was being demolished for a bridge and all I could do was watch from a tiny screen halfway around the world.

It is midnight in Wisconsin and I am FaceTiming my cousin, asking her to show me what remains of the family home. With her phone held up by shaky hands, I make out from the pixels what is left of our neighborhood. I could see steel sticking out of the walls of bulldozed homes, busted concrete on top of uneven asphalt, and uneven cement holding puddles of rainwater. I could see my neighbors walking around the remains. Under KN95 masks, laughter gushes from their eyes and the split-second recognition of kin emanates. They ask me how life in America is and when I'll come home. We are people who have lived next to each other for decades. And now, we mourn the same loss.

But once, amid the carcinogen and smoke of Metropolitan Manila, beside the swarthy Pasig River and plywood houses held together by scaffoldings of steel, somewhere between the narrow streets of bumper-to-bumper traffic running around the clock, our house stood. We were at home here, despite the sadness of poverty, the monsoon that blew against our windows, and the fact that this wasn't ours forever. The government owned that land but we believed that we did too.

I was ten when my family moved here when my parents bought a strip of land in front of the run-down Noah's Ark Sugar Refinery in Mandaluyong because it was cheap because we didn't have our own house because we were too poor for that. Exhibit A: we were so poor that for my school's Halloween party, my mom, instead of being a normal mom who could have clad me in a brand-new store-bought princess ball gown with the face of the cartooned Cinderella or Princess Aurora sewn into its chest area, draped me in white cloth, teased the crap out of my hair, smothered my face in baby powder, and dressed me up as Sadako, the killer ghost from the Japanese horror film *The Ring*. I was in kindergarten. I was laughed at by my princess classmates and my superhero peers. But thank God, I now had the chance to start a new life far from the embarrassing memories of my childhood.

The new house was approximately three miles away from my grandparents' house in San Juan, where my family and my uncle's family shared a roof, and where we had lived ever since I was born. It was the family's house. My grandfather drove passenger jeepneys around Manila for a living while my grandmother, Nanay, stayed at home to take care of their four sons, childbearing, and childrearing.

They were so poor my father had to start driving the jeep at sixteen. They were so poor my uncle was shot dead in cold blood and there was no trial. No justice was served. All because they were too poor to get a lawyer. Still, they were able to get this house because Tito Nelson worked in Manhattan for five years driving a Dunkin' Donuts delivery bus around the city. I would later find out that he got here with his wife with a fake visa. He was deported and can never set foot in this country again.

My grandfather died of diabetes when I was five. Before he was cremated in the city where I was born, I scratched my back with his backscratcher then watched it, and him, go up in flames. All of my memories of him existed in the confines of this house. His disease swallowed up the wholeness of his existence. He was in that wheelchair ever since I breathed my first breath and he breathed his last. Sometimes, in my dreams, he's still there, smiling at me, stretching out his backscratcher for me, beside the dining table on the ground floor where his wheelchair was always parked. I did not cry when he died. I was too young and too small to hold grief in my hands.

When we were living in San Juan, for the first decade of my life, I did not know boundaries. I had no understanding of space. This was because my family had lived in one single bedroom with no windows for ten years, where half of the space was given over to a queen-sized bed that my sister and I shared. Nevertheless, this was home to us.

Back then, I walked home from preschool with my father carrying my glittery pink backpack behind me after class. We passed through a narrow pathway built right under our neighbors' houses, all of which were crowded and compact, void of front facades, and organized with no clear demarcations as to where properties end. This explains why the walkway became a de facto communal space where I spent morning after morning saying hi to every person who sat at the doors of their houses.

This was how I met Agassi, my childhood best friend, a pudgy little boy who always had crumbs lining the corners of his mouth. Our houses shared a firewall because we lived next door to each other. He lived with his grandmother, a devout Catholic who exclusively wore flowy duster dresses, who had an altar of the Virgin Mary right next to her doorstep, welcoming everyone who graced their humble abode.

Agassi and I shared a fondness for pretending to be adults, prematurely drinking coffee with my aunt on the first floor of my house while watching Japanese anime like *One Piece* and *Sailor Moon* with dubbed Filipino voices. We spent afternoons watching people on the terrace of my house, stuffing our mouths with buttered and sugared bread, wired from the glucose high. When he left for Dubai, I stopped watching anime. I started walking to the bakery by myself with a single piece of bread in hand and then on the way back, I'd pass by his house, watching the candles burn at the feet of Mary, wondering what he was doing with his parents overseas, if he felt at home. When he left, I named a pen and made it my best friend to make up for the loss. I left, too, eventually.

My first memories of Mandaluyong smelled like fresh paint, newness. Churchmates and family came for the house blessing with jaws dropped, chatting among themselves with mouthfuls of noodles, admiring the unscathed beige walls, following the pastor around while he smeared holy oil at the corners of our new home. It was unfamiliar, my feet hitting the smoothness of the cold tiled floor. Even here, I am not. I miss the splintering wooden stairs, the shared firewall, and the refrigerator that whirred loudly after being soaked in floodwater. Gone is San Juan. Gone are Agassi and the bakery of sugared bread. Gone are the neighborly hellos. The guests left. We bid our goodbyes. Just like that, our house was empty.

From the terrace, I watched the Whirlybird ventilators turning on the green roof of the abandoned sugar refinery. I watched the uniformed construction workers with their neon orange hard hats as they played at the basketball court in front of our house. I watched the twinkling skyline of the urban jungle, the one across the river, sparkling with light pollution, ridden with buildings of cement and metal with little square windows illuminated from the inside. It was a new world, one with clear demarcations. And I did not know where I stood.

"[Exile] is the unhealable rift forced between a human being and a native place, between the self and its true home," Edward Said says in his essay "Reflections on Exile." I first read it in the bleak midwinter of my third year in America, holed up in the bedroom of my family's rented apartment in South Central Wisconsin after testing positive for COVID-19. I haven't been home since I got here. I left without even knowing that it was going to be the last time I would see the house of my teenage rebellion.

I am twenty-one. It's almost been a year since my house was demolished, since I FaceTimed my cousin to show me what was left of the place I called home, the rubble, the ripped-out plywood, the broken-down walls of cement. 861 MRR Track

Barangka Ibaba no longer exists. It has been replaced by a billion-peso bridge which serves as a de facto runway for the cars of rich people who use it to cross into their utopia.

I am crouched over my laptop, furiously typing on a wooden table that my dad found in the dumpster of one of the apartments he cleans, looking for footage of the newly built Estrella-Pantaleon Bridge, obsessively reading through the comments of strangers saying things like, "The bridge looks so beautiful!!! It's like you're in a different country!!! :)" I am in a different country and the beauty that they are describing is absent.

Am I really in the first world? My family's house in Whitewater is falling apart at the seams. There are soft rags made from old shirts lying on the kitchen floor. I was showering once and the bathwater leaked into the other side of the duplex, my Filipino neighbor's bedroom. Every two weeks, the heater stops working, having its self-declared labor strike, and I walk down the stairs to a freezing living room.

"For an exile, habits of life, expression or activity in the new environment inevitably occur against the memory of these things in another environment," Said says. "Thus both the new and the old environments are vivid, actual, occurring together contrapuntally." *Exile* comes from the Old French word *essillier* which means "banish, expel, drive off," which could belong to the Proto-Indo-European *helh*. It is the root of the Greek word *elauno* which means "to drive" or one "who is driven out."

I never had to worry about the cold in Manila. Whenever I walked outside there would be heat on my face, a stinging genial heat that I grew up with, a heat that can raise bananas from shoots on the ground. The distance from home is suffocating, this lonely enterprise of existence.

I find myself crying in the banana aisle in Walmart because the produce sticker says that every banana sold helps educate the Philippines. I am receiving my college diploma in America. I put my bananas on the cold countertop of the self-checkout machine. The scanner beeps. The white woman speaks through blared speakers with a robotic voice. The child in me mourns for the bananas, none of which are ever enough.

*

At the peak of rural-to-urban migration, the industrialization of cities, and the nation's formidable recovery from the tyranny of a fourteen-year martial law, Noah's Ark Sugar Refinery was built. It was a time of nationwide financial turmoil since everyone was reeling from the presidential dictatorship. This was why when the sugar giant opened up positions for factory workers who were in charge of monitoring daily deliveries and inspecting raw and refined sugar quality, my aunt, a newly converted urbanite, didn't say no.

Tita Joevie along with my mother and her siblings started their exodus from the farmlands of Cagayan Valley to Metro Manila in order to get a college diploma. Their parents were farmers, rice planters who woke up at four in the morning to fetch water, cook breakfast, and dig the soles of their feet into the soft mud and murky waters of the fields so that they could earn something come harvest time. If someone wanted to escape a life of grueling labor, one without dirt underneath their fingernails, then Manila was the place to be. They left for the city when my mother was seventeen. They never looked back.

Because Tita Joevie's uncle worked for a Visayan glass company, they had a place to stay when they first moved to Manila. Their apartment was at the mercy of their uncle's boss, who, after allowing their family to live rent-free on their land basically as informal settlers for ten years, eventually kicked them out as soon as they needed the space. The owners sold the land to the local government to get out of paying taxes. This pushed my aunt and my uncle to settle at MRR Track Barangka Ibaba, a small plot of land owned by the government next to the 3.9-hectare land where the gargantuan factory of Noah's Ark stood. By painstakingly packing fine cane sugar grains into clear plastic bags for the company's supermarket clients, she was able to buy a two-story house at the heart of Manila where her family of six lived, including Lola Daling, who would sweep the front of their house with a coffee in hand in the morning, who I would find smoking a cigarette while reading a book in the afternoon. Their family was ours too.

It was perfect. Their house was near a public basketball court where neighborhood moms would synchronically dance to Zumba over grounded speakers, where during Lent, two ladies, with sweaty cotton towelettes slung on their shoulders, would do an uninterrupted chanting of the *Pasyón*, an early sixteenth-century epic poem narrating the life, passion, death, and resurrection of Jesus Christ. It was also a makeshift stage for amateur singing competitions, barangay-wide beauty pageants, and several local government politicians' electoral campaigns.

Their house was near a public elementary school, a public high school, a barbershop, a street fried-chicken stall, a McDonald's, a dental office, a bank, a tricycle terminal, a train station, and most importantly, it was a bridge away from the country's financial center, a shopping mall, and a red-light district. This working-class community consists mostly of minimum-wage earners, stay-at-home housewives, and low-income families. I wouldn't say we were poor but a plant blog said aratilis grow like mushrooms in underdeveloped areas of the metropolis. There was an aratilis tree in front of our house planted before we got there.

Even so, we were still rich because our houses were right in the middle of where life was happening in the big city, standing lowly right alongside gated subdivisions and opulent celebrity houses. Our wealth was defined by the land around us. I will appreciate this later on when I am old enough to feel confident walking around the neighborhood on my own. This is when I have saved enough lunch money to buy rice porridge and fried chicken skin and grilled pig intestines, and pay for my own cheap haircuts. This is when I can use the liberties that I have as someone who was living in the city. Everything was within arm's length. Everything was possible.

In 2009, my father, with the money he earned from driving a taxi around Manila, bought the lot next to Tita Joevie's house, the same year Noah's Ark stopped its operations after failing to settle a 900-million-peso loan with the United Coconut Planters Bank. This pushed her to open a small neighborhood retail store on the ground floor of her house, where construction workers would go for a cigarette, candy, and soda packaged in clear glass bottles. Looming over her business is the empty shell of the sugar factory's former glory.

In 2015, the Supreme Court ruled for the deportation of the Chinese sugar magnate Jimmy T. Go back to his home country after being convicted of the ownership of several illegal businesses. With that, the Ark went off. Still, the people remained. Their heads were barely above water.

It isn't too bad, not for my eleven-year-old self, especially when I know of Gabriel. There is a reason for me to stay. What a dreamy and sweaty shirtless boy. He goes out to play basketball only after ten at night, when he has the court to himself and he can do as many free throws as he wants, and I will sit on the terrace of my house, admiring this sweaty shirtless boy at the cusp of puberty do as many free throws as he wants. As if on cue, the drunken neighborhood dads, with their plastic Monobloc chairs laid out at the front of their houses, sing Whitney's "I Will Always Love You" over staticky speakers with their breath reeking of chicken oil, Marlboro Lights, and alcohol-fueled confidence.

I am ten and my only understanding of love is from Sunday school. Love is patient. Love is kind. It does not envy so we can live our life here in Noah's Ark in the middle of the city of our dreams. On our way to church, Ate Eunice asks me about Gabriel. She asks me what mattered more to me, if it was love or money.

"Love," I answer, too young to understand how expensive it is to stay alive. I still believed that poverty was something one transcended. This was because when I was six, I picked up a book of anthologized biographies of the richest people in the Philippines. The rags-to-riches narrative was the easiest lie to believe. I wanted to be a businessman then. I wanted to compete with the Ayalas, the Gokongweis, and the Sys—the country's multibillion-dollar business tycoons. I wanted an air-conditioned house. I wanted my own room. I wanted a car so my dad wouldn't have to pick me up from school with a bike. But as I grew up, the gap grew and each day would pass, the rift between me and the people I read about stretched, impossible to cross.

I am ten and the life I imagine with Gabriel is one of lack. We are still in Noah's Ark. We share a bed. We have a small electric fan keeping us cool in the corner of our room, a small cabinet for our clothes, and a small kitchen where we cook over a gas stove and I am so inexplicably happy.

It is 2022. I am far from Gabriel, far from the ten-year-old version of myself that was ridden with prepubescent hormones that made me delusional. He is in a five-year relationship with a beautiful girl and I am happy for him. His grandmother, Tita Cors, who I know from morning conversations in front of my house where she used to sweep a lot, tells me he's doing well, that she's proud of him, and that he's still a good boy.

I am crossing continents over Facebook Messenger to ask Tita Cors how they've been, if they like the new place they're staying in, if rent is expensive, and if water and electricity still cost too much. I ask her what she misses about their house. She says everything, she says the pesky neighbors, the noise, the exchange of homecooked meals in clear plastic Tupperware, helping one another and the fact that during Christmas you are morally obliged to give money to children who need new clothes, the nonstop karaoke, the fighting couples who chase each other down the street with a knife, greeting one another Merry Christmas and Happy New Year, the carols. She misses the Marisas, the Marians, and all the other Mariteses. The demolition has colored every single one of our conversations, the antithesis of an elephant in the room, always acknowledged.

Tita Cors has lived on our street since 1974, after moving from the province of Zambales. The house she lived in for forty-seven years before it was demolished was left to her by her sister, who immigrated to America, and she made a life supporting herself through college, hopping from one contractual job to another, crossing the bridge to Makati to hang at the back of fully-packed jeepneys just to get to work.

Tita Cors tells me of the train after which our street was named that used to lull her to sleep, the train that went in and out of the sugar factory, back when it was still Insular Sugar Central. She tells me that from the window of her house, she could see pesky children going inside the factory to get sugar. The workers didn't mind until the company was changed to Noah's Ark and everything was fenced in. She tells me there used to be a field of grass where her neighbors would hang their clothes on multicolored plastic hangers out in the open, where the kids were free to run and play and be kids, and I wonder if we could have that space again in a city that prides itself for its callousness. Gabriel doesn't even have a basketball court to play at. Tita Cors tells me she'll talk to her grandson about me. I thank her for her time and say goodbye.

It was paradise. The building, with its foliage sprawling over into the otherwise desolate urban inferno, housed man-made waterfalls, five-foot chandeliers, and a rooftop that made the skyline look like a blanket of Swarovski crystals, all luxury and pomp. Its hundred-story towers were named after some of the world's most beautiful waterfalls—Niagara, Sutherland, Dettifoss, Iguazu, and Livingstone—and its design reflected that ornateness, inspired by the French industrial designer Philippe Starck, designer of the Mondrian Hotel in West Hollywood, Paramount Hotel in New York City, and the Delano in Miami. It was the country's first residential Eden.

A hundred stories down, our house stood at the east of Eden, on the outskirts of paradise. In Sunday school, I learned that it was where God banished Cain after he killed his brother. I wonder if God has banished us here in the same way. After having been left by the Ark, we are now being cast out of paradise.

It had its perks, living that closely to middle-class affluence. My sister, who studied at a public high school beside the basketball court in front of my house, gushed to me about their AC units, all of which were donated by the owners of Acqua. They replaced the decades-old electric fans that were ridden with rust. While the towers were being built, the neighborhood drowned in the sound of construction, of steel clanking on steel, of construction canes lifting blocks of cement off the ground. But now, she could study trigonometry in peace, all thanks to Acqua.

Because of Acqua, the kids in our neighborhood could play on a small strip of concrete where all the 10-wheeler construction trucks would pass through to enter the site. It was also where our community church held its summer Vacation Bible School, where they talked about Adam and Eve and the Garden of Eden. They talked about paradise, how the consequence of disobedience is exile, and I wonder if God hears our prayers for the land to be ours.

All we desired was to have our share of paradise. All we desired was to not be exiled to the outskirts of the metropolis.

I think back to the time before our house was demolished when we held Bible studies every Tuesday night in the garage underneath my house. My aunt and I would bring down a Thermos of black coffee, and a tray of sugared bread, and lay out long wooden chairs for the neighborhood moms who religiously came, despite being exhausted from the long labors. I would lead worship with an acoustic guitar slung over my shoulder, singing about the goodness of God in spite of the hardships of life, despite the thorns in our flesh. The neighborhood moms would sing along with me, their voices shy and shaking, and in the parking space, we found God. We found the sovereignty present amidst the suffering we never understood.

The problem now was that we were out of Eden and the temptation now was to curse God and die. Did the promise still hold true in exile?

I was sixteen when President Rodrigo Roa Duterte was elected into national office. During his campaign, he proposed the implementation of the "No Relocation, No Demolition" policy, which meant he would not allow the demolition of informal settlers' dwellings if there is no available relocation site for them. He explicitly told the developers to make sure their urban projects would not displace settlers.

The Estrella-Pantaleon Bridge that connected Makati to Mandaluyong was first built in 2011 and then rebuilt in 2017 to accommodate the heavy traffic going into the Makati City Central Business District. This meant widening the roads on the Mandaluyong side to make way for a four-lane bridge, which entailed the demolition of a neighborhood of Noah's Ark where our house belonged.

The bridge expansion is a part of the Build! Build! Build! Infrastructure Program, the government's attempt to conceal the disconcerting squalor of the entire nation, especially in Metro

Manila, wherein it tries to hide its stench through the construction of bridges, train stations, and the useless Manila Baywalk Dolomite Beach that cost 389 million pesos, and opened to the public in the thick of a global pandemic, only to be washed away by the climate-change-induced tropical storms.

In Mong Palatino's essay "The Rise and Rise of Manila's Informal Settlers," he says, "Metro Manila's embarrassing poverty is partly hidden by the frenzied construction of residential condominiums, call center hubs, and malls. They are false icons of progress but quite effective in masking the burgeoning poverty in the metropolis." Absurdly enough, the government didn't even have the money to support its own project, since the Estrella-Pantaleon Bridge, which prides itself on having wider sidewalks and being able to withstand high-intensity earthquakes, was funded by a grant from Imperial China.

"I'd also like to express our gratitude to the government of the People's Republic of China for financing the project," the president said in a keynote speech before the unveiling of the bridge marker at its inauguration. "The 1.46-billion-peso funding that they have extended highlights the goodwill of the Chinese people and its government and further cements the good relations between our two countries." I read these statements while I am exiled from home, far from my own country and everyone and everything I hold dear in the homeland, and am filled with profound loneliness, the one that Edward Said describes as a "fundamentally discontinuous state of being" when one is in exile. There is a slow and calculated way in which the urban poor are pushed to the margins until they no longer have a place to call their own.

"Destroy their house and they will have nowhere to go," the president said in a speech in Malacanang in 2016. "Will they be like dogs? Where will the people go?"

There I was again, sitting on the roof of my house with my father's pigeons next to me, with wet laundry drying overhead in the city's smog, breathing in the un-fresh air, surveying the bright buildings on the other side of the bridge, the amber sunset behind it. I feel the zinc roofing sheet's cool surface on my thighs, and hear the distant sounds of teenagers yelling expletives at each other on the basketball court. I am twelve years old and I remember it all so clearly.

Because I live in the middle of everything, I am suffocated by the presence of everything in close proximity and I find that being on top of the world is the only way I can be alone. I mean, sure, this isn't the top of the world, but at least I can hide from my mother, my father, my older sister, my aunt, and my three cousins sitting two floors beneath me, and for once, in the dark rooftop, I can see the light.

Last midnight, my grandmother died in the arms of my mother. She gave her a shower, combing her dripping wet hair when she stopped breathing. Nanay had just gotten out of the hospital, one chemotherapy session after another, to extract a brain tumor that paralyzed half of her face. When none of the treatments worked, the doctors decided to send her home.

I walked down the stairs half-awake at three in the morning to see my mother sitting at the dining table with tears in her eyes and at that moment, I already knew she was gone. I opened the door to the room where she stayed. Under the ashen moonlight, she sat lifeless yet peaceful, her head hanging to the side, blanket slung over her atrophied arms hooked to an IV, the hollow frame of Nanay in the dark. I didn't cry when I went back to bed, the shock of grief was so immediate it was paralyzing. I just lay there, closed my eyes, and wondered if my father knew he built the house where his mother would breathe her last.

Four days before I was born, the Payatas landslide killed 232 people. Because of a slope of accumulated garbage, a wall of trash collapsed, causing a fire that razed about one hundred squatters' homes. A squatter is defined by the *Collins Dictionary of Law* as "one who settles on the lands of others without any legal authority, applied particularly to those who settle on public land." Not everyone swallowed up by the weight of the mountain caving in was found. The official data reported three hundred missing people. Other sources reported close to a thousand dead.

The residents of the Payatas dumpsite were migrants from Smokey Mountain, a landfill located in the middle of Manila. After its shutdown in 1995, the community that mostly made a living out of scavenging moved to Payatas. Because of the incident, six hundred homeless families were relocated to Rizal. The United Nations Human Settlements Program defines "informal settlements" as those consisting of structures built without legal tenure security or structures not conforming to building regulations.

"Life in the relocation site is more miserable than it was in Payatas. For a year, the children were forced to stop their education because there is no school inside the relocation," says Delia Badion, chairwoman of the July 10 Payatas Victims Organization. Violence awaited those who resisted. In 2011, a quarter of Metro Manila's population were informal settlers, the Department of Interior and Local Government says, and I wonder if the violence is inescapable, and if we cannot choose to shun suffering, and if we only get to choose which is the lesser violence in the same way one chooses the lesser evil. The local government of Mandaluyong gave the residents of Noah's Ark a choice. It was either money or being relocated to a substandard governmental condominium on the outskirts of Manila. Of course, the people chose money.

After the demolition of our house, the Department of Interior and Local Government paid for the damages. Century Properties, the company that owns Acqua, should have also paid for the damages because they were building another residential tower next to the bridge. But after seeing that the house was owned by immigrants to the United States, they refused to pay. My aunt, to whom the house was left, was yelled at by the representative of Acqua after she repeatedly came back to their office in the thick of a global pandemic, begging for our share of the land's worth. Our name was erased from the list of subsidy recipients. After hours of video calls between Manila and Wisconsin, we never got the money.

When the Payatas landslide happened in the year 2000, then-president Joseph Estrada ordered the immediate closing of the dumping ground. It was opened weeks later by the city mayor to inhibit the epidemic caused by uncollected garbage in the metropolis. The bodies underneath the rubble of metropolitan waste were left without a proper burial, pushed deeper into the earth by an accumulation of detritus. The violence in Payatas was quiet, peaceful even. No one heard the wrong that was done.

I was nine when the demolition drive happened in Baclaran. Backing the demolition team, the riot police came with guns blazing, with anti-riot armor and hard-shell shields, with skull-breaking batons, ready to pounce on informal settlers who pelted the officials with huge stones and glass bottles, dropping them from atop the concrete walls of the mosque. The authorities wanted to demolish the informal settlements in order to pave the way for the construction of a public transport terminal.

"Even if we all die, we won't leave this place," says Carmina, one of the residents. "Don't [the cops] have hearts? Do they feel nothing?" According to the residents, three died in the riot, including a seven-year-old boy. The Southern Police District Chief Superintendent denied the fatalities.

Four years later, the mosque itself was demolished because this, too, was built on private property. In 2007, the Philippine Reclamation Authority promised the Muslim community that they would not tear down their holy place of worship. Instead, they would help "beautify" it. In 2013, the mosque was bulldozed to make way for a shopping mall.

Demolish was coined in the 1560s, and its original meaning was "to destroy the structural character of (a building, wall, etc.), by violently pulling it to pieces," from the French word *demoliss*, which means "to destroy, tear down."

My father was nine when the demolition of his two-story childhood home in San Juan happened. They lived beside the Pasig River in a makeshift house of plywood tied together by wooden planks and tin roofs weighed down by spare car tires. I never saw it. He stayed there until he was eight before the government came for it and replaced it with a bridge. When our house was demolished, I told him we were gentrified. He told me he does not know what it means. I did not try to explain it to him. I do not know where to start.

Three days before I left for America, my family, my cousins, my aunts, and I checked into one of the rooms in the Dettifoss Tower in Acqua for a staycation. The beds were soft. The bathroom smelled of fresh paint and lemon air freshener. The floor-to-ceiling windows showed us the city I spent most of my life in—the one I called home and will call home whenever someone asks me where I am from.

One of the last memories I have of Manila was spent on the terrace of that building. That night I counted streetlights from where I stood. I watched the slow procession of cars inching their way through heavy traffic. In three days, I would be shipped off to a part of a different continent, where the smog is nonexistent and the roads are empty.

Noah's Ark Sugar Refinery died, for real this time, in 2016. Since it was practically defunct and occupied too much space, Century Properties decided to buy the land and tear down the unused factory to make way for Acqua, a six-tower riverfront residential community.

It was perfect. The condo was near a bridge that led to luxury shopping malls, exclusive private schools, and restaurants with valet parking services. It was a utopia totally unknown to those who lived outside of it. I could only look from the outside in.

At six in the morning, my sister and I, clad in our branded overruns, would start our journey to the other side of the bridge. On gray concrete, we walked past the low-rise apartments in our neighborhood, past the speeding motorcycles who were on the bridge with us, past the Pasig River and the school of janitor fish—all this for a taste of affluence.

With our wired Skullcandy earphones plugged into our phones, both of us would jog around Rockwell Drive, pretending to be one of the residents in the area, most of whom are either rich, white, or both. Then, after pretending to exercise, after fantasizing about a life where we are rich enough to live on this side of the city, my sister would buy two pancakes at the McDonald's in the basement of the shopping mall, where uniformed maids get their food while the people who pay them eat at illy Caffè or the Starbucks Reserve. This fantasy is made obsolete as soon as I remember that our small family business of delivering medical supplies to hospitals across the metro cannot support this lifestyle.

We will live and die lower middle class, but who can stop me from living out this delusion? PowerPlant Mall was built in the year 2000 over the site of the former Rockwell Thermal Power-Plant, named after James Chapman Rockwell, the first president of Manila Electric Company, which was a subsidiary of New York's General Public Utilities. Now it is a site for the rich, luxuriating in indoor waterfalls and faux coconut trees wrapped in Christmas lights that stand four stories high, with Swarovski and Porsche stores nearby. As soon as I walk in, the security guard clad in a stiff bleach-white polo with his fake gun in his back pocket uses a wooden stick to check the inside of my bag. I am reminded that I do not belong here.

This isn't the first time I have felt this way. I am sixteen, studying in a private Catholic school at the mercy of a merit scholarship, face-to-face with lack every time my father drops me off at the gates of my university with his beat-up motorcycle, next to my classmates ushered in with the latest iPhones, clad in Zara and H&M, stepping out of their shiny little cars with their maids holding umbrellas over their heads.

I had classmates who lived on the rich side of the city, trust-fund babies, born with bread and butter shoved into their mouths. They spent their summers in Bali, Tokyo, and Copenhagen, and never had to worry about elbowing someone in the face while on public transportation during rush hour because they had their personal chauffeurs who lived according to their temperaments. Of course, not all of my classmates were spoiled brats, but even they could not deny their privilege.

When my family first moved to our house in Noah's Ark, I studied at a public elementary school that had Greek columns at its front facade. Well, don't let that fool you. In one classroom, sixty sweaty kids sat shoulder to shoulder in cramped wooden armchairs while an overworked and underpaid teacher for thirty years yelled at the top of her lungs to teach Maths, Science, English, and History for eight hours straight. It was a school that mostly catered to the poor, the children of housewives, jeepney drivers, call center agents, and laundresses. For the first time, I felt better off than I really was.

In this school, my classmates ostracized me for being "rich," just because my house had three stories, because my family had a car, and because I came from a private school—which only allowed me in because of an academic merit scholarship. They made me cry and I begged my mother to make us poor, not understanding the privilege I had to even say that, but now I am six years away from that incident and I could not understand why I hid in the bottom aisle in Zara whenever I ran into someone I knew inside the mall, as if there'd been a crack in the simulation, a glitch in the system. It brings me back to being amazed that my friend from first grade had her own house and not just a single room where their whole life existed.

Rockwell had everything one needed, even a paid musician with a ceramic bowl at the hood of the baby grand, playing jazz for those shopping at the organic supermarket that prided itself on ethically sourced products but couldn't pay their workers enough to shop at the store they worked in. I guess this is what growing up poor did to me. I was raised to have a myopic obsession with the stupefaction of wealth. And now, I can't help but compare the price of tomatoes at the grocery, or order anything but tap water when I eat out. I'm always out of place no matter where I go, both sides of the bridge. I'm always at the threshold, exiled from both environments.

Still, whenever I cross that bridge, I tell myself I will do anything to prove I belong here. When I walk around H&M, flipping through shirts that I cannot buy, sporting a cheap thrifted outfit, I casually wave my hand-me-down iPhone 5S, ask where the fitting room is in straight English, unflinchingly, as if somebody's watching from the corner of my eye, waiting to banish me from paradise as soon as I make a wrong move.

In her article "Metro Manila Through the Gentrification Lens: Disparities in Urban Planning and Displacement Risks," Dr. Narae Choi says that during the colonial rule of Spain from 1521 to 1898, traditional communal land in what we now know as the present Metro Manila area and the land granted to religious friars became private estates, giving over ownership into the hands of a select few individuals.

In 1956, the prestigious Bel-Air Village, a gated subdivision on the same street as PowerPlant Mall and the high-rise Rockwell residences, was gifted by Ayala Corporation, the country's oldest and largest multibillion-dollar conglomerate, to two hundred former Philippine Air Force and US Air Force pilots. And now, the place stands within minutes from five-star hotels, elite private schools, shopping malls, and corporate offices for international companies.

In our Tuesday night Bible studies, the missionary read from the book of James. It contained God's warning to rich oppressors. He told them to "weep and wail because of the misery that is coming." And I think about the curse coming upon all who have lived on earth in luxury and self-indulgence, who have fattened themselves on the day of slaughter.

I see burning on the horizon. I smell smoke.

On February 4, 2021, a fire annihilated the homes of one hundred families at the end of our street. Facebook Live showed men throwing paint buckets filled with water. The houses were due for demolition since the property had already been bought and paid for by the land developer. The news said it was caused by a gas stove malfunction. When I was ten, while driving through the neighborhood home from school, my father told me that when the squatters refused to leave despite the orders of private landowners, their houses would be annihilated by arsonists. I do not know what to believe. How does one explain the flames?

Exile is "like death, but without death's ultimate mercy," Said says. My father watches the news and Manila is on fire again. We lost the house, and in that, lost our home.

Yet, even when it no longer stands, even when the house of my youth is mere fiction, a myth underneath the bridge that demolished it, I still go on Google Maps at one a.m. with a demented pull to its documented existence, zooming in to the gate of my sister's high school, the neighborhood sundry store that sold rice porridge to my high school self, the aratilis tree in front of the only house my family has ever owned.

Once again, I am sixteen, thirteen, ten, in the backseat of my dad's car knowing the exact moment when I've arrived home because I know the orange tint of the streetlights in front of the ghost of Noah's Ark.

I could see it. It is there, even with my eyes closed.

EULA BISS

Love and Murder in South Africa
FROM *The Believer*

MY FIRST encounter with South Africa was a book, *My Traitor's Heart*, which I read when I was twenty, and it was because of this book that I traveled to South Africa twenty years later. I don't know where I thought I was going then, but it might have been further into the book, which was a reckoning with what it means to be white. The author, Rian Malan, is a white South African who worked as a crime reporter during the death throes of apartheid, and he told the story of his country through a series of murders.

South Africa had the world's second-highest murder rate in 1990, when *My Traitor's Heart* was published. Those were the days of burning tire necklaces and cursory executions. Murder in apartheid-era South Africa wasn't like murder in other countries, according to Malan. "Elsewhere in the world, murder was just another function of ordinary social relationships," he observed. "In the vast majority of cases, murderers killed someone they knew—wives, bosses, fellow drunkards, rivals in business or love. In South Africa, it wasn't like that. In South Africa, you could be walking down the street, minding your own business, when white trash boiled off the back of a passing pick-up and kicked your head in, simply because your skin was black." Re-reading that passage on the plane to Johannesburg, I could think of at least one other country where murder was like that, the only country I really knew. But when I read *My Traitor's Heart* at twenty, it wasn't the murders I recognized—it was the psychological state of the author.

He was disturbed by his country and confused about his

place in it. He had grown up in a middle-class suburb of Johannesburg, where he saw very little of the violence that enforced apartheid. But he read the news, and he wondered who he was. His people, in South African terms, were Afrikaners, an ethnic group descended from Dutch colonists. "The white tribe of Africa" is how Malan described Afrikaners, "arrogant, xenophobic, and 'full of blood,' as the Zulus say of tyrants." His family, the Malans, had been in South Africa since 1688. A Malan died in a massacre of Afrikaners by King Dingane ka Senzangakhona's Zulu warriors, and the brother of that Malan massacred Zulus. A Malan fought in the first war against the British, and a Malan died in the second war against the British, the war in which Afrikaners were held in concentration camps.

There was one Malan buried in the archives who haunted Rian Malan more than the others. This Dawid Malan was the master, until 1788, of the finest estate in the Cape Colony. He owned slaves and vast vineyards, which he abandoned to run away with his neighbor's slave, a black woman named Sara. Taking nothing with them but two horses, Dawid and Sara disappeared from the colony and the historical record. Sara never reappeared on paper, but Dawid resurfaced several decades later, on trial for violently defending an Afrikaner's right to beat his black servant. "The man who abandoned his birthright for the love of a black woman had become what would one day be called a white supremacist," Malan wrote, "willing to die rather than accord black people equality before the law."

More than a century later, in 1948, another Malan, Daniel François Malan, led the Afrikaner nationalists to power on the promise of a "final solution." This was apartheid, a gridlock of laws that divided the population into racial groups and intervened in every aspect of life, from sex and marriage to work, housing, and education. Apartheid eliminated mixed neighborhoods, mandated segregation, and separated families. A byzantine system, the Pass Laws, controlled the movement of black South Africans within the country, and hundreds of thousands of black people were arrested each year for violations of these laws.

The young Rian Malan opposed apartheid, but not in any way that he would later consider meaningful. "We believed that apartheid was stupid and vicious," he wrote of himself and his teenage friends, "but we also believed that growing our hair long undermined it." He and his friends spray-painted SAY IT LOUD, I'M BLACK & I'M PROUD in six-foot letters on an embankment in their suburb, and Malan showed a photo to his family's black maid. Her response: "Ah, *suka.*" Get lost. Malan had never heard the James Brown song, but he'd read about it in *Time.* He knew more about American culture than he knew about the culture of the people who lived in his backyard, in shacks. "The strangest thing about my African childhood," he wrote, "is that it wasn't really African at all." Malan was more Western than he was African—because he was, more than anything, a product of apartheid.

At twenty, I recognized myself in the young Malan. I saw my own undeveloped politics, my own failings and my own frustrations, my own crisis of conscience. I saw the deficiencies in my education, which was, in many ways, an apartheid education. I had been fed mostly platitudes about race in America and I was hungry for real talk, so I was drawn to Malan's impatience with empty gestures and his intolerance of pious pronouncements.

At forty, when I traveled across South Africa carrying *My Traitor's Heart,* I read the book at more of a remove. I saw how often Malan describes black Africans as unknowable and inscrutable, with customs and conflicts that could never be comprehended, and of Africa itself as unfathomable and otherworldly. He compares white South Africa to a moon base, by which he means that it was insular and artificially maintained. But outside that base, in the townships and homelands of black South Africa, everything is alien to him. His book is the artifact of a mind still half-entrenched in apartheid.

The young Malan believed that he loved the black people in his life, the gardener Piet and the maid Miriam, who raised him. "Maybe it was the love of a prince for his loyal subjects," he later recognized, "and conditional on their remaining loyal and subservient." In high school he broke apartheid law when he slept with a black woman, but he didn't know her name, and his most frequent contact with his black compatriots was when he bought dope. "I yearned for black friends," he wrote, ". . . and in the end I was given some." These were his colleagues at a progressive newspaper.

Malan was working as a reporter for Johannesburg's *Star* in 1976, the year of the student uprising in the neighboring township of Soweto. On June 16, twenty thousand students walked out of the schools to protest apartheid, and were met by the police, who fired tear gas and live ammunition, killing hundreds of children. The next day, helicopters and armored cars were called into Soweto, but the uprising continued, and spread. White South Africa was on edge. "Whenever my telephone rang, some white paranoiac came on the line to pass along another rumor," Malan recalled. Someone had heard that tomorrow was kill-a-white day, for instance, or that black maids had been told to poison their employers' tea. While the black people of Soweto were mourning their children, the white people of Johannesburg were preoccupied with fears of imagined vengeance. In the midst of this paranoia, Malan answered a call reporting a real act of vengeance, a black man shouting, "Africa! Africa!" and swinging an axe at whites on the streets of Johannesburg.

Malan's first thought was that if he himself had been in that axman's path, all the good he'd ever done would not have saved him. He had disdain for the white paranoiacs, but he shared with them a fear that he was not safe. Fear, as he came to understand, was "the force that held the white tribe together." He sympathized with the axman's cause, but still, he didn't want to be killed. He wanted to be seen and recognized for who he was. He wanted, in other words, to be loved. He wanted this for all the reasons people want to be loved, but for another reason, too, a reason intimately tied to his race—he wanted proof that he was good, because he knew the system he was embedded within was bad.

I have to wonder now why I keep returning to this book. Beyond the spectacle of the murders—beyond the melodrama of Malan's tortured relationship with his country, beyond the unanswerable question of what it means to be white—is a problem that continues to captivate me: the problem of love under apartheid, which is now the problem of love in the ruins of apartheid.

*

The emotional landscape of *My Traitor's Heart* was so familiar to me at twenty, that when I boarded a plane at forty, I was still under the impression that I was going somewhere familiar. I was disabused of that notion even before I left the airport in Johannesburg. Dizzy with sleeplessness, I stood before a sign on the bathroom door and wondered what it meant. The sign was wordless, like the falling figure that indicates a wet floor, but it was communicating something else, in a universal visual language I did not understand. The sign was a reminder that I was not well traveled. Of the eleven official languages of South Africa, I spoke only one. This was an expansive country of wide velds and high deserts, mountain ranges and coastline, surrounded by three oceans, with a history that stretched back to the very beginning of humankind, and I knew next to nothing about it.

I stepped into the city feeling chastened. Flowers I couldn't name poured over brightly painted fences topped with razor wire. That first evening, I walked the streets of Johannesburg with Glen Retief, a white South African writer. He was the only South African I knew, and I didn't know him well—not well enough to have asked him to bring me along when he traveled back to his country from the United States. But here we were, both of us stopping and turning when we reached the edges of the neighborhoods that were familiar to him. If Glen was an imperfect guide to a country where less than 10 percent of the population was white, I was a more imperfect student. I had arrived with an independent study in mind, but I was doubting the whole endeavor already. I'd made a mistake, I confessed. It was crazy of me to have thought that by going to Africa I was somehow going deeper into my own country, into a place that would help me understand the place I came from. Glen, who had been living in the United States for most of his adult life, did not think this was crazy. What the United States and South Africa have in common, he said, is that they are both postapartheid states.

WELCOME HOME read a sign at the entrance to the Apartheid Museum. The museum was located between the city center of Johannesburg, which had been designated a white area under apartheid, and Soweto, the township that became, under apartheid, the largest black city in South Africa. The surrounding landscape was scrubby and arid, scarred by mining. This place was home, in that human life first evolved here, with all humans sharing one common ancestor, a woman who lived hundreds of thousands of years ago in what is now South Africa.

The museum was packed with schoolchildren, each group in matching uniforms, entirely purple, from the slacks to the shirts; or entirely blue; or entirely red. They were a beautiful sight, these children, streaming around us in their bright colors with their excited chatter. They were all black and all "born free," as they say in South Africa—born after the first democratic election that marked the end of apartheid, in 1994. Glen was moving quickly through an exhibit of anti-apartheid posters, looking for one that he might have pasted on a wall himself, but he stopped abruptly at the sight of a heavily armored vehicle topped by a machine gun and surrounded by a crowd of children. It was a sight that called to mind the Soweto Uprising, the children fired on by the police, and the armored cars that had rolled into Soweto the next day.

This armored car was a Casspir, which the police used to patrol the townships of black South Africa in the final decades of apartheid. Later, South Africa sold Casspirs to the United States, which used them in Iraq and Afghanistan, and in the War on Drugs, a war on our own people. In 2014, a Casspir, or one of its cousins, showed up at the protests in Ferguson, Missouri.

This Casspir emanated a metallic scent of use as we climbed through the narrow door. The interior was dark, with small windows, one cracked. Probably by a rock, Glen said. Rocks were the weapons with which the children of the townships fought the police, in uprising after uprising. Rocks and bricks and Molotov cocktails. This vehicle would have been manned by white boys just out of high school, afraid and unprepared, doing their mandatory military service. Glen had refused that service, and left the country in his twenties. Now he lingered inside the Casspir and said quietly, "Imagine being one of those boys." This armored car was like white South Africa, he told me—a confined space that was heavily protected, a psychological prison, but a safe one.

There were 131 nooses hanging from the ceiling of a small

room just beyond the Casspir. When I saw them through the doorway, I felt dislocated, as if they had followed me there, as if lynching were in the air I carried. Each noose represented the execution of a political prisoner who had been sentenced to death by hanging. The list of names on the wall did not include those who were killed without having been tried and sentenced, so it did not include the name Bantu Stephen Biko.

Biko was a leader of the Black Consciousness Movement, which emerged in the silence following the Sharpeville massacre of 1960. Informed by a diaspora of thinkers, from W.E.B. Du Bois and Marcus Garvey to Aimé Césaire and Frantz Fanon, Biko was a philosopher of the psychic impact of apartheid. "Not only have they kicked the black," he wrote of the Afrikaner nationalist government, "but they have also told him how to react to the kick." Refusing to cower before the kick was the foundation of Biko's philosophy. Black Consciousness, as he saw it, was not a means to an end. It was an end in and of itself—to live with dignity. "The most potent weapon in the hands of the oppressor," he wrote, "is the mind of the oppressed." And so to be "conscientized" was to reclaim your own mind.

From Johannesburg we flew to Port Elizabeth (now Gqeberha), where Biko had been imprisoned before his death. There we began driving across the Eastern Cape province into one of South Africa's former "homelands." These were reservations designated for native Africans, who could obtain passes to work in white South Africa but could not live there. "Sophisticated concentration camps" is what Biko called the homelands, where 80 percent of the nation's people were forced onto 13 percent of the land. Over three decades, 3.5 million people were relocated to the homelands, one of the largest mass removals in modern history.

Each homeland was the designated territory of a particular ethnic group, as defined by the government. We were in the former Transkei, which was Xhosa territory. The Xhosa were historically farmers and herders, and they migrated to this part of Africa before the Dutch arrived, making this something of an actual homeland. In 1976, the year before Biko was killed, the Transkei was declared an independent country and its occupants were stripped of their South African citizenship. This allowed the South African government, the only government that recognized the Transkei, to divest itself of responsibility to the people who lived there. "Separate development" is what this strategy was called—segregation on an enormous scale.

We drove three hundred miles into the former Transkei, past King William's Town (now Qonce), where Steve Biko was born, and through Mvezo, where Nelson Mandela was born. The landscape was a graceful grassland, lightly tattered. There were corrugated metal shacks along the roadsides, and barbed wire fences that had caught bits of trash. Women traveled on paths next to the road, carrying thirty-gallon barrels on their heads. In some places, gashes of erosion had opened in the hillsides, where the land had been overgrazed. Apartheid had starved this region of resources.

The drive took most of a day, the last three hours on unpaved, unmarked roads. When we arrived at a dirt lot on the edge of the village of Nqileni, dusk was turning to dark, and we walked the rest of the way down an unlit path, led by a young boy who did not speak English. There were no roads in Nqileni, just a handful of dirt tracks. Almost nobody in the village owned a car, and most everyone traveled on foot. The sky was wide and uninterrupted by telephone poles or electrical wires. In the velvety darkness, I could hear waves breaking on the edge of the black expanse that was the Indian Ocean.

Morning revealed a place of extraordinary beauty. The village was located between the Xhora River and the Bulungula River, on rolling hills that overlooked the ocean. The mouth of the Bulungula opened onto long stretches of sand, and mist rose off the shoreline through the mangroves on the bluffs. Low tide exposed rocks crusted with mussel beds, where women carried buckets of mussels on their heads.

The hills above the shore were dotted with smooth round huts, rondavels, painted peach or turquoise or butter yellow. Many were thatched with grass, and others had roofs of corrugated metal. Solar panels were mounted on some, to my surprise. These homes did not have running water or toilets, but they had enough solar energy to charge smartphones.

A woman nicknamed Jabu served as my guide to the village, and frequently as my translator. She was a lively conversationalist who spoke English, which she had learned from tourists in the backpackers' lodge, where women from the village cooked dinners of goat meat and pumpkin leaves for hikers making their way along the Wild Coast. "What is it like for women in your culture?" Jabu asked as we set off down the path leading from the lodge into the village. I fumbled my answer, getting lost in the minutiae of pay differentials and workplace discrimination. After listening patiently for a few moments, she asked, "Can a woman in your culture choose not to marry?" She knew the answer to this already, as well as the answer to her next question: "If a woman is married, can she have a job?"

Jabu was in her twenties and was the mother of a young child, but had no intention of marrying. Marriage would mean she could not leave the village for work or education. She would be confined to women's work as it was defined there, and she would be expected to wear the traditional dress of a married woman. Three older women sitting in the grass by the side of the path served as her example. Like most people in the village, they spoke only isiXhosa, but they smiled at us and took their role as an exhibit with good humor. They wore scarves knotted over their hair, and long, full skirts, with cloths tied around their waists. Those cloths, Jabu noted, were hot and scratchy.

Jabu wore knit shorts with leggings and ankle boots. Glen had given her a hat emblazoned with the name of the college where he taught, which she tucked over her hair. She would have looked at home in a coffee shop in the college town where I lived, except that she had demonstrated for me the traditional use of river clay as a cosmetic, so her face was covered in white clay. Ghost-faced, in her college-spirit-wear, Jabu knelt on the floor of her mother's rondavel and ground corn with a large rock, then laughed gently as I struggled to heft the same rock and crush a single kernel.

Women's work in Nqileni involved a considerable amount

of heavy lifting. There was the carrying of water, the collecting of firewood, the lugging of buckets of cow dung to resurface the floors, and the excavation of mud to make the bricks from which the rondavels were constructed. This was all the routine maintenance of life. There was little work in the village that wasn't women's work, but there weren't very many men. When I asked Jabu where the men were, she answered simply, "The mines." Except for the young and the old, most men left the village for work, as they had under apartheid.

"A culture is essentially the society's composite answer to the varied problems of life," Biko wrote in an essay about African theology. The culture Jabu called "my culture" was postapartheid Xhosa culture, which answered problems introduced by apartheid, among other problems. It was a way of life that had been disrupted and undermined, but still maintained. I wanted to blame apartheid for burdening the women of Nqileni, but Jabu understood the source of her outrage to be something far older.

The village headman explained to me, with Jabu as his interpreter, that the crates he used as chairs were reserved for men, and women should sit on the floor. His home was a small rondavel like all the others, mostly empty inside, with a single kerosene burner for cooking, an eroded dirt yard, and a few wandering chickens. The headman was responsible for allocating land and settling disputes in the village. One of my traveling companions asked if people like us, white Americans, would be allowed to move to this village. We could seek permission from the tribal council, the headman responded tactfully, and then added something that made Jabu smirk. If we moved here, we would have to be prepared to open up our private bank accounts, as the members of this village shared everything.

I watched Jabu's face as she listened, alert to every word and every implication. The spotlight of my limited understanding was trained on her, and it was from this position, as Jabu's foreign audience, that I admired her. I didn't know her, but I felt that I recognized her. I saw the little dance move she did to express enthusiastic agreement, and the posture of quiet deference she assumed when translating. I saw the way she expanded her vocabulary, learning and practicing the term *umbilical cord* over the course of several days. Eventually, she'd like to complete her secondary education, she said, but that would require leaving the village. For now, she had a child to raise, and she wanted to send him to university.

I spent my days in Nqileni walking the paths that rose and fell over the hills. I visited the local radio station where Jabu hosted several radio shows, and I traded polite greetings with one of Jabu's cousins, who wore a red leather jacket with metal studs on the shoulders and red clay on her face. I practiced my four or five words of Xhosa intermittently, with no improvement. After dark, I returned to my rondavel by the lodge, where the dung floor and the thatched roof had filled the room with a grassy scent. I opened a window to the wind coming off the ocean and lay down to read *My Traitor's Heart* with a flashlight. I read without interest then, finding the book suddenly dim and hard to follow. At the far edge of what had once been an unrecognized country, Malan's concerns seemed to belong to another world, the world of white South Africa.

"Mike was my friend, but he didn't trust me," Malan writes. This was his colleague at the paper, a black man who quoted Milton and hummed Handel. They drank together after work, before returning to their segregated neighborhoods, and talked about everything but politics. "If we had talked politics, I would have had to creep and crawl and beg forgiveness for what my people were doing to his. I would have turned into a worm, and Mike into a cripple, a victim." It seems unlikely to me now that Mike would have allowed for that—Mike was a Biko man, a Black Consciousness man. But I don't doubt that the politics of the moment freighted their friendship.

Malan, who shared a last name with the minister of defense, had been assigned to cover crime in part because he spoke Afrikaans, the language of the police. Working for the newspaper allowed Malan to temporarily defer his military service. When the time came to serve, he left the country. "I ran because I wouldn't carry a gun for apartheid, and because I wouldn't carry a gun against it," he writes. "I ran away because I hated Afrikaners and loved blacks. I ran away because I was an Afrikaner and feared blacks." He fled in a confusion of love and fear. When he returned eight years later, he looked up his old friend Mike. Those years had been hard years in South Africa, years of violent struggle, and Mike was weary. He had been drinking himself to death, he told Malan as they headed to Soweto for a *jol*, a bender.

At the shebeen where they drank, Mike told anyone who asked that he would vouch for this white man, that he would "go the whole hog for him." This moved Malan, who was always searching Mike for signs of affection. But the night got darker as Mike got drunker. Someone asked if "this whitey was ripe for the picking," and Mike chuckled. Malan asked his drinking companions if this, his whiteness, really needed to come between them. One of them told him that every white man was an enemy, and then affably made an exception for Malan. But Mike was not in the mood to release Malan from his whiteness, and he would not tell him the lie he wanted to hear—that it didn't mean anything.

I felt done with Malan then, after a day of watching people make the most of the starved land that apartheid had left behind. I was tired of Malan's need to be exonerated, and his fixation on being understood as good. I felt far from his desperate desire to be loved by his fellow country people. But that was when I was still in Africa, reading by flashlight. Now, years later, back home under electric lights, I don't feel so far away from Malan's desires. I know what it is to be a tourist in your own country, and I know that's much worse than being a tourist anywhere else.

Jabu marked the conclusion of her tour of women's work by painting the faces of her tourists in the manner that female initiates in the village are painted during the ceremony that marks their transition to adulthood. There was some sly humor to this, as if we Americans had remained children in our insular lives and were awaiting passage into true adulthood even as we entered middle age. But it was an embarrassing spectacle, too, this sacred ritual repurposed as a tourist attraction.

I wanted no part in a fake initiation, but I wanted to be close to Jabu. I wanted to feel the warmth of her breath on my face as she painted my eyelids. In the darkness behind my eyes, that warmth flooded a vast subterranean cavern of teenage loneliness, a loneliness punctuated by an occasional sleepover, a brief encounter with a girl who might give me a tour of her life, dress me in her clothes, and apply makeup to my face, her touch a flicker of intimacy.

Jabu had no reason to trust me, and I knew that, or I would not have hesitated to ask her the question I asked before I left Nqileni. I had avoided this question for as long as I could, until my last day in the village, when we were walking down the path toward the lodge.

"You can write about me," Jabu answered quickly, unconcerned. Then she added, "But I think you should write about Steve Biko." She gave his name the proper isiXhosa pronunciation, "Beekaw," so I wasn't sure I understood. "He was killed by the police?" I asked. "Yes," she said. "You should write a poem about Biko. About what they did to him, what they did to people during apartheid."

What the security police did to Biko was detain him for interrogation and then inflict a head injury that caused him to die of brain damage. What the government had already done, years earlier, was declare Biko a banned person. He was confined to the township where he grew up, could not speak in public, could not publish his writing, and could not be quoted in the press.

In the year before his death, Biko was called as a witness in the trial of nine young black men who were accused of treason, not for their actions as much as for their ideas. Black Consciousness itself was on trial. Biko was asked to explain the slogan "Black is beautiful," and several pages of trial transcript were dedicated to an interrogation of the word *black*, during which the judge asked, "But now why do you refer to you people as blacks? Why not brown people?"

Biko used the term *black* expansively, not just for Indigenous Africans. *Black* was an inversion of *non-white*, the collective term used by the government for an ever-increasing array of racial categories, including Colored, Bantu, Indian, and Malay. These categories were, Biko recognized, a divisive strategy. *Black* was a gesture of solidarity, whereas *non-white* was a term of exclusion. To be called *non-white* was to be defined in the negative, Biko argued, defined by what you weren't. To choose *black* was to define yourself in the positive.

Under apartheid logic, being pro-black could only mean being anti-white. This is what Donald Woods, a white newspaper editor, feared when he first met Biko. Woods was opposed to apartheid, but he was also opposed to Black Consciousness. He misunderstood it as a claim to cultural superiority. Black pride, he thought, was as racist as Afrikaner nationalism. And he resented being reduced to his race. "I don't have to bloody well apologize for being born white or for racial policies I don't support!" Woods told Biko during their first meeting. At this, Biko grinned and settled back into his chair.

Biko wasn't asking for any apologies, and he wasn't interested in reproducing apartheid with black tyrants in place of white tyrants. He wanted more than "a mere change of face" in the government—he wanted an entirely new system of governance. Biko had nothing against white liberals as individuals, he explained, but he didn't believe that black liberation could be achieved under white leadership. White liberals were too comfortable, and their goals were too limited. He wouldn't compromise on his most basic rights, and whatever hurt feelings this caused couldn't be his concern.

By the end of that first meeting, Woods had agreed to hire a black reporter to write a column on Black Consciousness. As Biko walked Woods to his car, he pretended to shield his eyes from the blinding glow of the Mercedes, one of the spoils of apartheid. They became friends, and Biko never stopped ribbing Woods about the Mercedes, which, Woods protested, was the "smallest, cheapest" Mercedes available.

Early in their friendship, Woods tried to impress Biko by offering to bring him to a restaurant where black people could not ordinarily dine with white people. Biko was not impressed, they did not go to the restaurant, and that, Woods noted, was his last act of "token integration," though it was not his last blunder. Both men had political ambitions and loved nothing more than long conversations about political strategy, so this was not an unlikely friendship. But it was opposed by every force in the country, including the police force.

To evade the security police, Woods and Biko sometimes used puns on isiXhosa words as a code when they arranged their meetings. Woods had grown up in the Transkei, where he'd learned to speak isiXhosa from his playmates. Those Xhosa children didn't have schools, so they couldn't read, and it had never occurred to Woods that his black playmates were his intellectual equals—not until he met Biko. Opposed to apartheid as he was, apartheid had nonetheless left a mark on his mind.

After Biko's death, Woods was declared a banned person for his association with Biko. He could not write for the newspaper or appear in public, he was surveilled and harassed, his family was threatened, and he eventually fled South Africa to publish his book *Biko*, which includes long passages of Biko's own words, smuggled out of a country that refused to print them. The book, like *My Traitor's Heart*, is an indictment of white liberalism, written by a white liberal.

Biko himself, writing under the name Frank Talk, had a few things to say about white liberals. They believed fervently in the "myth of integration" and were eager to promote integration alone as the solution to a problem that would, in the end, long outlast apartheid. This problem was the concentration of wealth and property in the hands of a white minority. The psychic shadow cast by the concept of racial superiority would also outlast apartheid. White liberals were preoccupied with maintaining their moral superiority, Biko wrote, and wasted too much energy proving their liberalness to one another and performing it for black people. "If they are true liberals," he insisted, "they must realize that they themselves are oppressed."

Biko was killed the year I was born, 1977, but none of what he writes about white liberals seems of the past to me, or of another place. Nor does the manner of his death: beaten by the police. Here in the suburbs of Chicago, the integration of the public schools is still commonly regarded as the solution to a much bigger problem. We are housed within this problem, in properties whose value has been artificially inflated or deflated by redlining and zoning laws. Not long ago, this historically progressive town had separate hospitals for white people and black people, and separate YMCAs. The aftermath of apartheid is still unfolding here, and the past is still playing out. One needs only to read the local papers, or listen in on conversations within the PTA, to witness amateur actors delivering poorly performed versions of Biko's first conversation with Donald Woods. I myself have rehearsed that conversation several times, sometimes playing Woods, and sometimes playing Biko.

Like Woods, I feel hurt when I'm not seen for who I am, and like Biko, I'm aware of more pressing concerns. The United States incarcerates more of its own people than South Africa did at the height of apartheid. I know this, but I don't feel it every day, in part because I'm protected from it. What I feel every day are the stresses in my relationships with friends and colleagues and neighbors. The assumptions, the misunderstandings, the discomfort that is spoken and unspoken. The reality that we are not equals before the law.

Unspooling alongside every interaction is a filmstrip of who we are, a supercut of unsteady footage. In one video, shot in a New Jersey mall, a fistfight begins between two teenagers when a light-skinned boy pushes a black boy. Police break up the fight and sit the light-skinned boy down on a couch while both officers kneel on the back of the black boy and handcuff him. The light-skinned boy, who will later clarify that he is not white and call the arrest of the other boy "plain old racist," watches from the couch. This viral video was texted to me by the father of one of my son's friends. An explanation followed, but I knew what he wanted me to see.

Friends Disappear is the title of a book about this town where we live. The author, Mary Barr, begins with a photo of her childhood friends sitting on the front steps of a house. They have all just graduated from eighth grade at the middle school where my son is now in eighth grade. The date of the photo is 1974, when the school district had been desegregated for five years. Six of the teenagers are black and seven are white. They are sitting shoulder to shoulder, two with their arms linked, one on another's lap. They are close. But the white kids and the black kids won't remain friends in high school. They will hardly see one another. By the time Barr tracks down every person in the photo, thirty years later, two of the black boys will be dead—one killed in a confrontation with the police, another in a crash during a police chase.

All but one of the teenagers in the photo "flirted with delinquency," according to Barr. They smoked pot, they drank, they skipped classes, they got bad grades. Two of the white kids dropped out and finished their degrees at night school, but all the white kids went on to prosperous futures. Only one of their black friends made it to the middle class.

There is a persistently naive belief, common among white liberals, that fostering friendships between children of different racial backgrounds will heal the division cleaved into this country by American apartheid. Friendship, in other words, is seen as the solution to a problem that threatens lasting friendship.

I once sat in a restorative-justice circle at my local elementary school, where a white parent new to the district told the circle that he wanted his children to have black friends. Asked if he had any black friends, he admitted in dismay, "No, not here." Within that circle, this was understood as a personal failure, rather than a consequence of the long aftermath of apartheid.

Love and friendship are undermined by the same policies that undermine education and homeownership. Redlining devalued black property and left American cities gutted—so, too, with interracial relationships. We have railroads running between us, highways, sanitary canals. This is part of the everyday agony of living in a postapartheid state. Is this agony the worst of it? Not by far. But it is agony, nonetheless.

"The American landscape was once graced with resplendent public swimming pools, some big enough to hold thousands of swimmers at a time," Heather McGhee writes in her book *The Sum of Us*. In the 1950s, under pressure to integrate those pools, some towns transformed them into members-only private swim clubs. Others drained their pools and let them sit empty. In St. Louis, the first integrated swim at the largest public pool in the country ended with a white mob attacking the black swimmers. In Montgomery, Alabama, the grand Oak Park pool was filled with dirt and paved over. I now think of the gaps in my life, in my relationships—the silences, the losses, the failures, the distances—as swimming pools filled with dirt.

Shortly before I left for South Africa, a friend told me that her wife, a banker, worked with a white man from South Africa who had once said, "It's hard to be a white man in South Africa." That phrase became a joke between my friend and her wife, something one of them would say if she happened to catch the other looking out of touch or self-involved: upset that the lawn service had failed to eradicate the dandelions, for instance. I found this joke funny even as I believed something of the earnest sentiment. Not that it is hard to be a white man in South Africa, but that it is hard to reclaim your own mind from apartheid.

"It was harder than ever to be white and conscious," Malan writes of the final years before the end of apartheid—meaning that many of the white people in his circle didn't know what to do with their consciousness. Understanding their position in what Biko called "the system" made them want to escape that position, but they saw no way out. A "people without a positive history is like a vehicle without an engine," as Biko put it, referring to an apartheid education that taught African history as a series of deficiencies and defeats. Malan, who recognized the history of his people in Africa as a history of hatred given and received, found himself without an engine. He hated Afrikaners for being bigots, and he hated liberal whites for being ineffectual. He had no tribe.

White people are, as a group, hard to love. We can also be difficult as individuals. When we look at one another, we don't always like what we see. There's a white South African woman in my town who runs a website that informs white residents about issues of relevance to black residents. I haven't met her, but I've seen her interviewed in a film, and even before she said anything, I was distancing myself from her in my mind. She had lived here for almost twenty years, she said, and she'd once thought she lived in a diverse community. But at some point she noticed that all her friends were white, and that she knew nothing about the black community or its history. As a child growing up under apartheid, she said, she felt guilty, and uncomfortable, and helpless. There, at the word *helpless*, the distance closed. I, too, felt helpless, and I hated to admit it.

"I have told you several murder stories, but the true subject of this narrative has been the divided state of my own heart," Malan confesses in his final chapter, the chapter he rewrote for the paperback published a year after the first edition. Mandela had been released from prison by then, and Malan was still revising a book that had already gone to print. Both endings read as an unsolved problem. The closest Malan comes to putting this problem into words is "I was searching for a way to live in this strange country."

I spent my last hours in South Africa walking the wide, pleasant paths of Green Point Park in Cape Town. The previous day, we had driven past miles and miles of tightly packed metal shacks flanked by rows of concrete outhouses near the edge of the highway, through the bleakest landscape I had ever seen, to a school in Makhaza township where children danced for us. At the end of the performance, Glen got up and danced the jive while I quietly wept, hiding my tears. Those tears were the product of the education I'd come for. And so, educated, I walked through the park in a rage. To hell with this country, I was thinking. A white woman came along the path with a child on a tricycle, trailing glittering red steamers from the handles, spangled by sunlight. I looked through the woman's smile into her skull, and thought, *How do you live with yourself?* The answer to this question came to me instantaneously. She lives with herself, my mind told me, in exactly the same way you do.

MOSAB ABU TOHA

The Pain of Travelling While Palestinian

FROM *The New Yorker*

THE FIRST time I travelled outside of Gaza, I was twenty-seven years old. Growing up, I had always thought of "travel" as riding a taxi, bus, or bike within the borders of the Gaza Strip. My family lived not far from Railway Street, but there were no trains there. I had heard stories about the Gaza International Airport, but Israel had bombed it when I was eight. I remember asking my childhood friend Izzat, a soccer fan, about the places he wanted to visit one day. "Barcelona," he told me. "I want to play alongside Messi, Xavi, and Iniesta." In 2014, a few days after Izzat graduated from college, he was killed in an Israeli air strike. Our freedom of movement was just another victim of the occupation.

The first place I tried to visit was Boston. I needed a US visa, but was not allowed to travel forty miles to the US embassy in Jerusalem, or to drive four hours through Israel to the US embassy in Amman, Jordan. Instead, my brother-in-law drove me to the Rafah border crossing with Egypt, in southern Gaza, so I could fly to Jordan for my visa interview. I remember standing in the travel hall in Rafah, surrounded by the young, the old, and the sick, and thinking that my suitcase, like me, had never been on a real journey before. When my plane took off from Cairo International Airport, I had the feeling that my legs were shrinking below me.

At the US embassy in Jordan, an officer handed me a list of personal information that I would need to provide: home addresses, phone numbers, and e-mail addresses, the names of my siblings and children. My fifteen-year travel history was blank. I did not know how long the decision would take—only that I could not go back to Gaza while I was waiting. After forty days of limbo, living in a rented apartment in Amman, I finally got the visa. In the years that followed, I was lucky to go on many trips.

Since October 7, it has been difficult to exit Gaza at all. My immediate family was able to leave in November because my youngest son, Mostafa, has a US passport. On our way to Egypt, however, Israeli soldiers separated me from my family, beat me, and interrogated me. In December, my mother applied to travel to Qatar with my twenty-year-old sister, Afnan, who needed medical care for a rare genetic disorder. They were not approved until late March. Afnan, who has the vocabulary of a four-year-old, could barely understand the broken Arabic of Israeli soldiers at a checkpoint. My mother nearly fainted during a four-kilometer walk in the sun. In Gaza, this is what travel means now.

In June, I took another trip. My family was relocating from Egypt to Syracuse, New York, and we planned to visit my mother and sister in Doha on the way there. We were excited. In the two-hour van ride to the airport, I took photos, and Yazzan, my eight-year-old son, looked out the window and asked questions. In Doha, my mother and sister greeted us at the entrance to their building. I laughed when I looked in their fridge, which was stocked with fresh foods that were impossible to find in wartime Gaza. "Look what you have!" I told my mother. "Mango, cherry, cucumber, cheese, and more."

She looked guilty, not happy. "I wish I stayed with your father and your siblings and their kids," she told me. She had waited months to come to Doha, only to wonder if she never should have left. She said that Afnan was so afraid of going home that she was refusing to leave the apartment for days on end.

We stayed for a week. Then, on the morning of June 18, we woke up early and collected our suitcases. My mother stood in silence, avoiding our eyes. I promised her that we would meet soon in Gaza, but both of us knew that we might be away from home for a long time.

On our way to the airport, the sun shone gracefully above the Persian Gulf. I felt proud that we had made it this far. We were sitting and waiting for our flight when a young man, who was tapping something into his phone, looked up at me and spoke in Arabic. "Are you Mosab? Mosab Abu Toha?"

I pretended not to know the name, but my kids gave me away. "Yes, this is Mosab!" my daughter Yaffa said. "He is kidding."

The man smiled. I smiled at the kids, then at him. "How do you know me?"

"I know your story. Is it not you who was detained by the Israeli Army?"

"Yes. In fact, I was kidnapped, not detained."

The young man was Palestinian, like us. He studied at MIT but had recently helped his family evacuate Gaza and resettle in Qatar. I was amazed that two Gazans could meet by accident, like two fish finding each other in an ocean. That is the nature of the diaspora: Palestinians who might once have met in Gaza now bump into one another in airports.

When my family landed in Boston, for a layover, Mostafa jumped on one of our carry-on suitcases and asked me to pull him along. This was becoming his favorite kind of travel. In line for immigration, he started to sneak under the stanchions, laughing, his little face triumphant. Then it was our turn to step up to a booth. I handed over our passports and visas to a woman in a uniform.

When I saw the woman's reaction, I started to wonder whether something was wrong. She spoke into a radio. Then a muscular young man with a metal badge, who had a Taser, a pistol, and handcuffs on his vest, escorted us to a waiting area. After my experience with Israeli soldiers, I was nervous, but I didn't want my family to notice. "We need to go to our new house," Yazzan said impatiently. Finally, a young customs officer came over to talk to me.

I was surprised by the officer's kindness. He seemed concerned about whether my family in Gaza was safe and had enough food.

When he was done asking questions, he gave our passports back and even offered to help us with our suitcases. I was starting to relax, and I texted a few friends. "All good," I wrote to them. "Collecting our bags."

Before we could board our connecting flight, we had to pass through security again. My boarding pass seemed to trigger another alert. The officer reached for a radio and said, "Supervisor!"

The supervisor appeared behind the officer and looked at the screen. They chatted in a low voice before eyeing me. It turned out that a string of four letters had been printed on my ticket: "SSSS," for Secondary Security Screening Selection. "Your wife and kids can proceed," the supervisor said. "I will have to ask you to follow me."

This time, I was told to pass through a metal detector and then a millimeter-wave scanner. Neither seemed to find anything. A TSA employee asked if he could pat me down. I said yes. The employee ran his fingers around my collar and down my chest. Bystanders seemed to avert their eyes. I scanned the crowd and spotted my wife, Maram, in the distance, seeming to look for me. I wanted to shout to her, to reassure her, but I feared that would only make things worse. Then, with the back of his hand, the officer touched my private parts and my bottom. I knew that this sometimes happened to travellers. But for a moment, I felt as upset as I had been in Israeli custody.

While the officer swabbed my palms for explosives, Yaffa finally spotted me and tried to beckon me over. "I will join you when Uncle is done," I said in Arabic, acting like the TSA agent was a relative so she would not be scared. Finally, the supervisor left to photocopy my passport. When he came back, he said we were done.

"Before I go, I have to tell you something," I replied. He listened.

"I was kidnapped by the Israeli Army in November, before being stripped of my clothes," I told him. "Today, you come and separate me from my wife and kids, just like the Army did a few months ago."

He nodded, looking embarrassed. I asked him whether he would do the same to travellers from Israel. I thought about how Israeli settlers, who live on Palestinian land in violation of international law, can travel to the US without a visa. "This is random selection," he told me. "It's not meant for you."

I fought back tears. My children could see me. "For me, it's not random," I said. "I travelled to the US three times before. Nothing like this happened to me." He gave me a business card for complaints to the TSA.

I carried my shoes, watch, and travel documents over to where my family was sitting. We ate some lunch. On the final leg of our flight, the kids quickly fell asleep. In Syracuse, five old friends picked us up and loaded our ten suitcases into their three cars. Their warmth, the smell of the trees outside, the hot meal that was waiting at our new home, pushed my exhaustion and frustration away.

I could not have guessed that my next trip would be much worse. Around noon on July 1, a friend took me back to the Syracuse airport. I was flying to a book festival in Sarajevo by way of Washington, DC, and Frankfurt. I was unable to access my boarding pass from my phone, so I tried a self-service kiosk, which told me that my travel document required verification. "Please alert the nearest United representative," the kiosk said.

The United representative at the check-in counter stared at her screen for so long that a colleague came over to help. Then, struggling to pronounce the name of my destination, she asked, "Where is Sarajevo?"

"It's the capital of Bosnia and Herzegovina."

Another moment of silence. I asked if there was a problem.

"We think you can't transit in Germany," one of them said. I was surprised. I had flown through Germany several times in the past.

The first woman pointed to my passport number. "They only allow numbers that start with four, eight, and nine," she said. "Yours begins with a six."

They found me a new route via Washington, DC, and Athens. I wasn't happy—the trip would be longer than before—but I didn't think I had a choice. I accepted my new boarding passes and walked to security.

The Pain of Travelling While Palestinian

The TSA agent who scanned my ticket looked me over, then called his supervisor. My ticket said "SSSS" again. A young man read me the secondary-screening rules—two pages of tiny print—very quickly.

My bags went through the scanner. I went through the metal detector and millimeter-wave machine. An officer asked me whether I had been patted down before. "Unfortunately," I said. I knew what to do. He ran his hands over every part of my body, and I thought again of Israeli soldiers. Finally, I was allowed to rejoin the other travellers.

I found my gate and pulled out my phone. When I looked up the rules for travel through Germany, I realized that the United representatives had made a mistake. They had been looking at a list of prohibited ID-card numbers, not passport numbers. The number on my ID card started with an eight; I was allowed to travel through Germany. But now it was too late. I needed to board or I would miss my flight.

When we landed in DC, I called United. An agent told me that I was still booked on a Lufthansa flight to Frankfurt. "Are you sure?" I said. The boarding pass in my hand said Athens. For a moment, I felt relieved. It was 5:20 p.m. and my flight to Frankfurt was at six.

At the gate, the Lufthansa staff had trouble printing my "new" boarding pass. They, too, called a manager, and I rushed through my story. I was now so frustrated that I was thinking about cancelling the entire trip. Then the manager told me, "You need to go and re-check in, I'm afraid." She pointed to my new boarding pass. It said "SSSS."

Shocked, I told her that I had been screened just three hours before. "I'm sorry," she said. "You cannot board the plane without this." It was now 5:33 p.m.

The directions to the TSA checkpoint were complicated, so a kind female staff member ran there with me as my backpack bounced on my back like a door knocker. A TSA supervisor confirmed that I would have to be screened again, and the officer who searched my bag appeared to touch every item in my luggage—tea bags, pens, a notebook, a comb. She put her hand into each of my socks, as though searching for something to justify the "SSSS" on my ticket. About five TSA employees stood around as I was patted down, watching me realize that my trip was already ruined.

After seventeen minutes, the supervisor stamped my boarding pass four times in red. When I told him that I had been treated unfairly, he told me about an online portal where I could complain. By the time I returned to the gate, it was 6:30 p.m. The plane was gone.

United gave me a convoluted new itinerary with a total of five legs: Syracuse to Washington, Washington to Munich, Munich to Frankfurt, Frankfurt to Zagreb, and Zagreb to Sarajevo. My next flight would not take off until after midnight, and I struggled to stay awake. I thought about giving up and flying back to Syracuse—a day of travel, wasted. But I reminded myself of the readers I would meet in Bosnia, of the excitement of signing my book of poems in Bosnian.

Two hours before the flight, I requested my boarding pass at the Lufthansa gate. Again, the staff could not print it and called a manager. When he arrived about an hour later, he asked me whether I had a Schengen visa for travel in the European Union.

"Why do I need a Schengen visa? I'm not staying in a country that needs one."

"You need a Schengen visa because you cannot transit in more than one Schengen country."

I could not believe this was happening. The airline had given me an itinerary that I was barred from following. "You have to find a solution for this," I said. I was twelve hours into my trip and I had not even left the United States. The manager seemed kind, but after making some calls he concluded that I would not be allowed to board. "Maybe you should try finding a flight where you don't have to transit in the Schengen area," he said.

When I called United and demanded a new flight, the woman on the other end of the line told me, "We can get you a trip to Sarajevo, but I cannot get you a stay in a hotel." She connected me with her supervisor. "It's your job to know whether I can take a flight or not," I told him.

I stayed on the phone for eighty-six minutes, until 1:55 a.m. I was tethered to an outlet so that my phone would not run out of charge. The only flight that could get me to the festival in time, the manager finally said, was leaving for Vienna in more than fifteen hours. The airline would not book me a hotel.

I was lucky that my new gate was near an airport chapel. I went inside and found a pile of prayer rugs in a closet. The room was empty, so I arranged them into a makeshift pillow and blanket, lay down, and slept on and off for more than twelve hours. Before walking to the gate, I made up for all the prayers that I had missed.

On July 3 at 2 p.m., I landed in Sarajevo. Forty-four hours had passed since I had arrived at the airport in Syracuse.

Sarajevo reminded me of Gaza. I saw bullet holes in the walls of some buildings and craters in several streets. I thought back to 2014, when Israeli forces had bombed my neighbor's house and my family had patched holes in our home. I thought of the day last year when Israeli strikes reduced our home to rubble.

In my four days in Sarajevo, I met many writers and artists. One of them invited me to an upcoming festival there, which several Gazan photographers and artists were expected to attend. At first I said that I would be glad to come. Then I thought about the airports and the screenings and the days away from my family, and I changed my mind. When I wrote to the editor of my forthcoming book about how difficult the trip had been, he told me, "For your book tour, maybe we should arrange events in cities near you so you don't have to enter airports." I had hoped that travel would make my world seem larger, but I felt like it had clipped my wings.

To my amazement, the return journey went smoothly. There was no "SSSS" on my tickets. When I checked in at the Sarajevo airport, an agent took a few minutes to confirm with a colleague that I could board, then waved me through. I made it to Syracuse as scheduled, feeling like I had got away with something. A friend picked me up at the airport. Later, I looked up an online ranking of passports from around the world. Israeli passports, which allow for visa-free travel to a hundred and seventy destinations, were ranked eighteenth in the world. Passports from the Palestinian Territories, which allow for visa-free travel to just forty destinations, were near the bottom of the list.

In the weeks after my trip, I tried to understand what had happened to me. My friend Hasan, a US citizen who spent most of his life in Gaza, told me that he is regularly stopped at airports and asked intrusive questions—for example, what he is doing in his own country of citizenship, or whether he is carrying a weapon. I also called three experts on the surveillance of travellers.

Shezza Abboushi Dallal, an attorney at an organization that works to hold law enforcement accountable, housed at the City University of New York, told me that the US government maintains a watch list, which includes travellers, that it calls the Terrorist Screening Dataset. The most famous part of the database is the no-fly list. "But there is also the selectee list," she said. People on this list are often pulled out of line for secondary screenings, as I was.

I learned from Faiza Patel, the senior director of the Liberty and National Security Program at the Brennan Center for Justice, that even experts don't know how many watch lists there are, or how people are added to them. A person can also experience secondary screenings without being on any list. Some passengers are flagged because of where they're going, or because they have a one-way ticket.

I kept wondering whether I was on a list because I come from Gaza, or because the Israeli government had wrongly labeled me a threat. Dallal said that many Palestinians have reported problems at US airports since October 7. "There's a lot of intelligence sharing between Israel and the United States," Patel told me. But we had no way of knowing whether that had played a role in my case. Saher Selod, the author of *Forever Suspect: Racialized Surveillance of Muslim Americans in the War on Terror*, connected my experience to the Bush era, when the screening database was expanded. She also mentioned another policy from that time, the now-defunct National Security Entry-Exit System, in which people from twenty-four Muslim-majority countries (and North Korea) were made to register for fingerprinting, photographing, and interviews. "If you're wondering if being Palestinian is part of this . . . absolutely," she said.

I kept checking the website where the Department of Homeland Security, which oversees the TSA, reviews complaints. For ten weeks, my case was "in progress." Then *The New Yorker* sent the TSA questions about my experience. Two and a half hours later, I received a "Final Determination Letter" from the DHS. It said, in part, that some airport screenings are random, and that the agency "can neither confirm nor deny any information about you which may be within federal watchlists." The letter referenced "systems which contain information from Federal, state, local and foreign sources" that can sometimes lead to the misidentification of travellers. It also said that the agency has "made any corrections to records that our inquiries determined were necessary, including, as appropriate, notations that may assist in avoiding incidents of misidentification."

In response to questions from *The New Yorker*, a spokesperson for the Israeli Army said, "We do not comment on information shared between Israel and its strategic partners." The TSA shared background information about secondary screenings and said, "TSA works closely with the intelligence and law enforcement communities to share information." It declined to comment on my experience at the airport.

On a Friday in August, I was at home in Syracuse when the doorbell rang. The kids were playing outside, and I heard a male voice ask them, "Is your father home?" Maram and I found two men at the door. For a moment, I thought they worked for the school district where we were trying to enroll the kids. Then I saw that one of them was wearing a badge and a pistol. "Hi. We're from the FBI."

One of the agents told me that he had heard about my experience with the TSA at Logan Airport. He asked if I had a few minutes to talk about it. They remained standing while I sat on the couch; one took notes on a tiny pad. I told them about my airport experiences. Then they started to ask about a wide variety of other topics—how we felt about the neighborhood, what we had done in Egypt and Qatar, what our lives were like in Gaza. Then they asked me about my "interaction" with the Israeli Army.

I told them that I had already described my experience in this magazine and on CNN, but they wanted me to talk about it. I was starting to explain how I was blindfolded and handcuffed when I realized that Yazzan was sitting next to me. I did not want him to experience my pain again, so I sent him upstairs before I continued. I explained that, since October 7, I had lost thirty-one members of my extended family in a single air strike, an Israeli sniper had killed one of Maram's uncles outside a school shelter, and Maram and I had each lost a grandparent to illnesses that were exacerbated by conditions in Gaza. Many of our relatives now live in tents. I got the feeling that they had not really come to ask me about my experience in the airport.

After nearly an hour, one of the agents asked me if I had any questions or concerns, or if I wanted to tell them anything. He sent me a text message and invited me to reach out. Before they left, I asked for help with my TSA complaint, or with removing my name from any watch list I might be on. They said that they couldn't help with other government agencies. They gave me a nameless business card for the local FBI office and left.

Maram came downstairs with Yazzan. We ate lunch together, but I was unable to enjoy it. She told me that when I had sent Yazzan upstairs, he had asked her, "Are they going to take Daddy?" When *The New Yorker* asked the FBI about my experience, a spokesperson declined to comment on where the agents had got my name or why they had visited me.

A couple of years ago, I wrote on Facebook that I was in Cairo for a visa interview, and my friend Ahmad saw my post. "I'm in Egypt, too," he messaged me. We spent a few serendipitous days together. Ahmad is a foodie, and one afternoon, we met for lunch in a restaurant that overlooked the Nile. Another day, we travelled together to the Red Sea—two Palestinians, exploring a place that was usually out of reach.

Earlier this year, I wrote to Ahmad in Gaza. "You just came into my mind yesterday," I told him in Arabic. "Do you remember our time together in Suez the summer before last? How are you doing?"

"I'm just doing some travelling, like you," he joked, wryly. "But I'm doing it from one school shelter to another." He had recently been in Rafah, where more than a million displaced Palestinians had taken refuge, and had tried to raise the money needed to leave Gaza with his family. Then Israeli forces had invaded Rafah, shuttering the border and displacing many families again. As of late August, Ahmad was living in a tent with his wife and three kids, in the Mawasi neighborhood of Khan Younis—the fifth place where they have stayed in the past year.

Ahmad begins each day at 6:30 a.m. "You cannot have a moment of sleep after that, because of the flies in the tent," he told me. He lines up to buy bread while his wife prepares breakfast, usually from canned food. "To make tea, I have to find someone who has lit a fire," Ahmad said. Then he spends about an hour and a half waiting to fill buckets of water. In photographs, he looks much thinner than he does in my memory.

Ahmad always dreamed of taking his wife and kids on a trip to Egypt, and beyond—to ride with them on trains, to try restaurants and cafés, to take pictures of new places. Now he dreams of adopting some other nationality, so he can escape in times like this. He is a refugee, not a traveller. "I've lost hope that we will return to our previous life," he told me. "I feel like we will remain refugees forever."

KHALIL ABUSHAREKH

Zeppole (aka Awama)

FROM *Your Impossible Voice*

I'D BEEN living in Houston for four years when a new restaurant opened in my neighborhood. Coppa created quite a buzz. The cuisine was Italian, and the waiter told me the pizza was made with Italian water. I didn't taste the Italian water, but after a delicious dinner, I asked the waiter what dessert he suggested to go with coffee. He replied that his favorite was zeppole. I didn't know what that zeppole was, but said I'd like to try it. When it arrived, it looked familiar—like the Palestinian dessert known as "awama" (donut balls), but this time topped with chocolate syrup. I took a bite. Immediately the taste transported me far, far away in time and place. I remembered I hadn't tasted this flavor for over fifteen years. At first, I couldn't remember why I had stopped eating this traditional tasty street dessert so common in Gaza. Then it came back to me. The taste conjured up a huge load of physical and emotional—especially emotional—pain.

A constant source of contention in our household had been that my mom would regularly buy new clothes for my two sisters but seldom for me. I would get angry and argue. Her standard answer was that girls must always look good and dress nicely. At age eleven, that response would just irritate me more. Later, I realized this phrase is the polite way of saying daughters get married, and they should always look nice to speed up the process. But I didn't care about that, and jealousy was eating at me like fire consuming wood. I decided to revolt against this injustice. I fine-tuned a master plan that would force my parents to buy me new shoes on a regular basis. I already knew how to wear out a pair of shoes in no time. No can, bottle, stone, wall, or even a street pole would be out of the reach of my kicks. I pummeled anything and everything in my path. If I didn't find an object, I kicked sand. I became a master at abusing shoes. By the end of a month, they would look pathetic, so Mom would buy me a new pair. It wasn't long before my dad suspected what was going on. He concluded that I needed to be taught a lesson. There would be no new shoes for me until the beginning of the new school year.

I looked at my pitiful shoes. There was no stitching in place. Air and water swirled in the space between my toes, and I couldn't distinguish between the color of my shoes and the color of the dust encasing them. But I shrugged my shoulders and said, "That's fine with me. When people see me, they will think I look homeless or like a beggar, and they know I am your son." Dad acted as if he hadn't heard me. I wanted to explode in anger, but he continued to ignore me. Months passed, and my hatred of humanity—all of it—accumulated. I couldn't bear being around my family, Dad, Mom, my sisters. Besides that, hot, sweaty summer was approaching.

Summer also would bring my dad's brother from the United Arab Emirates to spend his vacation with us. Uncle Marwan was and still is a generous gentleman. His visit meant gifts of French perfumes, colorful T-shirts, and lots of little gadgets powered by the Energizer Bunny. I figured that after my uncle arrived. I would be relieved of my dirty, tattered shoes, that they would be replaced in no time. *Just give him a day or two*, I thought, *and he will insist my mom buy me a new pair.*

Three days passed and he said not a word. To speed things up, I complimented his shoes. "Thank you. They are the Clark brand. It is known for comfort," he replied.

I thought to myself, *I don't care one whit about your shoe brand. Actually, they are a bit ugly. The point is, look at my shoes!* But of course, I didn't say anything. Instead, I dropped other hints to direct his attention to my feet, but more days passed. I came to believe that Uncle Marwan was deliberately ignoring my dilemma. That led me to add my favorite uncle to the tyrant category, next to my parents. I forgot about the perfumes, T-shirts, and gadgets. I forgot about any extra cash that he gave me; I stripped him of the title of being generous and a gentleman. Now I considered him a cheap man who didn't listen to me or help me solve my problem.

One night after a long, hot day, as usual I closed the family grocery store at the front of the house. When I entered our living quarters, everyone was already sitting in the courtyard, including many guests who had come to spend time with my uncle. Sitting in a circle on Monobloc chairs, they were listening to my uncle's stories and his perspective on matters big and small. With the stars twinkling overhead and a cool Mediterranean breeze, it was a very pleasant setting. I pulled up a chair and joined the circle, a little behind the elders. A fresh breeze wafted over us, but this time it was loaded with an awful smell. At first everyone ignored it. But then it came again. Individuals began searching with their eyes where it could have originated.

When the third wave hit, someone asked, "What is this smell? What can it be? Is it trash burning?" Another said, "Maybe it is a dead rat." Someone else asked, "Where is it coming from?" All the faces were questioning, except mine. I was immune to that smell. It was just my feet after I took off my shoes. Not a big deal.

Then, all eyes turned to the source of the smell. My uncle said to me, "Are you an idiot? You take off your shoes here, where we will be eating? Get up! Go wash your feet and put those shoes as far away from us as possible."

I stood up slowly, my face looking as if I didn't comprehend the problem. Then my uncle told my dad, "Do you like how he looks? What do you think people say about us after your son looks and smells like this?" My father tried to explain the situation to his brother, but my uncle cut him off. I turned my face aside to hide my smile. Filled with satisfaction, I wanted to do a victory dance then and there. Instead, I continued to play the role of a sad, miserable son as my uncle continued rebuking my dad for his actions. I washed my feet and returned to the group. Then Uncle Marwan said, "Mister, prepare yourself to go with me tomorrow to the market. I am going to buy you new shoes."

I continued my dopey look, and I asked, "But, who is going to sit in the store if I go with you?"

My uncle said, "Omar, tomorrow you sit in the store until we come back from the market." I managed to continue looking like a boy who had no power but to obey his uncle's orders, but that night I couldn't sleep. I kept imagining what brand, what style, what color my new shoes would be. And what if my uncle would buy me two pairs of shoes? One scenario followed another.

We didn't go to the old city market. Instead, Uncle Marwan took me to the new market. What a great start! This was the place Mom avoided because of the more expensive, luxurious brands. My eyes were scanning the windows while trying to keep up with my uncle's giant strides. After we stepped into one of the shops, Uncle Marwan's attitude made me think he must already know the store owner. Gradually, however, I realized it was a trick of his to act as if he were a celebrity, someone everyone knows. Because of his accent, it was instantly obvious that Uncle Marwan was not from Gaza. The owner welcomed my uncle and flattered him by announcing, "You sound as if you are not from here. May I ask where you are from?"

With a big smile, my uncle responded, "I can't believe you picked up on my accent so quickly. I am from Gaza, but I've been working in Abu Dhabi, in the Emirates, for over twenty years." Whenever my uncle meets someone new in Gaza, he immediately tries to make a connection. He wants to find someone who knows someone who has worked with him in the Emirates or who studied with him in Egypt. The store owner was no exception. My uncle began digging into his memory, trying to remember the one guy he knew in Egypt with the same last name as the store owner, but that person's first name did not come to him. Uncle Marwan started a description—a man about my uncle's age who was fair-skinned with black hair, not too skinny, but maybe he had gained weight by now. Eventually, the name Mohammed came to him. The store owner's face remained blank. My uncle came back with a question. "Maybe I'm thinking of his younger brother? Maybe it's not Mohammed. Is there a Mahmoud?"

I just wanted all Mohammeds and Mahmouds to die. I wanted my uncle to end this useless dialogue. We were in the store to buy me shoes, not for an ancestry discussion. But I had no say in the matter. I sighed now and then or tapped my filthy shoes on a chair leg. My thoughts wandered to how I would burn these shoes with gasoline as soon as I got my hands on a new pair. Finally, after tea and the journey through extensive family histories and my uncle slipping details of his travels and adventures into the conversation, he mentioned me. "My nephew Khalil needs new shoes. Would you please find him something of excellent quality that also looks good?"

Soon I was trying on one shoe after another. I asked for the brands I coveted and tried on only those shoes that appealed to me. My mom wasn't there, and I could choose what style, what color of shoes to buy. Price was not an issue. Plus, for the first time ever I would have a pair of shoes that actually fit like a glove. Mom always insisted on buying a size too big so my feet would have room to grow. But this day I didn't need to think about the future. This day I could choose exactly what I wanted! I picked suede shoes because they were just what my mom would never consider buying.

Walking home, I tried to keep a considerable distance between me and anyone else so that no harm would come to my new shoes. I knew I was wearing the coolest brown suede shoes ever. I even believed I was a better human being because of the shoes I was wearing. Mom, of course, had a completely different opinion. She looked at me and said, "You are an absolute idiot! You picked suede shoes! What good are they on the camp's dusty, dirty streets?" I was convinced she said those things because of how expensive the shoes were and because she was jealous.

My uncle paid thirty-five shekels for the shoes. With thirty-five shekels my mom could buy me sufficient clothes for a full year.

In the meantime, since my grandparents lived less than a block from us, as did many aunts and uncles on my mother's side, Riad, my youngest uncle, spent a lot of time at our house. I considered him more a friend than an uncle. He let me listen to his tapes of Western music, especially George Michael and Ace of Base. On rainy winter nights we would be in his dark room listening to the music of Fairuz while reading pulp fiction pocket novels for hours on end. No conversation necessary.

That "new shoes" summer, my mom asked her younger brother to go to Naser Street to buy some awama to be shared that night with my Uncle Marwan and other guests. Riad planned to ride his bike to the store and asked if I wanted to join him. Immediately I said yes, especially since it would be an excellent opportunity to show off my new shoes on the trendy, clean sidewalks of Naser Street. I rode on the middle bar of the bike, not a comfortable place to sit, but better for the biker. The added weight is in the center, and the person pedaling enjoys better control of the bike. As for me, I knew I would enjoy the ride no matter what, since I could feel superior to the kids we passed who were walking.

The ride became harder when we approached the steep slope by Shanti's mosque. That hill is every biker's nightmare. I offered to get off the bike and walk up the slope, but Riad was stubborn. I remained on the bike. His breathing became more labored, but at the same time he tried to suppress it and act cool. The bike continued to slow down. Soon, it was barely moving, but Riad was up to the challenge. Once he reached the summit, with his voice barely audible, he announced, "It wasn't that bad. It was easy except for your heavy weight."

Now the road was flat, and Riad wanted to make up the time lost on the slope. He started to go faster and faster. Turning to me, he asked if I was afraid. "Of course not," I responded. "Actually, you are still going slow!" Though he pedaled still faster I couldn't resist asking, "Is this the best you can do?"

My scream pierced the heavens. The bike was on top of us, and I felt the hot asphalt under me. Riad asked me not to move as he pulled my foot out of the bicycle's wheel. After I was freed, I kept jumping on one leg, holding my other bare foot and squealing like a stuck pig. Riad shouted at me to stop moving around. Then he carried me to the sidewalk and sat me down. "Don't move. Let me see if your foot is broken," he said. That scared me even more, and my crying became more intense. He gently manipulated my foot, examining it like an expert. Then Riad said, "No broken bones." I felt good, even though pain ripped through one foot.

But then I remembered my new shoes. I didn't want to look, even though I knew I had to. My right shoe had been ripped to pieces, with one big flap barely hanging onto the sole. My heart stopped as Riad looked at me and smiled. "That's a very good quality shoe. It saved your foot and absorbed the hit."

Time froze. Voices faded away. Nothing else existed except me and my shattered shoe. First anger and then the sense of defeat crept into my being. I had worn those beautiful shoes only a few days. It would have been better if my flesh had been destroyed or my ankle broken if it meant my shoe had not been harmed. I concluded that day that mankind was involved in a conspiracy. My heart was on fire, filled with rage. I needed to seek revenge against all mankind, especially the evil forces that had taken from me my most precious shoes.

Days passed, and my sense of outrage slowly receded. I forgave my Uncle Riad and his bike, concluding that zeppole, awama, was the cause of this disaster. If no one had craved this dessert, I would have stayed home, and this disaster would never have occurred.

None of the donut balls—in my memory awama, but now zeppole—were left on my plate. I had devoured all six pieces as I finished my coffee. It was getting late, so I beckoned the waiter for my bill. He asked me, what did I think of my dessert? I produced a wide smile. He said, "I take it you liked it."

SUMMER HAMMOND

A Little Slice of the Moon

FROM *New Letters*

The McDonald's Girl

It is June 1995, and the clouds break. The sun pours into the Strafford, Missouri, truck stop McDonald's, known to townsfolk as McStop. The sun makes luminous the fry station, turns the bubbling grease into glitter, magics to gold the fluffy ponytail poofing out from behind the blue mustard-stained visor of the McDonald's girl.

Watch her.

That smile she is smiling is solid, has weight, an anchor to keep her from lifting off, as she scrubs a splat of ketchup from the countertop. She scrubs and scrubs, though the stain is long gone. She is dreaming. She is floating. *That sun!* Her cash register wears a halo.

There are some moments that are cathedrals. The dreamy nineteen-year-old McDonald's girl, adorned in her blue polo, black pants, nonslip restaurant shoes, mustard-stained visor—she knows this. She knows, too, that she is, right now, inside one of those cathedral moments, and though she is standing, she is on her knees, praying for the moment to stretch, out and out and out, so she never has to step outside its holy sweetness.

The McDonald's girl has just said *yes*. Barely. In a whisper. But she did it, she said *yes*. She has said *yes* when her whole life has been built upon *no*, every bone in her body trained for *no*, her very skeleton, a fortress raised. And yet, only a few minutes before, a small *yes*, a hush of wings, a little silver moth escaping into daylight, from between the solid bars.

She is trying to savor the escape—before the fear seeps in.

The door swings open and a big voice belts, "I hear there's a movie star working today! A movie star, you heard me! Oh, look! There she is!"

The McDonald's girl stops scrubbing, her smile erased. Her coworkers freeze in various poses, reaching for a Quarter Pounder in the warming bin, scooping fries into a container, pressing the nozzle of the soda machine—a McDonald's vogue. They shift their gaze between her, the man, her, the man.

They have friends come in, all the time, big groups swinging through the doors, shouting for them, cajoling them for a hot apple pie, on the house. But not the McDonald's girl. No one ever comes to see her, to flirt, to invite her to the movie, the party, the big game. No boyfriends, no girlfriends, no family even—none they've ever seen. Her customers adore her, particularly the old farmer who will *only* stand in her line. The McDonald's girl stubbornly bestows extra swirls on his ice cream cone, no matter how many times, or how frustratedly, the managers remind her of the three-swirl regulation.

Otherwise, it's like the McDonald's girl doesn't exist in the outside world. Where does she go when she leaves at the end of the day? What is she going toward when she walks, in her uniform, along the side of the highway, the 18-wheelers whooshing by, her big ponytail lifting? Does she live in the sky? *She is nineteen*, they whisper behind her back, *and she doesn't even drive. Is it because she's part of that religion? She's a Jehovah, you know, doesn't even celebrate her own birthday.*

Yet here is this man, calling *her* a movie star! And he, himself, is arresting. A big man, but not in the way of the long-haul truckers who pull up in their flat beds layered with pipe, swaggering in and hiking up jeans that will never win against that formidable gladiator of a belly. The men who bellow, *"Give me a twenty-piece meal and as many honey mustards as you can throw in the bag—and Supersize me!"*

No, this man is *built,* jaw droppingly, with biceps big and round as camel humps. He wears a shiny red shirt pulled taut against his massive chest, enormous sunglasses, and from beneath a camouflage cap flows an audacious mullet of white-blond hair.

And it's *her* he goes to. Right up to her register, leaning his elbows on the countertop.

"Hi, darlin'," he says to the McDonald's girl, whose cathedral moment now lays, in broken stained-glass glimmers, at her feet. He slips off his sunglasses. "Remember me?"

Me

Uncle Ronnie was not a man you could forget.

Nicknamed *Mr. Hollywood* in the small Mississippi River town of Princeton, Iowa, where my mother and her siblings grew up, and where my sister and I grew up, until we moved four hundred miles away, exchanging one terribly small town for another: Strafford, population 800, in the Ozarks of southwest Missouri. Before we moved, I thought the town was called *Stratford.* The name sounded rich. I'd imagined a river with swans in it, and our lives changing.

Uncle Ronnie.

A pro bodybuilder, he scored scads of trophies, and was named Mr. Midwest in 1981.

His hugs haunted my nightmares.

Bear hugs, the family called them, laughing. As if bears aren't terrifying huggers. And, as bears went, Uncle Ronnie was a grizzly. He should have known his immensity, the power he had to crush a child in his grip. He didn't seem to know.

That day, when I went to hug him, though I was nineteen, and not six, it happened again. All the breath pressed out of me, my lungs, my very bones gasping, crackling, begging for air.

Uncle Ronnie laughed, thundering, boisterous, full of glee.

I walked home that day, not alone. With a secret.

The 18-wheelers blew past, lifting my ponytail, and I, in my blue polo, black pants, black nonslip restaurant shoes, tore off my mustard-stained visor and, by the side of the road, danced.

The belted cattle we called Oreo cows—a startled audience to my little outburst of joy.

At last I ascended the steep hill in our neighborhood, and caught sight of our house, the long ranch with stone columns, the white porch swing, and my mother's beloved herb garden.

Her Sweet Annie, a constellation of tiny yellow stars, set to dancing by a breeze.

Only then did I break into a cold sweat, crushing my visor in my hands.

Grandma had come, too.

Uncle Ronnie had accomplished the near impossible and convinced her, in spite of her myriad prohibitive fears (heart attack, tornados, car wreck) to travel with him. He'd picked her up from her decrepit house perched on the Mississippi in Princeton, Iowa, and delivered her here to us, in Strafford. Reunited with Grandma, my sister and I were delirious as the bees, drunk on the squash blossoms in the garden. We pressed our faces into the space below her neck, breathed in her crepey skin aromatic with sweet face powder. Her purse smelled the same way, and her jewelry, too, only with a metallic tang. We cried so our tears ran down into her bra, and she lifted our faces and kissed them, and she cried, too, so all our tears were tangled up together, and she called us *girls*.

I wondered if she could see that my sister, twenty-six, and still living at home, had withered from slender to bony, her lovely ivory complexion now sallow, her trademark waist length and wavy hair having thinned, dramatically, to mere wisps she now gathered into a meager ponytail that never stayed.

That past year, my sister had suffered mysterious and brutal seizures, robbing her ability to talk, then walk. The seizures had nearly taken her life.

My mother and father had concealed all this from relatives. They had not sought medical treatment. My father insisted, *The doctors would drug her, turn her into a vegetable.*

Instead, our parents had become a vigilante medical team, as they'd done for so many years. The home we'd left behind in rural Iowa, a double-wide trailer, had poisoned us with high levels of formaldehyde, off-gassed from the cheap petrochemical products—the walls, the floors, the cabinets—used to manufacture the home. We had been diagnosed with environmental illness, multiple chemical sensitivities, and chronic fatigue syndrome linked to carcinogenic exposure, both formaldehyde and the pesticides sprayed lavishly on the farmland surrounding our trailer. In the 1980s, few knew about environmental illness, and few believed in it. Doctors dismissed our symptoms as *all in the head*, while our Jehovah's Witness religious community shunned us for low meeting attendance—their perfumes, colognes, and hairsprays made us sick.

We'd fled to the Missouri countryside, hoping for a fresh start. Now isolated, it was easy enough to keep my sister's seizures—her head shaking so fast in the dark of her room she looked possessed—a secret.

My mother had turned to her vast collection of nutritional cookbooks, herbs and other natural remedies, the whirr of her blender, day and night, becoming the panicked heartbeat of our household.

My father had scoured his ever growing contact list—those who believed in, and treated, the environmentally ill. Through his network, he unearthed a health practitioner who claimed to heal stroke and seizure patients with educational kinesiology, also known as Brain Gym. Brain Gym had been introduced in some schools as "brain training" to improve academic performance and support students with learning disorders, which, in our situation, didn't sound promising. But my father was desperate. He flew the Brain Gym therapist from Houston, Texas, to stay with us, and treat my sister.

Against all odds, Brain Gym therapy had worked. Though weak and depleted, my sister had slowly regained her ability first to walk, then talk. She managed her seizures with "the cross crawl," the exercise that, according to the practitioner, connected the two hemispheres of the brain, restoring the transference of electrical impulses and information. *Imagine it*, he'd said, *like turning all the lights on in a house.*

We had been told, before Grandma and Uncle Ronnie's visit, not to speak of what had occurred.

Grandma, eagle-eyeing my sister with a frown, perhaps knew better than to ask questions. She simply declared, "Well, sweetheart, you still got it! In all the *right* places!"

Grandma's familiar belly laugh filled the house in a minute, with more warmth than it had known in four long years.

That night, in the living room, Uncle Ronnie learned to cross crawl.

This was the reason for his visit. Though he and Grandma were unaware of the back story, they knew my father was no longer cleaning carpets. He was now a certified Brain Gym practitioner. He had an impressive new office, business cards, and a growing clientele at an alternative health-care clinic in downtown Springfield.

Under my father's tutelage, Uncle Ronnie moved his eyes to the top left, top right, lower left, lower right, while simultaneously his massive arms crossed to pat one knee, then the other, and his Thor-like legs marched in place, feet smashing down, making a racket in the floorboards. All the while, he hummed, a rich bass that permeated every corner, reaching my ears as I sat at my desk in my room, fresh from a shower, wearing my favorite tee. Ronald McDonald, grinning in his yellow jumpsuit, arms spread wide. From his palms, shamrocks bloomed, forming a leafy green double arch over his head. Though as a Jehovah's Witness I didn't partake in the holiday myself, I'd taken secret joy in my customers' delight over Shamrock shakes. The shirt, soft and worn, had become my comfort shirt.

A giant *thud!* from the living room shook the walls and rattled the pencil jar on my desk. An expletive flew through the house. I could hear my father explaining, in the gentle coaching voice he now used for his clients, that losing balance in the beginning was normal. It was okay. He encouraged Uncle Ronnie to start again.

Uncle Ronnie had been in a bad accident. Sitting in a parked car, he'd been struck from behind by an 18-wheeler. He had sustained a brain injury, significant enough to impair his livelihood as a hunting and fishing guide.

But Uncle Ronnie was struggling with another, deeper problem.

Uncle Ronnie, my father said, couldn't keep a key in his pocket. Every key would warp slightly, become defunct. In the past year, he'd thrown away at least a half dozen keys.

My father had revealed this while driving me to McDonald's on a stormy morning when I couldn't walk. He'd said, "I think he's bending the keys himself." At my puzzled look, he'd clarified, "With his energy. His rage."

My father believed he'd found his mission in life. Thwarted in his efforts to become a Jehovah's Witness elder, his carpet-cleaning business pushed to the brink of bankruptcy while caretaking my sister, he was buoyed by new optimism. All the tragedy had led him to this place—to heal our family.

In the living room, Uncle Ronnie's humming and marching resumed.

Rage.

I closed my eyes. I knew what I had to do.

I would have to recapture the moth—turn my *yes* to *no*.

The McDonald's Girl

It happens like this:

Not one, but *two* tour buses, pull into McStop. The squeal and gasp of brakes. A shadow falling across the restaurant. Old folks, decked out in spangles and fringe, on their way to see Andy Williams, Shoji Tabuchi, and the famous Baldknobbers show in Branson, spill from the twin buses. They stream—hungry, grumpy, and sparkling up a country neon storm—across the parking lot.

The McDonald's girl, just starting to dismantle the soda machine nozzles for a deep clean, rotates them back in, swiftly.

Donna, the manager who hired her, stands on tiptoes to look out. She grabs her hair, screams.

They are short-staffed that day.

Donna turns to face the only two cashiers: the McDonald's

girl, and the new hire—timid Jenny—who has literally started to shake.

"Welp!" Donna throws her hands in the air. "We're dead." She flees to the kitchen to help the two cooks, one of whom, Becky, is swearing, throwing pans, and threatening to quit.

The McDonald's girl has struggled hard to stay with her job. Her first few months, she was slow, bumbling, couldn't make sense of the cash register, gave customers the wrong orders, spilled drinks, pissed off the truck drivers, the tourists, her co-workers, *everyone*—except for the shy old farmer who always believed in her, stood in her line even if it was the longest, and for whom, in gratitude, ignoring Donna's censures, she devotedly made extra twist cones.

Now, two lines form, snaking through the restaurant, twisting and turning, out the door into the parking lot, and all those faces watching her—ready to be mad, prepping for a conniption over cold fries and a broken shake machine.

The McDonald's girl straightens her visor. Rolls her shoulders back. Takes the first order, the second, the third—no tomato, extra cheese, hold the mayo, add bacon—her fingers flying, tapping keys like a concert pianist. *Are these her fingers?* She thinks maybe, after all, there is something redemptive and praiseworthy about a surplus of adrenaline.

She's in the flow, smiling, greeting, slapping down red trays one after another *smack! smack! smack!* She rushes back and forth between her register and timid Jenny's, trying to help. Tufty gray-haired men in ANDY WILLIAMS MOON RIVER THEATRE T-shirts groan with complaint, like old wood floors. At the same time, she expertly fills up and caps drinks with that soul-satisfying lid crinkle, shovels fries into cartons, hands them to customers like golden, greasy bouquets.

One by one, satisfaction cards are filled out with a flourish, and winks. "This girl is top-notch!" One of the ladies in a pink sequin Dolly Parton ball cap cries out, lifting the girl's arm, champ-like. "Give her a raise!"

The McDonald's girl feels bright and shiny. Precious, like gold.

Finally, they file out to board their buses, rubbing their bellies and cracking jokes, festive moods restored. The McDonald's girl falls back against the counter, plucks off her visor, and wipes her sweaty hairline with the back of her arm. "How are you?" Checking in with timid Jenny, slumped over her register.

Timid Jenny raises her head, braids frayed. "How do you do it? That was a *nightmare*."

"If you stick it out, I promise it'll get better."

Donna hurries out from the kitchen and shocks her, pulling her into a big, warm hug. "I had my doubts about you," she says. "We all did. But you've surprised us." Donna takes hold of her shoulders and looks her right in the eye, beaming. "You're a *real* McDonald's girl."

She can't breathe. Those words, like coming out of the wilderness after a hundred years lost. She hunts out a dish rag, dips it in a bucket of fresh, soapy water, and begins scrubbing the countertop, all those ketchup splats, just to keep herself from flying to pieces.

That's when he sneaks up on her. "Howdy."

Dane, the other grill cook. The even-tempered one.

The tall one. With all the dark hair. The dimpled chin.

The one—she's a little bit in love with.

"You were amazing out here, rock star," he says. And then, "You saved us."

The way he holds her eyes, both gentle and intense.

When has the McDonald's girl ever been looked at that way? Never.

And she knows, she already knows, what's coming next.

"I've been wanting to ask for a long time. Would you like to go out with me?"

She knows, too, the word she has to say. It starts up from her gut—and gets stuck.

Out instead, this tiny little fluttering whisper of a thing:

Yes.

Me

My mother and her little brother, Ronnie, were seven years apart, yet mistaken for twins.

Towheads, my mother called them. They shared platinum hair and—for small town rural Iowa—preternatural good looks.

Ronnie was *Mr. Hollywood*, and my mother—*Marilyn*.

My sister and I were struck speechless by my mother's youthful photographs, that stunning updo of blond hair, red lipstick, movie-star pout. What was invisible—was the violence she'd been subjected to from childhood. The heart shattering that happened behind closed doors, at the hands of a raging alcoholic father.

After my sister recuperated, my father turned his attention to my mother. She, too, marched in place and hummed. My father muscle tested her for herbal anxiety and depression tonics—valerian root, kava, passionflower. He massaged lavender oil into her wrists. He pressed tiny magnets to acupressure points on my mother's face, arms, legs, securing them with Band-Aids.

The Brain Gym therapist had picked up on the deep turmoil splintering the family. He attributed the rifts to trauma, caused by my sister's life-threatening illness, our history with formaldehyde poisoning, and the shunning we'd experienced from members of our faith. He led us about the house, muscle testing each of us in various rooms, and applying magnets to hidden corners in the kitchen, the dining room, our bedrooms. He explained that the magnets would balance *polarities* throughout the house, and within us, opening invisible internal pathways that would allow us to reconnect, and heal. He also introduced us to frequencies that could be played during times of acute stress, inducing mental calm.

Therefore, my father instituted a new ritual—pressing play on the cassette player in the kitchen when my mother called Grandma on Sundays. *Brain tones* shrilled, purred, buzzed, and thrummed in the background while my mother and Grandma chatted about seemingly innocuous topics: clearance sales, recipes, a cardinal's hilarious frenzy in the bird bath. But my mother's weekly conversations with her own mother always left her rattled, simmering, ready for a knockdown drag 'em out.

Not just conversations with Grandma. A whole host of things could trigger what my sister whisperingly referred to, through the years, as *Big Kahuna*.

A Little Slice of the Moon

I was a dedicated student of my mother, an expert navigator of her mine-filled psyche.

After triggering a blow up, I carefully memorized the places that were ripped and torn. And I learned from them, what not to do.

In third grade, I'd written about my first crush, the boy with all the curls, in my little red diary with the silver lock. One day, I came home from school to find my mother fuming, and without enough time to fathom my misstep, she'd cornered me, eyes in slits, shaking the little red diary in my face, the broken lock jangling.

In sixth grade, I tasted the deeper ache of first love, and finding the feeling immense, too much to hold on my own, I longed to share it with my mother. She picked me up from school, on a day when he had nearly broken me with his smile, his unexpected touch, moving a wisp of hair from my face with a quiet tenderness I'd never known. I was stupid with hope, confiding to my mother, both shy and scared, "I *like* him."

No one passing by on the Iowa rural road, rolling cornfields on one side, pine trees and pig farms on the other, could hear the *BAM!* No farmer on a tractor could detect the explosion rocking the small blue Honda Accord. No one could see pieces of a girl tearing away, flying out the window, catching in the branches of the pine trees, pieces of herself she could never find again.

Seven years later, I ran to my sister, hysterical.

No one was home but her, alone in her room, as usual. She sat on her bed, cross-legged with a calculator, pencil scratching across paper, working on high school algebra. We had moved to Missouri, in part, to homeschool, because homeschooling was legal there. Still, at nineteen and twenty-six, neither of us had graduated.

I fell to my knees on the floor beside her bed, in my blue polo, black pants, sobbing into my mustard-stained visor, once again crushed between my hands. In an instant, she was beside me, ordering me to calm down. Gratitude for her "big sister" voice, silenced during a year of seizures, only made me cry harder. Frustrated, she threw a box of Kleenex at me, demanded

I blow my nose. I did, then wailed, "I got asked on a date—and I said *yes!*"

"You did *what?*"

Her face. The fear.

I jumped to my feet, ran to my room across the hall. I tried to shut the door but she was hot on my heels, wouldn't let me, pushing and prying until I surrendered and she cornered me.

"You've got to tell Mom," my sister said. She looked me dead in the eye.

"No, no, no." I pushed my face in my hands.

She grabbed my shoulders, shook. "You've *got* to. As soon as she gets home. It will be worse if you wait. You know that."

The sound of an engine made us swivel to the window.

My mother's silver car crested the hill.

"*Tell* her!" my sister shook my shoulders again.

I tore from her grip and ran to the bathroom, where I sunk to the floor.

A minute later, my sister's footsteps pounded past, down the hallway.

A soft June breeze rippled the curtain, carrying the bright chirps and trills of a goldfinch, perched in the cottonwood tree outside.

Then a slam.

Heavy footsteps, getting nearer, stopping outside the bathroom.

Bash! Bash! Bash!

A fist, smashing the door, against my spine.

The goldfinch leapt from the branch, flew away.

The McDonald's Girl

The McDonald's girl is curled up in a ball at the bottom of her clothes closet.

Look, she is a *real* McDonald's girl. After the explosion, the shattering, limbs flying—look, she is still in her uniform! Her blue polo, sweat and snot and tear drenched, she clasps her mustard-stained visor to her chest.

This is where her sister finds her.

She makes the McDonald's girl get up, makes her walk into her room, the adjoining bathroom, pushes her shoulders down, until the McDonald's girl is seated on the toilet.

The McDonald's girl watches, blank and numb, as her sister flings open drawers, digs for makeup containers, which she throws onto the countertop with a rattle. There is the little chalkboard her sister used to communicate, when she couldn't speak. A broken chalk lies next to a lipstick tube. "He'll be here soon. You have to get ready."

"I'm not going," the McDonald's girl says.

"Yes, you are." Her sister opens a bag of cotton balls with a soft *pop*.

The McDonald's girl presses the toes of her nonslip restaurant shoes together, draws her shoulders closer, a trembling huddle. "I can't." She doesn't understand why her sister told on her. She doesn't understand why, now, her sister is lifting her chin, patting foundation onto her face, the cotton ball so soft, the liquid so cool, her sister's touch—gentle enough to return her to tears. "I can't!"

"You have to."

"If I go, she'll hate me forever." The McDonald's girl wonders, with a stab—is this what her sister hopes will happen?

Her sister has always borne the brunt of their mother's rage.

Her mother's favoritism, not only transparent—weaponized.

The McDonald's girl winces at a memory. The Brain Gym therapist, in his side quest to repair the family's emotional dynamics, had muscle tested them while they looked in each other's eyes. Muscle testing, he'd explained, revealed whether a food or supplement would be beneficial or detrimental. Furthermore, it could expose the underlying nature of a relationship.

Her mother's arm had sunk like a leaky boat, looking at her sister.

Then, she and her mother had faced each other. Her mother's arm had stayed solid, rooted as a tree, looking at her.

She remembers her mother's smile.

She remembers—her sister's shattered face.

This, the McDonald's girl thinks, must be revenge.

Then her sister takes hold of her chin. "If you don't go, you'll hate *yourself* forever." Her voice, fierce and trembling. She is twenty-six, and has never had a job. Never dressed up for a date.

Her sister holds up two lipsticks.

And the McDonald's girl—chooses the pink.

Me

I returned home that night to a dark house. Not even the barest glimmer in the window.

No one waiting up.

Aching, I stuck the key in the door.

I tip-toed past where Uncle Ronnie snored, his colossal frame sprawled on the living room couch that rolled out into a bed. I flicked on the light in the bathroom. There on the floor, my Scrunchie. I'd knelt, picking it up, cupping it in my hands. My frizzy hairs, still clinging to it. I held the Scrunchie with grave tenderness, like a wounded bird.

The soft knock on the door sent me to my feet, blood zinging.

It was Grandma.

She was staying in my parents' bedroom, while they slept in the RV. Wordlessly, she took me by the arm and pulled me to her room, closing the door with a firm *click*, and twist of the lock. I knew how my mother would interpret this moment—her mother and daughter, teaming up, double-crossing her, in *her* room.

In the pretty little jacket and frilled shirt, the clothes my sister had lent me, and dressed me in, I went rigid with guilt.

Yet when Grandma set her hand on my arm, and whispered, "Tell me all about it," my firm obedience gave way.

And so it was my grandma, who just happened to be visiting, captive audience to the details of my first date. She oohed and aahed, sighed and smiled, leaned in to giggle. Her presence was fortifying, consoling, and at the same time, devastating. Her presence made me painfully conscious of an absence. The awakening was sharp. Mothers engaged in this intimate sharing with their daughters, after a date.

I did not have that mother.

My mother, in spite of my persistent hope, had never become that mother. I was nineteen, and though living like a child was not a child and when, *when would my mother be that mother?*

If there had ever been any hope, my choice to go that night had destroyed it.

I was sure of that.

A loss opened up in me, a no-going-back abyss.

The McDonald's Girl

She'd stunned herself, the way she'd walked into McDonald's that late fall day.

She'd marched right up to the counter and asked for an application.

Where had that come from?

It was the first time she'd even been *inside* a McDonald's.

Formaldehyde exposure had compromised her family's immune system, so her mother insisted on natural foods, even forbidding the consumption of chocolate milk in kindergarten. Once, she'd snuck it during snack time, dribbling the tiniest chocolate spot on her pink sweater. Her keen-eyed mother had found it at once, interrogated her. Terrified, she'd told her first lie—a rambunctious classmate had spilled it, she said. However, she was too guilty, too obedient, to sustain the lie. Shoulders slumping, she'd caved, told the truth, and could never have chocolate milk again, without feeling a dark stain.

Walking into McDonald's that day, asking for an application, also weighed like sacrilege. She couldn't explain why. No one had told her she couldn't get a job. And yet, along with so many other parts of growing up—a driver's license, a car, a high school diploma—a job seemed forgotten. Or was it forbidden?

Her grandma suspected her religion.

The Jehovah's Witness cult, she said, had stunted her granddaughters, shut down their lives.

Or was it that bizarre illness?

There was so much to point at. Too many places for secrets to hide.

When Donna called, offered her the job, told her to come pick up her uniform the next day—*her uniform!* The McDonald's girl had thrilled, toes curling in her shoes with elation and pride. Then, she had quietly gathered crumbs of courage in her room, before heading outside, to her mother, hanging bedsheets on the line.

It was a crisp September day with a breeze, and the sheets were playful, winding around her mother's legs. Her mother laughed, a clothespin in her mouth. She handed the McDonald's girl a pillowcase, and they clipped it to the line, together. A quiet and sublime moment—she was about to risk blowing to smithereens.

"Mom. I have a job."

Her mother's eyes blew open. "Wow," she said. "Look at you. The stealthy one. Didn't say a word, did you?"

And later, "Better not catch you eating that bad food!"

The warning, small, but to the McDonald's girl, piquant, raising the hairs on the back of her neck.

Look at her now. The stealthy one. In truth, the shaky-legged chicken, poised on the porch with her pink lipstick and jacket (*for later, when it gets cooler,* her sister had said) folded over her arms.

Her mother in the house, laughing with Grandma, too loud, sending her a message: *Don't go, and maybe I can forgive you.*

Dane's blue pickup rattles into view.

The McDonald's girl jumps.

She scrambles off the porch, stumbling, racing up the hill, tearing the threads, *tearing them,* screaming through her teeth. She doesn't stop, doesn't turn around.

Dane hops from his truck, striding toward her in dark jeans, cowboy boots, fancy black shirt embroidered with shiny silver lassos. He opens his arms with a big grin—and she swooshes right past, throwing herself into the passenger side of his truck.

He side-eyes her, wary, when he climbs in.

As they pull away, her teeth start chattering—

And thinking it's cold, he cranks the window up, fast.

Me

But I loved her.

She read to me. One of the symptoms of "mobile home sickness" is frequent and inordinately severe infections. As a child, before we knew about the formaldehyde, I often caught colds that turned into monsters. Once, I was absent from school for nine weeks. During that time, I cuddled in her lap and she read me *The Cat in the Hat*. My mother confessed later, she grew sick of the story, wincing inside when I begged her to read it again. Yet each time, she picked up that book and read using the same funny voices, the same dramatic energy, that made me laugh, and brought me comfort. It wasn't the story. It was *her* I wanted, without ceasing.

My father learned what was called "The Truth" from a bunkmate, while training for Vietnam. He brought home the Jehovah's Witness faith to my mother—an unwanted souvenir. No more birthday parties. No more Christmas trees. My mother cherished Christmas. For her, as a child, it had been the one peaceful day of the year. The one day her father stayed sober, and remembered her name. When she caught herself singing Christmas songs at the mall, she would apologize, her face full of longing.

She tried to make up for the lack of celebrations by inventing new ones. One June, she invited the neighborhood kids to a Strawberry Shortcake party, serving homemade shortcake topped with garden-grown strawberries and pink whipped cream. She perched Strawberry Shortcake dolls beside each plate. During the winter, she made sugar cookies in the shape of mittens, held together by thin red licorice laces, tied in a bow. We decorated the mittens together in the kitchen while the snow blew outside, and the kids in my class were surprised and charmed, made gleeful by the cookies, appearing on an otherwise dull January day with no holidays in sight.

These were forms of resistance.

My mother had grown up poor and never wanted to be poor again. She tried to decorate the trailer as though it were the big, old farmhouse she'd dreamed of in her childhood, lace curtains dancing in the windows, whimsical chicken and rooster plates, wildflower murals on the walls she painted by hand.

But the Jehovah's Witness faith empowered hardship, encouraging members to reject higher education, and worldly high-paying careers. *The Watchtower* praised brothers and sisters who purchased cheap homes and old cars, imparting a halo to these things, conflating low socioeconomic status with spiritual virtue.

Then there were the traumas, exacerbated by the religion's insistence that *everyone* knock on doors and preach, get yelled at by strangers, threatened, chased—persecution being a fruit of the spirit. Jesus's injunction to "go therefore," for one with complex PTSD, a nightmarish command. And later, the congregation's rejection of our family for an illness that lowered our meeting attendance and therefore cast us, according to the Watchtower rule book, as "spiritually weak"—compounding the psychological wounds of rejection and abandonment, with a heap of spiritual shunning and isolation.

All the things my mother hoped to escape, she couldn't.

Over time, the tragedy of her life became embodied by the vacuum cleaner—one my father had retrieved from the dump, and patched up with duct tape.

Still, it was always falling apart.

My parents' twenty-fifth wedding anniversary fell during Uncle Ronnie's visit.

Wedding anniversaries were the only celebration allowed by the Watchtower Society. For years, my family poured pent-up celebratory energy into them, with balloons, streamers, cake, and gifts—lavishly wrapped—for everyone.

That year was different.

Numb, I found myself wandering a Walmart Supercenter with Uncle Ronnie and my sister, a few stupefying days after the date.

Uncle Ronnie was exuberant as always, drawing attention with his loud voice, boisterous laugh, and bulging muscles in yet another skin-tight shirt, this one sleeveless and camouflage. He was on the hunt for an anniversary gift, and growing frustrated. "Girls, tell me! What does your mother *want?*"

The question that guided my life. My North Star.
She hadn't spoken a word to me, since.
"What does she want?" Uncle Ronnie cried again, swiping off his ball cap, driving a hand through his shock of blond hair.
"A vacuum cleaner." My own voice surprised me.
Uncle Ronnie swiveled, snapped his fingers.
He bought her the best in the store.
My sister and I adorned it with a large pink bow, the color of pink roses—our parents' wedding flower.
"A vacuum, eh?" my mother said, eyeing us, during the unveiling. "Who thought of this?"
Uncle Ronnie grabbed me, squished me to his side, warping my spine like a key in his pocket. "The movie star here!"
I watched the slow sneer move across my mother's face.
Which snapped back quickly into a smile—when Grandma handed her a piece of cake.

The McDonald's Girl

The McDonald's girl never knew the barn was there.
Look at it. Just look! All lit up in twinkle lights, tucked deep into the trees, glittering, and crying out fiddles, the small thunder of stomping boots.
She gazes, awestruck, as they pull up, and park.
Now if only her hands would stop shaking.
Inside the barn a wide, wood floor, the swirl of lights, spin of skirts, boots shuffling, kicking.
Dane stands close, tries to teach her the steps. He is patient and kind as a date, just like he is as a grill cook.
And she—she's just like she was her first few months on the job. Can't think straight. Keeps messing up. Gently, to guide her, Dane takes her forearm. She flinches away. He follows her edgy eyes to the bank of windows. Smiling uncertainly, he glances from the windows, to her. "Girl, is somebody after you?"

Dirty little rat! Her mother's rage-filled face, eyes seething, spittle gathering at the corners of her mouth.

You've ruined me. Grabbing her ponytail, yanking her up from the floor. The McDonald's girl's Scrunchie torn out, her hair flying wild, all over the place.

Clean up your filth before you go on your date! Her mother, whipping open the closet doors, seizing her old vacuum cleaner—

Throwing it.

The McDonald's girl, falling to the floor, shielding her face.

The vacuum cleaner crumbling before her, parts rolling.

"Girl—you okay?"

He can't feel the savage raw ache of her scalp.

Can't see the ragged explosion wounds, pouring blood.

No one can see the way she's been hurt, without her words.

The way he's looking at her.

What if—she told him the truth?

Instead, she puts her hand in his, and tries to dance.

Me

There were times I questioned my sister's seizures.

Mostly, when she screamed.

Haunting, blood-curdling horror movie.

My father said, screaming could occur with seizures.

Yet, I could never shake the sense, her screams carried anguish and rage.

Blasted it through the house, smeared the walls with it, speared us in place.

Forced her family to freeze, listen to, absorb and reckon with— all that pain.

On the last day of Uncle Ronnie's visit, my mother prepared a big lunch.

She followed a favorite recipe, one she called "fancy," a salad with roast chicken, chives, roasted almonds, and mayonnaise, served in a garden-grown cantaloupe, hollowed out. On the top of the salad, perfect and artfully placed melon balls, like little sunrises. Grandma raved over my mother's creative culinary skills. My mother beamed, passing a cantaloupe chicken salad bowl to everyone—but me.

Grandma glanced at me.

She had taken me aside once to whisper: "Don't ruffle her feathers, and be sure to apologize. She'll get over it."

During the farewell feast, my mother engaged with the warmest parts of her personality, cracking jokes, laughing big—her face going still, eyes blank as a dead woman, whenever I spoke.

My father had only spoken to me once, reminding me of the two Gods I had violated: Jehovah and my mother.

Pointedly, Grandma turned to me, asked about my job. The story poured out: The Branson tour groups. My manager's praise. *Real McDonald's girl.* I could feel, saying that name, my shoulders rising, my spine straightening, the light coming through my eyes again.

But what I saw across the table stopped me cold.

My mother, wagging her head and ugly mouthing—*blah blah blah.*

Grandma was engrossed in my story. Uncle Ronnie, pouring more drinks.

My father, refusing to see.

My sister, though, slammed down her fork. She spat, "*I'm* proud of you!"

Instantly, my mother turned on her a look of hate.

I shot up from the table, darted outside, into the garden.

My sister followed.

"What's happening?" I hugged myself.

My sister, turned me to face her. "You have to be strong, okay? You have to prepare yourself. After they leave, Mom might come after you. She'll burst into your room. She'll bring gifts you've given her, and break them. She'll tell you that you lied, that you never loved her. She'll scream at you, and keep screaming. Even if you go mute. Even if you curl up in a ball. Even if you crawl under the bed. She'll sweep everything off your desk. She might rip up your stuff to lure you out. Don't come out! Don't fight back . . ."

She advised me, on and on, like an old war vet.

We had to go back, quickly, to avoid looking like an alliance.

I picked a bouquet of Lily of the Valley to bring to Grandma. It happened, amidst the drifting shadows of the laundry room. Our mother was there to meet us.

My sister and I stumbled backward, together. We pressed into the wall like one creature, shoulder to shoulder. Our mother edged in. I caught the sharp sweetness of the delicate white flowers, crushed in my grip. Pushing her face close to ours, her lips tore away from her teeth.

"I'll get you," she hissed, eyes darting rapid fire between us. "I'll get you both."

The McDonald's Girl

To dance, you have to let go.

You can't be afraid.

The McDonald's girl is pretty sure her first date is a bust.

Sitting outside, she tears at grass. A breeze moves through, and the pines sing. A *hush hush* that raises goosebumps, the good kind, on her arms and legs.

Dane emerges from the barn, looks around, then smiles, taking long strides toward her. He crouches beside her on the cool grass. Hands her a cup. "Thank you," she says. The cup is chilled, and quiets her hand.

Dane doesn't answer, just raises his cup.

The McDonald's girl is thankful for him. Not just here, now, but at work together, every day. He is the serenest grill cook in the world. No fussing. No cursing. No fit throwing. No grill-cook drama.

Just the special order slid down the warming bin, and your name, softly called.

She marvels at the beauty of him, like the serene strength of the sunset. She wonders how many times she's sat alone, in her room, in the garden, on the front porch swing, and just over here, across the trees, around the bend, down the gravel lane, were all these people, dancing out loud? She never heard them.

Dane stands, then jogs off a little ways. He returns, wearing a dimpled grin.

It takes her a moment to process what he's holding out to her. Oh, a horseshoe!
It gleams, a perfect, poignant slice of silver.
She reaches out to take it.
And it's like—he's handed her a little slice of the moon.

Me

Uncle Ronnie told my sister and I to jump in the car.

"One last adventure," he said, "before I leave."

He laughed and chatted, but with an edge, glancing at us in the rearview mirror.

We drove past McDonald's. The arches, the way they shone, set longing deep in my chest. I pictured my cash register, how the late afternoon light, about that time, set it aglow, like a fire in a fireplace. Like a home.

Uncle Ronnie started talking then. He talked fast.

"When I was a kid, my old man was always drunk. Your mother and me, we never saw him sober, except on Christmas. After work, he'd go to the tavern, get drunk, then stumble home just in time for dinner. At the dinner table, he picked fights with us kids. He called me names. *Sissy. Pussy. Weakling.*"

He flicked the turn signal, took a back road. One I'd never been on before, the road dipping and rising, forest on either side, tree-filtered light, dappling the asphalt.

"If I didn't sit there and take it, if I talked back, he'd reach for me fast, like lightning, grab me by throat. It was no use fighting. He was right. I wasn't strong enough. He'd pull me by the hair down the basement steps. Then he'd swipe off his belt. Beat me bloody."

The road straightened through a field of wildflowers, black-eyed Susans and blue sage.

"I started bodybuilding so I could fight my old man and win. And you know what? I did. There was a time he came after me and I laughed, rolling up my sleeves, said, 'You sure, old man? You wanna fight this sissy? Okay, come take it.' I bashed in his face, threw him against the wall. Oh yeah, I had that old man on his knees, spitting teeth, begging for mercy."

He pulled the car over, gravel spraying out from under the tires. He cut the engine. All we could hear for a long time was him, breathing hard. "Your mother," he finally said, "she tried to save me from him. Every time. She tried but she couldn't. Your mother always—" his voice broke—"she was my protector."

He turned in his seat to face us, eyes red, chin trembling. "Girls, I saw what she did to you. I saw her corner you. I was there, behind you, but it was dark, you didn't see me. I heard what she said—" He rubbed his eyes, then shook his head, hard. "I can't believe it. I can't believe that was my sister."

We got out of the car. We waded the creek that ran alongside the road.

My sister and I splintered, going in different directions. Didn't speak.

The water was so clear, you could see every rock, every shape—bright, focused.

Uncle Ronnie took a picture of me, and mailed it a few weeks later.

My blue jeans rolled up, my McDonald's shirt with the shamrocks.

I looked so tall.

I had never in my life looked so tall.

The McDonald's Girl

The old farmer scoots over to her line, even though it's long and raucous—full of army guys in camouflage.

The farmer waits a long time for his turn, hands woven together, head down.

At her register, he unrolls a few dollars, orders his usual.

The McDonald's girl, smiling, gives him *five* extra twists.

Her largest, most exquisitely beautiful cone yet.

When he takes it from her, he stops for a moment, meets her gaze. "You're my favorite." He says it, shy, before shuffling away.

The McDonald's girl watches him go, her eyes blurring with tears.

He will never know, the gift he's given her.
Just that morning, her mother had packed her bags.

She'd left.
The McDonald's girl picks up her cleaning rag, scrubs that clean countertop with all her might, a fight.
"Hey."
She looks up, takes in a breath.
It's his day off, and she didn't expect to see him.
He's wearing blue jeans, a cowboy hat.
He peels some money from his wallet. "Can I get one of those anti-regulation cones?" He winks.
She makes it, heartbeat vibrating in rhythm with the ice cream machine.
When she hands it to him, not able to meet his eyes, he lets his hand linger on hers.
"I really had fun the other night."
"You *did?*"
"Yeah. I did. Did you?"
The horseshoe he brought her, shining in her hand.
When she finally looks at him, he sees what she feels, clear as light.
And he smiles. "Would you like to do it again?"

She thinks of her mother. Thinks of her first.

Her mother listening, in some dark room, with a suitcase at her feet.
Her mother, waiting for her response.

And the McDonald's girl says it.
Only this time, less like a moth, and more like an eagle.

Yes.

JOHN JEREMIAH SULLIVAN

Corona

FROM *The Sewanee Review*

THE FJORDS of Norway are one of the places I always hoped to see before I die. If you had told me thirty years ago that when I finally experienced them, I would find myself so racked with the fever and chills of coronavirus that my sweat soaked through to the mattress and my very eyeballs twitched, I would probably only have nodded—in sadness, maybe. Not in surprise. My life has been a succession of illnesses in interesting places. The first time I ever traveled abroad anywhere besides Canada—to Dakar, Senegal, in West Africa, as part of a foreign-exchange program in high school, a trip that changed my life in ways unrelated to health, as well—I caught a bug of some kind that played hell on my digestive system and caused me to miss a big part of my junior year. They never did figure out what it was. I learned the strange fact that some doctors get mad at you when they can't determine what's wrong with you. A specialist who had looked at my bowels thought it was "atypical Crohn's." Everyone else said no. My doctor at the time, Dr. Jeff, gave a paper on me at a conference. "My mystery patient," he called me. They wound up megadosing me with horse pills of antibiotics and apparently nuking the thing, without having successfully identified it. Before that ambiguous closure, I underwent a string of ghastly procedures: colonoscopies, sigmoidoscopies, and barium enemas, along with simpler, cruder forms of invasion. The doctor who gave me the sigmoidoscopies was wonderful. Older, Jewish, I don't remember his name, but I remember that at the beginning of every visit, as he was sliding his lubed-up index finger into my rectum, he would cheerfully call out, "Here comes the arthritic knuckle!" That was an important year for me as a writer, because I spent so much time in bed. The attacks of pain were worst at night. My mother would sit there with me, feeding me ice chips, the only thing that gave relief. There were no cellphones, of course, and I have always hated video games, so I read books—classics and trash—and wrote unreadable prose poems in my notebook. My stomach has been more or less permanently fucked since then. It was never great. I was one of those kids who are always throwing up. Every year on my birthday. It became a tradition. Once I ate a can of pineapple and barfed it all over the side of our car. Kids in the neighborhood saw it and asked me about it afterward. I told some strange lie about what it had been. The next time I made it back to Africa, in my early twenties—Morocco this time, in a place called El Jadida, where Orson Welles shot his *Othello*—a spider bit me during the night, on my right side, just below my armpit. I saw the spider in the morning and made the connection to the bite. I must have rolled over onto it and killed it. The spider was black, and relatively small, but somehow not as small as one would prefer. Over the course of three days, I developed a bubo at the site of the bite. A local pharmacist prescribed me a tube of curious coal-black cream that seemed only to accelerate the infection. I was traveling with my friend Ben, a tall kid from New York with brown hair and brown eyes. We had been on a few trips together already, and he knew to expect medical mishaps. Even so, I could tell he was tired of visiting pharmacies. We decided to press on, to keep moving toward more obscure towns in the interior. By this point the pain was such that I had to keep my arm sort of cocked to one side, straight out at ninety degrees, because if the inside of my bicep were to brush the swelling, I would cringe and howl. The bus we rode on got stopped at a military roadblock in the middle of the desert. The soldiers had machines guns. They made everybody get off, checked our papers. They seemed displeased to find foreigners but eventually let us pass with an indifferent wave. I remember a Berber woman throwing up into a big plastic bottle that she had cut in half for the purpose. On the seat across from mine lay Ben, curled up fetally with diarrhea. Bad moment, though not as bad as maybe five nights later, when I woke up lying in a tent-clinic somewhere, I don't remember the name of the place. I was delirious with pain and fever. The surgeon was, I think, very good. A slender man in his late fifties, with bifocals. He wore no coat, only a clean white shirt. His face was stubbled—it was the middle of the night. I saw the corona of a bright lamp behind the dark silhouette of his head. He existed for me in that holy glow healers have when you really need them. He apologized to me about the local anesthesia. My French wasn't good enough to tell if he was saying he had the wrong one, or that he had none. Certainly I felt every jostle of the scalpel exquisitely. I had tears in my eyes but my face and body were rigid. At one point he held up a little spoonful of pus, to show me what progress he was making. "*C'est du pus!*" he said. "*C'est du pus!*" I gave the thumbs-up. He wrote me a bill for fifty dollars and told me to send it when I got back to the States. I hope I did. I hope I sent all of them the money, all of the excellent dignified foreign doctors over the decades, when they waved their hands and told me to send the money when I got home. I can be very generous in the moment but am terrible at remembering debts. Right now I think of the doctor in San Blas, in the Mexican state of Nayarit. I was traveling with my friend Kitchen, a scholar of Spanish with wild, thick hair and a booming voice. He basically carried me into the clinic. Some sort of horrific spasm had taken over my body, starting at the neck, a creeping paralysis that colonized more and more of my torso. The doctor, a stout Mexican man with a full mustache and tinted spectacles, feared meningitis at first. He laid me on the table, put one hand on my back and one beneath my legs, and bent me together. I wanted to roar with pain but could only whimper. He apologized and explained that he had to do it. Then he prepared a cartoonishly large syringe full of horse tranquilizer and stuck the needle into my ass cheek. I all but instantly went noodly. He gave me a packet of Soma muscle relaxants and told me to send him the money when I got home. I took too many of the Soma and slept for twenty-two hours. Kitchen sat beside me and nudged me every now and then to make sure I was breathing. In Peru, ten years before, I had gone to the mountains with Mariana, to Cajamarca, where the Spanish captured Atahualpa, a brief side-excursion from a year in Lima. As we waited for our bus back to the capital, standing around in the afternoon, I was dizzy with hangover. The night before, there had been a festival in the plaza. Brass bands, hundred-foot-tall shadows dancing against the walls of the cathedral, fire balloons floating off into a starry Andean sky. At the bus stop I did what I knew was stupid and bought some cookies from a girl who sold them in the street. Homemade cookies in a baggie. About halfway through the trip the vomiting came, preceded by its green death-bearing aura. I didn't have anything in my stomach. It was all retching and bile. Other passengers, all Peruvian, brought me a succession of plastic bags. "He ate the girl's cookies," Mariana told them. "Ah, he shouldn't have done that!" they said. My head in her lap, my face against the jolting. At one point in the middle of the night I sat up to look at the driver. The bus lumbered down an extremely steep and winding mountain road. It was exactly the scenario you read about in the news articles about the buses in Peru that plunge off mountain roads. The driver kept crossing himself. He appeared to be having trouble staying awake. The whole trip took about eighteen hours, but it seemed to take so long that time lost meaning. Things got worse at Mariana's apartment. She ran out to buy a bottle of electrolytes and came back to find me on the bathroom floor with my hands sort of palsied up. She was in Peru on a government grant, and they had given her a little card for use in medical emergencies. It had a number to call, and a code you were supposed to read aloud when they answered, something gratuitously spy-sounding like *Tiger Alpha Honey*. That got you picked up in a private ambulance and taken to the Anglo-American hospital. In the emergency room there, I had that strange experience people talk about, where at a moment of danger you suddenly speak a foreign language much better than you thought you could, or than you could, really, at any other time. My Spanish was childlike, but I found myself saying with perfect grammar such things as, "I lost sensation in my hands and feet several hours ago." They got me into a room, where they kept me for a few nights and treated me for whatever the bug was. On the second day, a nurse walked in to check my levels. She was petite, with a dark bob. As she was messing with the IV and what-not, something must have happened. She reversed the flow, or a tube came loose. I remember the moment very clearly because she had been talking to me about a lake, in the United States, the only place she had ever visited there (some church camp), Lake Lagerón. I kept telling her I'd never heard of it. She kept saying, no, it's huge, you've definitely heard of it. Then she went over to the desk and wrote something on a notepad, brought it to me. I looked down: *Lago Hurón.* She'd been saying Lake Huron. I looked down again. My sheets were blooming red. I cried out, "Oh!" My blood had been flowing out of my body throughout our long exchange over the lake, enough to soak into the mattress. The nurse immediately ran to the door and closed it, a worrisome reaction. I fainted and came to in a chair. She was cleaning everything up. "*No se preocupe,*" I said absurdly. A custodial worker brought a new mattress in. I heard the nurse say, "Don't say anything." He smiled, and I remember his smile was nice, a little flirtatious but not unseemly. "Of course," he said. The hospital did not invite me to send the money later. They wanted cash in hand. Anyway, the list goes on. If I have been there, I had something go sideways healthwise there, and I have been all over the world. The hideous crusty rash all over my face in Azerbaijan. Knocked unconscious and shoulder busted by a tree limb while riding a trail horse in Cuba. Appendix removed in Cork City, Ireland, where I wound up in a bed next to a homeless man whom I actually knew from the neighborhood park, from giving him change and cigarettes. Bernard, pronounce the way the Irish do, like BAIR-nerd. He talked through the night in a croaky voice about the misfortunes of his journey, with me there to interject the occasional, "Jesus Christ, Bairnerd!" Finally my surgeon came, my marvelous doctor, he was Jewish and tall and sported a beautiful red afro, told me I would be okay as long as we moved fast. A young nurse put her finger in my butt, part of some test, and her finger was so different than the old proctologist's had been, back in high school. Something went wrong during the surgery, or not "wrong," but there was a complication. They tried to do the procedure laparoscopically, with the high-tech camera-scalpels, but found that nature had placed my appendix strangely on my colon (who could have foreseen?), sort of hidden behind it, and they failed to remove the whole thing. The surgeon was forced to sew up the little puncture wounds and do the traditional cut, instead, the one that leaves a long scar beneath your stomach, on the right side. I woke up in agony, feeling shot full of holes, and started to curse loudly, which, this being Ireland in the early nineties, earned me a talking-to from the nurses. When I saw Bernard in the park a couple of weeks later and tried to reminisce about our shared hospital experience, he professed to have no idea what I was talking about. I remember, though. I remember all of it. I have passed kidney stones on multiple continents. Cluster migraines—those are the worst, believe it or not; they take you back into caves of pain where you become a different person. All of those hours on the floor of the bathroom, when death is right there. It's odd, too, because in the most general terms, I would describe myself as a healthy person. My check-ups tend to go well. My body likes to wait until it can feel me changing time zones and longitudes. Now it had brought me to the majestic fjords of western Norway, and the coronavirus, which I had avoided for the entirety of the pandemic, nearly four years, found me there, in a little fishing village. A scary case. The shaking grew seizure-like. I fell in the bath, actually fell from the shaking. I was supposed to be there for only two days. The doctor in the village came and said that I would need to stay at least ten. I can't remember his face, I was so out of it, and this was not even a year ago. The room where I quarantined looked out over a fjord. They really are as a beautiful as people say, the fjords. The water has that deep, basaltic, glacial northern sublimity. Every so often a boat would enter the window frame and silently pass. The teenagers who seemed to operate the hotel without any direct supervision were sweet and never intrusive. I suppose I was a very easy guest. I lay there under the blankets and drank unsweet lemonade and watched the light change on the fjord, and gradually I came to feel that particular fondness for the world, which sickness has so often brought me, or the gift it leaves, rather, when you realize it won't be this time, and a calm descends. And it turns out this was all you had wanted, or what you had wanted most. That never lasts.

NAMWALI SERPELL

Navel-Gazing

FROM *The Yale Review*

YOU CAN find a lot in a navel. Lint. Grime. The meaning of life, the uncanny remainder of the cord that once bound me to my mother? Incredible. Why not gaze at it? Why not let sight spin into its depths the way water twists down the drain that becomes an eye in the shower scene in Hitchcock's *Psycho*? Yes, you can find all sorts of things in a navel. A flower. A button. (Tender button?) A tiny vortex. The knot at the end of a balloon. In medieval times, it was thought to be the "seat of wantonness," the source of pleasure for a woman. (Tender button!) An understandable error, almost more geographical than biological.

Another few centuries had to pass before we got "navel-gazing," or *omphaloskepsis*. At first, it just meant "to meditate," because *omphalos* invoked the rounded stone in the shrine at Delphi, once believed to be the center of the ancient world. The derisive word *omphalopsychite* was coined in the nineteenth century to describe the Hesychasts, a group of thirteenth-century monks who fixed their eyes on "the middle of the body" in order to "attach the prayer to their breathing." When we navel-gaze now, we are in communion with only ourselves. In our current usage of the term, these ancient spiritual and erotic ideas around "navel-gazing" coincide, clash—and somehow burst, deflating into something masturbatory, bathetic, even distasteful if we notice the implicit ableism.

Where were we? Ah, yes. The state of criticism today. Criticism—if by that we mean writing about our experiences, interpretations, and judgments of aesthetic objects—has always been a bit *omphaloskeptical*. You can trace this self-consciousness across some of its favorite forms: the apologia, the defense, the treatise, the manifesto, and now (dread word) the think piece. Well, the think piece doth protest too much, methinks. Our tendency to reflect on our work—the theories, the methods, the artworks—has devolved into a strained bleating about our "relevance" and "value." Criticism has become, in a word, *meta*critical: making a case for itself, prophesying its own demise, nostalgically musing on its halcyon days, decrying yet another crisis in the conditions of its production.

Perhaps we should start calling it crisis-ism. Endlessly diagnosing a crisis—etymologically, the point in a fever where either it breaks or we do—is in fact a symptom of something worse. We could see it as a kind of hypochondria. Everything from media illiteracy to what the French call *le wokisme* to plunging enrollments can be read as a sign of what's wrong with criticism. But isn't it getting tiring? This ritualistic navel-gazing, this fatalistic fetal position? The neck begins to ache, the hunched back twinges, the gazing eyes cross, a hiccup grows like a bubble in the ribcage. The hiccup is a thought; the thought is this: *Why can't we all just do our jobs?* Why talk about criticism, why talk up criticism, instead of just doing criticism?

Criticism has never thrived because of its marketing. Students did not pile into seminars led by Fredric Jameson, lectures delivered by Roland Barthes, or classes taught by I. A. Richards because their metacritical accounts of their critical practices were enticing, reasonable, or even comprehensible. The work itself and its effects on us were advertisement enough. Criticism lit people up, stirred them, made them reconsider what they value and how. If that is no longer the case, it isn't because we don't try to sell our product anymore. I would submit that it is precisely because we do, desperately, and in the wrong way.

I recently saw a series of ads placed by a well-known university press in a well-established vehicle for serious criticism, highlighting the titles *How to Get Over a Breakup: An Ancient Guide to Moving On* (a translation of Ovid's *Remedies for Love*); *How to Care about Animals: An Ancient Guide to Creatures Great and Small*

(Porphyry, Aesop, Ovid); and *How to Be Queer: An Ancient Guide to Sexuality* ("Sappho, Plato, and Other Lovers"). Now, I don't mind advertising as such—it has been, and has led to, great art. But the logic behind this way of selling our critical wares strikes me, again, as the kind of begging that begs the question: Why pretend that great works of philosophy and literature are self-help books?

It is not our job to convince "consumers" that "creative content" is a "good purchase." It is not our job to explain our relevance by asserting—spuriously, I might add—that great works in the humanities can help grow brain cells, work empathy muscles, foster good vibes, or manifest good politics. And it is not our job to convince companies like Condé Nast or universities like Yale or institutions like the Museum of Modern Art to devote funds to art or criticism by promising them a high return on investment.

The so-called crisis of the humanities is in fact not our responsibility—neither in the sense of our fault nor in the sense of our job to fix. The degradation of artistic practice and reception is the endpoint of political and economic forces that are way beyond our reach and our pay grade, somewhere up in that vast, mechanical realm of neoliberalism, the *modus operandi* of which has always been clear: it's easier to turn people into profitable consumers and tireless workers if they're deprived of literacy and culture.

This longstanding, insidious project in effect co-opts our aesthetic impulses. Just look around. No one wants to read. They want to get published. No one wants to look at paintings or sculptures or installations. They want to collect "views" on social media posts. No one wants to watch films or plays or dance performances, or to discuss what they mean. They want to make viral TikTok loops and reaction videos that pantomime the occasion. No one wants to listen to music. They want to stream the latest release and ride the unfurling "long tail" of cultural products.

These claims may sound like hyperbole, and you will no doubt have evidence (statistical or merely anecdotal) to contest them. But what we used to call art and culture—the movements of words, images, sounds, and gestures among people—bears little relation to what we now call being a "fan," a "media consumer," or a "creative." These ersatz versions of making and experiencing art are based on satisfying "preferences," on the idea of art as comfort, tool, or escape—in sum, art as something you buy and sell or that you use in some "productive" way.

Criticism and art have never exactly been lucrative or serviceable, so why are we pouring our energies into marketing instead of, say, unionizing? To convert our earnest navel-gazing into mercenary self-promotion, the "careerism" that Christian Lorentzen has named "the dominant style of American life," is not to resist but to capitulate to the logic of a machine that is indifferently masticating us to smithereens.

Despite my aversion to tap-dancing for institutional pennies, I do think we have a job to do. Critics, too, are *homo faber*, even if all we make are arguments. The question is not whether we should work and for how much. It is whether we can find work that doesn't alienate us from itself, and from each other. What might this non-alienated work look like? Well, it still involves "navel-gazing," but in two other ways. The first is to historicize, to gaze at ourselves but from a distance, instead of remaining in the reflexive circularity of a presentist "state" or perpetual "crisis." The second is to pay better and closer attention to the art that we claim to be so interested in, to zoom in on it with a formalist lens.

In his 2021 book, *Authority and Freedom: A Defense of the Arts*, Jed Perl refers to "authority and freedom" as "the lifeblood of the arts." He then opens out to a grand theory: "Whether reading a novel, looking at a painting, or listening to music, we are feeling the push and pull of these two forces as they shape the creator's work. Authority is the ordering impulse. Freedom is the love of experiment and play. They coexist. They compete." Yes, I thought upon reading this. Exactly.

Then I realized that my *yes* was more of a *déjà vu*. Wasn't this just Friedrich Nietzsche's distinction between Apollonian and Dionysian aesthetics? Or Roland Barthes's account of readerly and writerly texts? Or Elena Ferrante's recent account of two modalities of writing: staying within the margins or scribbling outside them; writing "neat narratives" while enticed by a "discordant clamor"; a "whirlpool" caught in a "cage"?

Looking back, a great variety of aesthetic models I've encountered over the years take recourse to this kind of division. Other examples, in roughly historical order, might include: tragedy/comedy; sublime/beautiful; matter/form; sensuous/rational; horror/terror; modernism/realism; novel/epic; invention/tradition; alienation/catharsis; dialogism/monologism; avant-garde/kitsch; *punctum/studium*; open/closed; experimental/lyrical realism.

It's as if criticism is always erecting opposed poles to describe art, to describe itself. It is not news that humans love to sort the world as Noah did, two by two. This is a given of contemporary philosophy, modern linguistics, critical theory, and cultural studies, as is the idea that every binary implies a hierarchy, unassailable if reversible. What is perhaps surprising is that all of these pairings can be mapped onto each other relatively smoothly, such that we can abstract from them a dynamic relation of what Mikhail Bakhtin called "centripetal" and "centrifugal" forces.

Between those forces that scatter and those that bind, Bakhtin suggests, there's a relation of adjacency. (They "go forward" "alongside" each other.) Friedrich Schiller, having reasoned his way through a set of "opposed drives" and "opposed principles" in aesthetic experience, describes their relation as "reciprocal action," "opposition," the "most perfect possible union," "equilibrium," and "the preponderance of the one element over the other," before finally landing on "oscillation," which he goes on to call "play." Oscillation appears in metacritical arguments as well. "In the final analysis," writes Barbara Johnson, "it is perhaps precisely as an apprenticeship in the repeated and inescapable oscillation between humanism and deconstruction that literature works its most rigorous and inexhaustible seductions."

The word for this, of course, is *dialectics*. One task historicist navel-gazery grants to criticism, then, is to describe what kind of dialectical relation obtains in an aesthetic experience or a critical analysis. In any given text, are we playfully bouncing between the two poles? Does that oscillation over time yield a kind of spiral? Is there a unifying synthesis or a destructive sublation of the two poles? What happens when the gap between them cannot be bridged, when we cannot make two positions match or meet or mate but must still account for their coexistence? Do we catch them in a parallax, as Slavoj Žižek has it? Are they stuck in a relation of non-relation, what Gilles Deleuze and Félix Guattari called a "disjunctive synthesis"? We may be stuck with twos, but the permutations of their dynamic relations are as endless as the computations programmers derive from ones and zeroes.

Another question we can extrapolate by looking at our past is: How do critics in turn judge the respective elements of those binaries? At the heart of any dialectic is an impulse to rank, to say, for example, that the beautiful is better than the sublime, experimental fiction better than lyrical realism. But history shows that artistic and critical values cannot be judged in any final way. (If they could, we would be out of a job.) When we take the long view, we see that while critics claim to judge aesthetic values, what we really do is argue about the relative worth of our respective indexes of value.

This is because every dialectical pairing has its own indexes of value (which of these two is more interesting? awe-inspiring? pleasing?), and these are often incommensurable with each other. Aristotle explained incommensurability by noting that we cannot judge how sharp a pencil, a wine, and a musical note are with reference to each other. Their respective sharpness lies on different planes of meaning; there is no universal scale of sharpness. And this is, often as not, true for the concept of beauty among artists or taste among critics. "Different strokes," as we say—but only if we mean the radical distinction between the breaststroke and a brain stroke, stroking a pet and the stroke of a pen.

This is one reason why trying to sell our project as critics is so futile. Our sense of value—the idea that it is dialectical and incommensurable—cannot be reconciled with capitalist logics of value. Capitalism calculates values by making them exchangeable, by reducing them all to the same scale of value, a general equivalent that we call money. For instance, capitalism might judge the respective worth of films by comparing how much money they make. We sometimes debate this metric as if it had anything to do with art. But whenever it is presented to viewers as bluntly as, say, the proposed Academy Award for Outstanding Achievement in Popular Film or the already extant Golden Globe Award for Cinematic and Box Office Achievement, we buck. Nobody actually wants a Box Office Oscar (BOO).

Most people understand, at some intuitive level, that the value of art cannot be reduced to how much money it makes or be measured according to capitalism's other main priorities: reproducibility, fungibility, and efficiency. While capitalism asserts that values can be compared and calculated through this kind of math, criticism is busy arguing endlessly about the differences in kind that make that math impossible. Our various indexes of value simply cannot be applied universally, cannot be generalized. Judging the beauty of Marvel movies makes as little sense as judging the sales records of Greek tragedies.

We already know about this contestation of incommensurable values in the world of art—it is what Herman Melville's "Bartleby, the Scrivener" is about; it is what Pierre Bourdieu's *Distinction* is about; it is what Andy Warhol's screen prints are about. And while I obviously prefer critics' and artists' version of value to bankers', that is a matter of my taste, my politics; the two systems are themselves incommensurable. Defending art in terms of how profitable it can be—how remunerative, how useful—is not just distasteful or banal or foolish. It is a contradiction in terms.

One definition of art may even be this: the exposure of incommensurable values. Whether aesthetic, ethical, or social, different values coexist within the work, both inviting and thwarting our efforts to weigh, reconcile, or unite them. Art gives us a picture of those forces at war. *Form* is our name for what surrounds or frames both material contradictions and the fission of distinct aesthetic techniques. Confronting this, criticism itself tends toward two poles: To bind and resolve art's contradictions, explain their emergence, and shape them into ideas. (This is historicism.) Or to allow art's contradictions to break over us, dissolve us, and then account for that experience as best we can. (This is formalism.)

Certain works of art epitomize this constitutive incommensurability. *Winged Victory of Samothrace*, the statue of the goddess Niké, stands headless at the Louvre. She has her own alcove at the base of a grand staircase, like an icon; the placard tells us she was stolen from Greece and reconstituted from three large broken pieces. She is human in shape, superhuman in size, both heavy and weightless. Her rounded flesh weights the air; her trailing drapery, which is somehow also her skin, seems lighter than air. She is missing a head, but we just know that it was lovely. Her robe flows against and behind her like the sea, rippling with the winds of her ancient isle; her feet are planted on a curving ship's bow, yet her wings, arcing above missing arms, are ready to raise her high. Her boundedness, the way she carves into space and time, we call beauty. Her breach, the way she cracks open time and space, we call sublimity.

She is perfection; she is a jumble of fragments. She is grace; she is a shatter. She manifests labor and freedom at once, too. To change the emphasis in Walter Benjamin's phrase "the work of art," *Victory* clearly took a lot of work. We cannot but recognize in her the anonymous labor of her making, even as it yielded an illusion of effortlessness. Her physical presence will not let us forget the time spent gathering the material to build, shape, and reconstruct her, nor the time that has passed since she was made, which yawns back into history even as she stands before us now, like the angel of history.

In an essay on photography, Walter Benjamin asks, "What is aura?" and answers with a riddle:

> A peculiar web of space and time: the unique manifestation of a distance, however near it may be. To follow, while reclining on a summer's noon, the outline of a mountain range on the horizon or a branch, which casts its shadow on the observer until the moment or the hour partakes of their presence—this is to breathe in the aura of these mountains, of this branch.

Web, manifestation, distance, near, follow, recline, outline, range, horizon, branch, shadow, moment, presence, breath: somewhere in the interstices of these opposed, even incommensurable, elements of Benjamin's conceit is the feeling of being with this statue. It's closer to a disturbance than a delight—less a free play of the mind than a jarring détente between senses distinct in kind.

Elsewhere, Benjamin says that "aura" is just our feeling that a work of art is looking back at us. Even without eyes to see, *Victory* glows with this returned gaze over the vastness of time—and with severance, too, the fracture of our alienation from her. After all, we are with her not on her breezy island but in the great hall of a famous museum whose grandeur and profits rest on the bones of the impoverished and the dead, our fellow victims of capitalism. (Niké/Nike.)

Yet our critical gaze need not be cowed by this monumental celebrity. Swept up in the collision of her incommensurabilities, our attention is drawn to her center, pulled there as if by a cord, or by accord. Or perhaps our attention is more like an arrow piercing her, pinning her still, as if in revenge for wrecking us. For there in her center is a wound, a whirlpool, a mystery: the slightly torqued recess of her navel. Omphalos. Something from the far reaches of the past, at the center of our own world, staring back at us.

LINDA KINSTLER

The Olive Branch of Oblivion

FROM *Liberties*

TO RUN out of memory, in the language of computing, is to have too much of it and also not enough. Such is our current situation: we once again find ourselves in a crisis of memory, this time marked not by death but by surplus. Simply put, we are running out of space. There is no longer enough room to store all of our data, our terabytes of history, our ever-accumulating archival detritus. As I type, my computer labors to log and compress my words, to convert each letter into a byte, each byte into a hexadecimal "memory address." This procedure is called "memory allocation," a process of sifting, sorting, and erasing without which our devices would cease to function. For new bytes to be remembered, older ones must be "freed"—which is to say, emptied but not destroyed—so as to prevent what are called "memory leaks." Leaks are to be avoided because, wherever they occur, blocks of precious computing memory are forever fated to remember the same stubborn information, and therefore rendered useless. For memory allocation to function smoothly, the start and finish of each memory block must be definitively marked. "In order to free memory, we need to keep better track of memory," one developer advises. Operating systems, unlike the humans for whom they were designed, are built to tolerate little ambiguity about where memory begins and where it ought to end.

The machinic lexicon is both a site of and a guide to the current memory crisis. We are living through the tail-end of the "memory boom," immersed in the memory-soaked culture that it coaxed into being, a culture now saturated with information, helplessly consumed by the unrelenting labor of data retrieval, recovery, and storage. Even the computers are confused, for deletion does not mean what it used to: when profiles, usernames, or files are erased they are often replaced by what are called "ghost" or "tombstone" versions of their former selves, and these empty markers of bygone selves haunt and clutter our hard drives. Fifty years ago, memory became a "best-seller in consumer society," as the great historian Jacques Le Goff lamented. The new prestige of memory, its special authority for us, was evident before the digital era, in culture and history and politics; but today, with the colossus of digital memory added, I suspect that we are watching as memory's hulking mass begins to collapse under its own weight.

It is a physical crisis as well as a philosophical one: the overdue reckoning with corrosive memorials—with the contemporary ideal and imperative of memorialization—has not been answered with a reappraisal of what memorials are for and what they can do, but rather with a rapid profusion of new ones. We all belong to the contemporary "cult of apology," in the words of the architect and scholar Valentina Rozas-Krause, who has observed that we have come perilously close to relying upon the built environment to speak on our behalf, to atone for our sins, to signal our moral transformation. Of course the cult of apology disfigures also our personal and social and political relations. "The more we commemorate what we did, the more we transform ourselves into people who did not do it," warns the novelist and historian Eelco Runia. A superabundance of bad memories has been answered only with more memory.

Our spatial coordinates are no longer primarily defined by our relation to physical memorials, municipal boundaries, and national borders, but ultimately by our proximity to data centers and "latency zones," geographical regions with sufficient power and water to keep us connected to the cloud, to track our live locations and feed our phones directions. (The cloud may be the controlling symbol of our time.) In the United States, the Commonwealth of Virginia is the site of the largest concentration of data centers: these bastions of memory are being built over Civil War battlefields, gravesites, and coal mines, next to schools and suburban cul-de-sacs, beside reservoirs and state parks. In Singapore, the proliferation of data centers led the government to impose a three-year moratorium on further construction. (The ban was imposed in 2019 and lifted in 2022; new data centers are subject to stricter sustainability rules.) In Ireland, which together with the Netherlands stores most of the European continent's data, similar measures are under consideration. Augustine described memory as a "spreading limitless room," an undefined space to which memories, things, people, and events are consigned for the sake of preservation, and we have made his theoretical fantasy all too real. These unforgetting archives suck up the water, energy, air, and silence; their server fields buzz, warm, and whir through the night. It is an unsustainable and ugly situation to which a bewildering solution has already been found: by 2030, virtual data will be stored in strands of synthetic DNA.

How did we get here? We are swimming in memory—sinking in it, really—devotees of what has become a secular religion of remembrance, consumed by the unyielding labor of excavating, archiving, recording, memorializing, prosecuting, processing, and reckoning with conflicting memories. We cannot keep going in this manner, for it is ecologically, politically, and morally unsustainable. There is no need to deploy metaphors here, for we are quite literally smothering the earth under the weight of all our memory.

What happened is that we forgot how to forget. Along the way, we also forgot why we remember—the invention of one-click data recovery, searchable histories, and all-knowing archives made our already accelerating powers of recollection reflexive, automatic, unthinking, foolproof. I am belaboring these contemporary technological mechanisms of recall because not only have they ensured that remembering has become the default setting of everyday life, but they have also tricked us into believing we can lay claim to a certain kind of forensic knowledge of the past—an illusion of perfect completeness and clarity. It is a dangerous posture, for it is one thing to say, as everyone well knows, that what's past is always present, and quite another to insist upon experiencing the present as if it is the past, and to attempt to understand the past in the language of the present.

Our commitment to remembrance at all costs is a historical anomaly: ever since there have been written records and rulers to endorse them, societies have sustained themselves on the basis of cyclical forgetting. Over the past two decades, as memory has become the primary stage upon which politics, culture, and personal life is played out, a handful of voices have attempted to call attention to this aberration. In 2004, the late French anthropologist Marc Augé declared: "I shall risk setting up a formula. Tell me what you forget and I will tell you who you are." In 2016, David Rieff asked, in a fine book called *In Praise of Forgetting*, on the political consequences of the cult of memory: "Is it not conceivable that were our societies to expend even a fraction of the energy on forgetting that they now do on remembering . . . peace in some of the worst places in the world might actually be a step closer?" He understood all too well that "everything must end, including the work of mourning," for "otherwise the blood never dries, the end of a great love becomes the end of love itself." In 2019, Lewis Hyde suggested that our inability to forget has crippled our capacity to sufficiently grieve. Reading Hesiod's *Theogony*, he observes that Mnemosyne, the mother of the Muses, ushers in both memory and forgetting in the service of imagination and preservation. "What drops into oblivion under the bardic spell is fatigue, wretchedness, and anxiety of the present moment, its unrefined particularity," Hyde writes, "and what rises into consciousness is knowledge of the better world that lies hidden beyond this one." A dose of forgetfulness allows us to put aside, if only temporarily, the sheer volume of all that we must mourn, to break the cycle of vengeance, to see through the fog of fury in moments of the most profound loss.

Prior to any of these pleas for forgetting, the French scholar Nicole Loraux demanded that we look back to the Greek world to rediscover the political power of oblivion. Her interest in the subject, she explains, began when she read of a simple question that an Athenian citizen posed to his warring neighbors after surviving the decisive battle of the civil war that ended the reign of the Thirty Tyrants. The man had sided with the vanquished oligarchs and followed them into exile: he had chosen the side of unfreedom. Facing defeat, he confronted the winning democratic army and asked, "You who share the city with us, why do you kill us?"

It was an "anachronistically familiar" question for Loraux in 2001 and remains so for us today. How to make the killing cease? How to quell the desire for vengeance? How to relinquish the resentments of old? How to reunite a riven family, city, or nation? Loraux pondered the Greek experience, which has become the paradigmatic example of political oblivion, a collective "founding forgetting" that diplomats and lawmakers would attempt to replicate for centuries to come. For once the Athenian democrats won the war and reclaimed their city, they did not seek to exact vengeance upon everyone who had supported the tyrannical reign, but rather only tried and expelled the Thirty themselves and their closest advisors. All of the Greeks, no matter what side they took in the war, swore an oath of forgetting, promising not to recall the wrongs of a war within the family, a civil war that had led its citizens to kill and jail and disenfranchise one another. They swore never to remember: to not think of, recollect, remind themselves of evils. Oblivion became an institution of peace: it amounted to a ban on public utterances, a prohibition against vindictive lawsuits and accusations over what occurred before and during the fighting. "After your return from Piraeus you resolved to let bygones be bygones, in spite of the opportunity for revenge," Andocides writes of this moment. An offering is said to have been made before the altar of Lethe, or oblivion, on the Acropolis; erasures cascaded across Athens as records of the civil war were destroyed, chiseled out, whitewashed. Memory was materially circumscribed, and democracy was re-founded upon the premise of negation. The Athenian approach, Loraux argues, "defined politics as the practice of forgetting." It ensured that from that moment onward, "*Politikos* is the name of one who knows how to agree to oblivion."

Oblivion: it is tempting to read the word as a mere synonym for *forgetting, erasure,* or *amnesty*. In practice, however, it has always been a far more complex commitment. When the Athenians swore never to remember, they were also swearing to always remember that which they had promised to forget. The Athenian example illustrates that the "unforgettable"—the civil war, or *stasis*, and the ensuing tyranny—is that "which must remain always possible in the city, yet which nonetheless must not be remembered through trials and resentments," as Giorgio Agamben observed in 2015. The terms of the peace agreement compelled its subjects to behave "as if" a given crime, transgression, or conflict never occurred, but also to always remember that it *did* occur and *may* occur again. It was a paradoxical promise to never remember and to always remember. The beauty of oblivion is that it reinforces the memory of the loss while prohibiting it from calcifying into resentment; it sanctions certain acts of vengeance, but also imposes strict formal and temporal limitations upon them, so that recrimination does not go on forever. In short, it mandates forgetting in service of the future. This is the upside of oblivion, and this is why, in our hyper-historicist moment, we must labor to remember its powers in the present, which for us is not easily done.

Doing so requires excavating the long-forgotten techniques of oblivion that, for centuries, regulated private and public life. A mutual commitment to oblivion was once the premise upon which all peacemaking was conducted, between states as well as between spouses. ("It is undoubtedly the general rule that marriage operates as an oblivion of all that has previously passed," the New York Supreme Court's Appellate Division ruled in 1896.) Today, the contemporary "right to be forgotten," which is practiced in a number of countries but not in the United States, is one of oblivion's most prominent, and promising, contemporary incarnations, providing the grace of forgottenness to those who long ago made full penance for past crimes. It is a testament to oblivion's power to combat cynicism and stubbornness and vindictiveness, to embrace the evolution of individual identity and belonging. Abiding by its rules, we acknowledge that who we have been is not the same as who we are, or who we may yet become.

"The only thing left is the remedy of forgetting and of abolition of injuries and offenses suffered on both sides, to erase everything as soon as possible, and proceed in such a way that nothing remains in the minds of men on either side, not to talk about it, and never to think about it." So spoke the French jurist Antoine Loisel in 1582 in his "Discourse on Oblivion," a document that has itself been almost entirely swallowed up by time. Loisel reminded his audience of the example of Cicero, who appears to have been the first to translate the Greek ban on forgetting into the Latin prescription for "oblivion," from *oblēvis*, meaning "to smooth over, efface, ground down." To erode, to erase. It is likely to Cicero that we owe the reconfiguration of the Athenian reconciliation agreement into a grand "Act of Oblivion." Tasked with reconstituting Rome after the assassination of Caesar, Cicero appears to have studied the terms of the Athenian agreement as a model for reconciling the republic:

> I have laid the foundation for peace and renewed the ancient example of the Athenians, even appropriating the Greek word which that city used in settling disputes, and so I have determined that all memory of our quarrels must be erased with an eternal oblivion.

Cicero recasts the terms of the Athenian reconciliation, and the attendant promise not to recall, as an *oblivione sempiterna*, an eternal oblivion. The Romans look to the Greeks to find a model for political reconciliation, which they adapt to suit their own ends. The oblivion is what erases "all memory" of Rome's quarrels and allows for the settling of disputes. Oblivion is an instrument of truce and amnesty.

Cicero turns oblivion into a legislative undertaking: "The senate passed acts of oblivion for what was past, and took measures to reconcile all parties," Plutarch reports. (Another translation reads: "The senate, too, trying to make a general amnesty and reconciliation, voted to give Caesar divine honors.") As a result, Brutus and his allies were protected from vengeful reprisals: oblivion becomes a legal, legislative mechanism for forgetting, amnestying, and reconciling. The Roman adoption of the Greek practice suggests that oblivion was not understood as a blanket amnesty, nor as an absolute commandment to forget, but rather something in between, a somewhat ambiguous legal, moral, and material commitment that enabled political communities to come back together while at the same time preserving—memorializing by means of a mandate to forget—the memory of what tore them apart.

Generations of statesmen, Loisel among them, have since followed Cicero's example of looking back to the Greek example and recasting its "unending oblivion" for their own ends. In 1689, for example, Russia and China signed the Treaty of Nerchinsk, in which Russia gave up part of its northeastern territory in exchange for expanded trade access to the Chinese mainland. The text of the treaty was inscribed upon stones laid along the new boundary line. The third clause of the Latin version of the treaty promises that "everything which has hitherto occurred is to be buried in eternal oblivion." (Interestingly, this clause does not appear in the Russian or Chinese versions of the treaty; the discrepancies between the different translations were one reason the treaty ultimately had to be revised.) During the early modern period, oblivion was a fixture of diplomatic speech: all over the world, powers swore to consign the grievances of wars and territorial disputes to "eternal oblivion." Russian rulers swore to *vechnoye zabveniye*, Germans to *ewige Vergessenheit*, French to an *oubli général*. So too did Chinese, Ottoman, and African rulers in treaties with Western powers. The Arabic phrase *mazâ-mâ-mazâ*, "let bygones be bygones," appears in Ottoman diplomatic correspondence dating from the thirteenth century as an element of customary law, and persists well into the nineteenth century in Ottoman and Western European diplomatic peace treaties. Oblivion was circulated, translated, and proclaimed as part of the ordinary business of statecraft. Rulers agreed to bury past wrongs as a way of signaling that their states belonged to the family of nations; forgetting the ills that members visited upon one another was a prerequisite for belonging to the family.

Modern states owe their foundations to the pragmatic promise of oblivion. When the newly installed Republican government of Oliver Cromwell sought to erase the English people's memory of the bloody civil war in 1651, his parliament passed an act to ensure "that all rancour and evil will, occasioned by the late differences, may be buried in perpetual oblivion." And when, nine years later, King Charles II sought to coax his subjects into forgetting the reign of Cromwell, he too declared an oblivion, forgiving everyone for their prior allegiances to the English Commonwealth except the men who beheaded his father, Charles I. (They were tried for treason and killed.) In France, policies of *oubliance* were widespread in the sixteenth and seventeenth centuries, and the Bourbon restoration of 1814 was marked by a new public law ending investigations into "opinions and votes given prior to the restoration" and stipulating that "the same oblivion is required from the tribunals and from citizens." In territories that would become the United States and Canada, European powers swore to oblivion in treaties with Indigenous peoples as part of the project of imperial expansion. Diplomatic exchanges between Indigenous leaders and European emissaries did not merely make mention of "burying the hatchet" or burying wrongs in oblivion—they were centered around these cyclical rituals of forgetfulness. French and English diplomats appealed to past oblivions whenever they desired to solidify an alliance with Indigenous peoples, securing their support against the encroachment of other white settler groups.

In the Revolutionary period, oblivions proliferated in the colonies, as the legal scholar Bernadette Meyler has documented. The Continental Congress invoked oblivion in its efforts to resolve a boundary dispute between Vermont and New Hampshire. North Carolina deployed one in 1783 to bring a cadre of seditionist residents back into the fold. Massachusetts passed one in 1766, Delaware in 1778. In 1784, Judge Aedanus Burke, a member of the South Carolina General Assembly, made one of the more forceful arguments for oblivion in American history when he delivered his pseudonymous "Address to the Freemen of the State of South Carolina." He wrote of how, during the Revolutionary War, he watched as a man walked over the "dead and the dying" bodies of "his former neighbors and old acquaintances, and as he saw signs of life in any of them, he ran his sword through and dispatched them. Those already dead, he stabbed again." The nature of the violence, he argued, far exceeded the capacity of law. And so a general clemency was the only way forward, for Burke, simply because "so many crimes had been committed that fewer than a thousand men in the state, he thought, could 'escape the Gallows.'" He declared that "the experience of all countries has shewn, that where a community splits into a faction, and has recourse to arms, and one finally gets the better, a law to bury in *oblivion* past transactions is absolutely necessary to restore tranquility." Oblivion was the only way that those who had been royalists could possibly still share the same ground with the revolutionaries they had fought: "Every part of Europe has had its share of affliction and usurpation or civil war, as we have had lately. But every one of them considered an act of oblivion as the first step on their return to peace and order."

Almost a century later, President Andrew Johnson marshalled similar language in his attempt to restore peace in the aftermath of the Civil War. In his first annual message after Lincoln's assassination, he advocated for a "spirit of mutual conciliation" among the people, explaining why he had invited the formerly rebellious states to participate in amending the Constitution. "It is not too much to ask," he argued, "in the name of the whole people, that on the one side the plan of restoration shall proceed in conformity with a willingness to cast the disorders of the past into oblivion, and that on the other the evidence of sincerity in the future maintenance of the Union shall be put beyond any doubt by the ratification of the proposed amendment to the Constitution, which provides for the abolition of slavery forever within the limits of our country." His speech casts the rewriting of the Constitution and the ratification of the Thirteenth Amendment as itself an Act of Oblivion, a way to "efface" the grounds upon which slavery had been legally sanctioned and defended.

And yet we live in the ruins of past peace treaties. We do not need to ask whether all these measures of imposed forgetting "worked," because we know that neither the oblivions nor the ceasefires nor the reconciliations that they were supposed to inaugurate ever held up for long (often for very good reasons). The more interesting question is why oblivion proliferated in the first place, and where the desire that is continuously revealed by the fact of its repetition originates. "Oblivion brings us back to the present, even if it is conjugated in every tense: in the future, to live the beginning; in the present, to live the moment; in the past, to live the return; in every case, in order not to be repeated," Marc Augé writes. The recursive calls for oblivion—pleas for a workable kind of forgetfulness, both legal and moral—can be found wherever people have quarreled, battled, and betrayed one another, only to subsequently discover that, even after all is said and done, they must share the same earth.

On September 19, 1946, as part of a world tour following the end of his first term at 10 Downing Street, Winston Churchill arrived at the University of Zurich and called for "an act of faith in the European family and an act of oblivion against all the crimes and follies of the past." Standing upon a dais set up outside the university building, he faced thousands of people gathered on the square before him and said:

> We all know that the two World Wars through which we have passed arose out of the vain passion of Germany to play a dominating part in the world. In this last struggle crimes and massacres have been committed for which there is no parallel since the Mongol invasion of the 13th century, no equal at any time in human history. The guilty must be punished. Germany must be deprived of the power to rearm and make another aggressive war. But when all this has been done, as it will be done, as it is being done, there must be an end to retribution. There must be what Mr. Gladstone many years ago called "a blessed act of oblivion."

As he spoke, the guilty were indeed on their way to being punished in occupied Germany, in Japan, and in the Soviet Union, where prosecutors had not waited for the battles to end to begin trying and sentencing German prisoners of war. The International Military Tribunal at Nuremberg was preparing for its 218th day in session, and in Tokyo the prosecution was still making its case. Much was still unknown about the nature and volume of German atrocities. Churchill acknowledged the unprecedented character of the crimes in question and underscored the imperative of punishing their perpetrators. He also established that everyone in the audience, having lived through the horrible years of war, was all too familiar with its nature, and that this familiarity was a kind of shared knowledge among them. Much was still to be discovered, unearthed, proven, and punished, yet everyone who had lived through the war in Europe, who had been proximate to its force, "knew" how it came to be—even those who had profited from it, and those who looked away. Otherwise, he feared that memory might be wielded to perpetuate the absence of peace.

Churchill did not shy away from retribution (he had once supported the creation of a "kill list" of high-ranking Nazis), but he also saw its limitations. He understood that the desire for vengeance could not be allowed to fester forever because it risked preventing Europeans from imagining a shared future together:

> We cannot afford to drag forward across the years to come hatreds and revenges which have sprung from the injuries of the past. If Europe is to be saved from infinite misery, and indeed from final doom, there must be this act of faith in the European family, this act of oblivion against all crimes and follies of the past. Can the peoples of Europe rise to the heights of the soul and of the instinct and spirit of man? If they could, the wrongs and injuries which have been inflicted would have been washed away on all sides by the miseries which have been endured. Is there any need for further floods of agony? Is the only lesson of history to be that mankind is unteachable? Let there be justice, mercy and freedom. The peoples have only to will it and all will achieve their heart's desire.

The stakes were high: letting the ills of the past "drag forward" was something that Europeans could not "afford" to do because that would mean "infinite misery" and "final doom" for the already imperiled and destroyed continent. The indefinite continuation of exercises in vengeance and recrimination would spell certain death not only for "Europe," as Churchill saw it, but also for the project of a "United States of Europe" that his speech called for. If the defeat of the Nazis had saved the continent from entering a new "Dark Age," then the practice of perpetual vengeance, he argued, threatened to bring it there anyway. A "United States of Europe," he argued, would return the continent to prosperity. But before that could occur, something else had to take place. "In order that this may be accomplished there must be an act of faith in which the millions of families speaking many languages must consciously take part," Churchill said. That "act of faith" was not a religious or spiritual rite but a political one: an act of oblivion.

The "Mr. Gladstone" to whom Churchill referred was the liberal politician William Gladstone, who served twelve non-consecutive years as British prime minister between 1868 and 1894. In 1886, Gladstone called for a "blessed oblivion of the past" to bury the memory of British Home Rule in Ireland and restore peaceful relations between England and Ireland. "Gladstone urged the MPs to grant the Irish a 'blessed oblivion' and permit them to forget about a tradition of hatred," the historian Judith Pollmann writes. Calling for oblivion, Gladstone implicitly referred back to the Act of Oblivion that had restored the British monarchy under Charles II. He was suggesting that the same tool that restored the British monarch in 1660 could serve quite the opposite purpose two centuries later, marking the erasure and forgetting of British rule in Ireland.

Oblivion in the aftermath of war and conflict is emotionally very exacting, and Churchill's remarks were at first poorly received. *The Manchester Guardian* called it an "ill-timed speech," and others thought that it was insensitive to the still-fresh wounds of war. (The paper did not argue that the speech insulted the memory of the slaughtered Jews of Europe, but rather the French, whom Churchill had dared ask to reconcile with the Germans.) Today, however, the speech is regarded as one of the first calls for the creation of the contemporary European Union, and Churchill is celebrated as one of its founding fathers. He called for a new collective commitment to oblivion, yet the half-century that followed was defined not by oblivion but by its opposite. The Nuremberg trials delivered partial justice for a select group of perpetrators, as did proceedings in the Soviet Union, Poland, Israel, Germany, France, Italy, Japan, and elsewhere. Retribution came in fits and starts, and it is still ongoing today. Memorials were erected all over the formerly occupied territories, part of an effort to ensure that passersby would always remember what had occurred there. But memorials also have an odd way of sanctioning forgetfulness: the more statues we build, the more we fortify the supposedly unbreachable gap between past and present. Is this not its own kind of oblivion?

In a moment of profound rupture, Churchill called for yet another repetition of the Greek model, for a new adaptation of the founding forgetting that supposedly bound the Athenians back together, if only for a short time. His call for an end to memory was far too premature. But his suggestion that, at some point, memory must cede ground to mercy—and, we might add, to the memories of other and not necessarily more recent crimes—is one that we are only now beginning to take up. The "United States of Europe" was ultimately founded not upon an Act of Oblivion but rather upon the myth that its constituent nations were bound together by a commitment to repudiate and remember the past, and to ensure that the atrocities of World War II would "never again" occur. We all know how that went. To consider the possibilities of oblivion requires accepting that there are some forms of memory production—prosecution, memorialization, truth and reconciliation, processing—that may effectively prolong and even exacerbate the wrongs they were intended to make right.

Oblivion is not a refusal of these efforts but rather a radical recognition of their limitations. It is an invitation not to endlessly participate in the "global theater of reconciliation," in the instrumentalization of survivor testimony, in what the literary scholar Marc Nichanian has called the "manipulation of mourning." It provides an opening through which we might attend to the moral ruptures that preceded the acts of wrongdoing; it creates space to engage in the kind of "unhinged mourning," that Nichanian locates "prior to any politics, prior to any foundation or restoration of democracy, prior to every accord, every contract, every pact and every reconciliation." Oblivion never speaks of forgiveness; indeed, it is the alternative to forgiveness. To forget a transgression is a distinct moral act that liberates its subject from the dueling imperatives to either avenge the wrong or to forgive it. It is, in this sense, an important rejection of the language of reconciliation, of loving one's enemy. It offers a path forward where this kind of "love" is unimaginable, if not impossible. Oblivion embeds the memory of the crime in the hearts of those whom it forbids from speaking about it. "This," Nichanian argues, "is what the Greeks, in their obsession, called *álaston penthos*, mourning that does not pass which nothing could make one forget."

Some years ago, I came across a scientific paper announcing that a group of computer scientists in Germany and New Zealand had come up with a "universal framework" that they called *Oblivion*. Its function was rather straightforward: it could identify and de-index links from online search engines at extreme speed, handling two hundred and seventy-eight removal requests per second. They promised nothing less than to make forgetting "scalable," as seamless and widespread as possible, and their citations refer to similar programs, including one called *Vanish* that makes "self-destructing data" and another, called the "ephemerizer" which also promised to make "data disappear." All of these efforts were designed in response to the inauguration, in 2011, of the European Right to Be Forgotten, or as it is officially called, the "Right to Erasure." This new European right affords individuals the ability to demand "data erasure," to require criminal databases and online sources to remove any personal data that is no longer "relevant" or in the "public interest."

The law is composed of two distinct but related ideas: first, that we have a "right to delete" the data that we leave behind as we move about the digital world, and second, that we also have a "right to oblivion" that endows us with what the scholar Meg Leta Ambrose calls "informational self-determination"— the right to control what everyone else is able to learn about us without our consent. Minor offenses, arrests, and dropped charges from the past may be deleted from internet articles and websites if they fit these criteria, such as in cases where criminal records have been sealed or expunged, and the penalties long ago fulfilled (or where no crime was found to have been committed in the first place). As Jeffrey Rosen has noted, the law derives from the French "'*droit à l'oubli*'—or the 'right of oblivion'—a right that allows a convicted criminal who has served his time and been rehabilitated to object to the publication of the facts of his conviction and incarceration."

The adoption of these new rights marks the most recent transfiguration of the ancient idea of oblivion. The Right to Be Forgotten is both a privacy protection and a rehabilitative mechanism, one which, like the Athenian oath, helps to restore individual membership to the civic family. It gives us the freedom to become someone else, to escape the unhappy past, provided that certain criteria are met. This new right extends far beyond the legal realm. For several years, European nations have been expanding the Right to Be Forgotten such that it protects cancer survivors and those with other chronic illnesses from facing penalties from insurance companies, banks, adoption agencies, and more because of their health troubles. It is a commitment to rehabilitation in the most comprehensive sense, a pledge to ensure that no one should be defined by their worst moments or their greatest misfortunes. You could call it a kind of grace. (The Russian word for these kinds of measures is *pomilovaniye*, derived from the word *milyy*, meaning "dear," "darling," "good." We wash away wrongs and choose to see only the best in ourselves, and in others.) To honor the right to oblivion is to submit to a particular performance of citizenship, one that may seem strange at first glance, and ubiquitous the next: for who among us cannot be said to be engaged in some studied act of forgetfulness, forgetting unhappy episodes from the past in order to prevent them from overtaking the future?

Like the oblivions of old, the Right to Be Forgotten has a paradoxically memorial function: those who ask for erasure have not yet forgotten their offenses, and their digital rehabilitation cannot alter the facts of their transgressions. I am thinking in particular here of a Belgium man named Olivier G., who killed two people in a drunk driving accident in 1994. In 2006, he was "rehabilitated" under Belgian law after serving out his conviction on multiple charges. In 2008, he sued a French paper for continuing to maintain records of his role in the accident online, and the European Court of Human Rights ultimately ruled that the paper had to delete his name from its past articles and replace it with the letter "X." Owing to the press coverage of the case, we all know very well that he is "X." And he himself is unlikely to forget it.

Yet his case still raises the inevitable question: What does oblivion mean for historical knowledge? By embracing its possibilities, do we also open ourselves up to the erasure of records, of historical truth? In *The Interpretation of History*, in 1909, Max Nordau lamented the "almost organic indifference of mankind to the past," and writes of the "stern law of oblivion" that limits the transmission of memory to no more than three generations. "It is in records, and not in the consciousness of man, that the historical part is preserved," he observed. And yet, as Nietzsche warned, an over-reliance upon record-keeping, upon archiving, preserving, and documenting—the features of his "superhistorical" person—can also snuff out our will to live in the present, our ability to see the world clearly before us. Every archivist knows that doing the job right requires a balance of preservation and destruction, that it is irresponsible and even unjust to save everything from obliteration. This is especially true in instances where penance has been paid, vengeance taken, time served, justice achieved so fully that it has begun to undermine its own wise and measured conclusions. "For with a certain excess of history, living crumbles away and degenerates," Nietzsche admonished. "Moreover, history itself also degenerates through this decay."

It is a mistake to understand history as operating in opposition to forgetting. Ernest Renan made this error when, in 1882, he famously observed that "the act of forgetting, I would even say, historical error, is an essential factor in the creation of a nation, which is why progress in historical studies often constitutes a danger for nationality." In fact, history is as much a vehicle for forgetting as it is for remembering: when we remind ourselves that histories are written by the victors, this is what we mean. History is always edited, and oblivion acts a kind of editorial force on the historical record, though of course history may be edited according to many criteria of significance and some historians may prefer one oblivion to another. To embrace the idea of oblivion, however, is to try to redirect the inevitable erasures of the historical record toward the pursuit of a more just and liberated future—to take moral advantage of the room, and the freedom, that we are granted by forgetfulness.

Besides, every act of forgetting, as Loraux reminds us, "leaves traces." There can be no absolute forgetting, just as there is no possibility of total memory. Every time I encounter a new Act of Oblivion in the archive, I take it as a marker that someone, somewhere, wanted its historical world to be forgotten. And yet there it is, staring back at me on the table. Almost always, whatever conflict prompted the oblivion in the first place is recounted in fine detail alongside the agreement to let bygones be bygones.

Where oblivion was once deployed to reconcile states with themselves and one another, today it is most often invoked in order to restore people to full political citizenship, to repair the relation between subject and sovereign. Oblivion has become individualized. To some extent, it always has been individualized. Every oath of forgetting required people to look past the transgressions of their neighbors, but not to forget them completely. Nichanian argues that this amounts only to a mere pragmatic performance of reconciliation, which should not be mistaken for absolution. "One should know with whom one is 'reconciling.' One should not confuse friendship and reconciliation," he cautions. "One should be capable of carrying out a 'politics of friendship' instead and in lieu of 'politics of reconciliation' . . . one must in any case know what will never be reconciled within reconciliation."

One must never forget with whom one is reconciling; one must forget what came before the reconciliation. These are the contradictory claims that the oath levied upon its swearers. It aimed to obliterate one form of memory while at the same time consecrating another. "I wonder," Loraux asks, "what if banning memory had no other consequences than to accentuate a hyperbolized, though fixed, memory?" The people are reconciled, but they see one another for who they were, and what they did, during the period of tyranny. Nothing is forgotten, and much is owed by one side to the other. This relation, Nichanian writes, is "the irony of being-together, the sole surviving language." What else is there? Oblivion is when one person says to another: I know who you have been, and what you have done, but I will pretend not to remember, and I offer you my friendship, and we will live amicably together. Call it pragmatism, call it decency, call it politics. (Call it quaint.) In the absence of forgiveness, which usually never comes, it may be our only hope.

JAREK STEELE

Nesting

FROM *Colorado Review*

THE SUMMER I was pregnant, I watched with growing detachment as my breasts asserted themselves and my spreading hips echoed my mother's. I had the urge to nest—procuring diapers and wet wipes, obsessively dusting, developing a sudden, unexpected interest in scrapbooking—and became, for a short while, someone I was not. That's not true. I was that person just as surely as I am this person, bald and bearded, typing at a dining room table. Unless that's not true either. If you asked me then, when I was nineteen, if I ever thought I'd be a man, I would have said it was impossible, but the truth shifts, and I suppose the space you're in shapes the person you are as much as you shape it.

When I had taken the Clearblue Easy pregnancy test five months earlier, I danced around the couch while my boyfriend, Tracy, sat on the bed with the test instructions in his hand. I'd thought that all the partying and all the infrequent and unpredictable periods and all the stress from not eating well had rendered me incapable of pregnancy. We hadn't tried for this, and I hadn't even thought of getting pregnant, but for the first few minutes, I was so happy to know I wasn't defective. Then the reality of being a parent with this man who didn't ask for any of this set in. I stopped smiling.

"I'm not trying to trap you," I said. "It's okay if you want to bail. I won't be mad." He got up from the bed and walked toward me. "Seriously. I can move in with Jo or something." He put his arms around me.

"I'm in," he said. It felt vaguely like a door closing.

Tracy and I lived in an old two-car garage in Vera, Illinois, a rough collection of houses just down the road from the Vandalia Correctional Center. He had converted it into a single paneled room, outfitted on one side with a sink, stove, and refrigerator. On the other side, a crib sat against the wall between the bed and the wood stove. A small window vent lurked at the back of the building by the bathroom. Tracy had installed one small window when he closed up the wall where the garage door had been. Another window was tucked into a storage closet that was now filled with amps, guitars, and a stool where he practiced Randy Rhoads solos and where I used to play my bass. I hadn't picked that up in a long time.

The old house that the garage belonged to still stood next to it. It was a destroyed monument to Tracy's old life. The roof and ceiling were collapsing. Huge blankets of insulation sagged onto the furniture that Tracy had never moved out. A lot of his old records and toys were still in his childhood bedroom, decomposing in the open air. Frames holding soggy pictures still populated the end tables, and broken plates and cups and moldering shoes littered the floors. In places, the carpet had turned to dust.

My teddy bear still sits next to my bed decades after I got him. If he were trapped in a collapsing house, I don't know if I could calmly sleep in the garage while it all fell down in slow motion, but Tracy didn't really ever look at the house after the tornado hit it. Or maybe he just told me it was a tornado, and what had really happened was that after his mom had been gone for twenty years, after his sisters had moved away and gotten married, and after his dad finally died of lung cancer, Tracy found himself alone with that house and its ghosts; maybe he kicked out the windows, tore off the front door, and left holes in the walls, then walked across the driveway to the garage and went inside. Maybe if it had been that way, he would have moved heavy equipment across the lawn, knocked down the whole thing, and made room for something new. We'd have parked a trailer on the concrete pad and maybe grown some tomatoes. Instead, the old house and the collapsed septic tank, buried under the burn pile in the backyard, rotted a few yards away from the garage-house, where I was now desperately cleaning.

The vacuum cleaner rattled and smelled like it was burning. A thread from the carpet had wound itself around the brushes a few weeks before, and I had tried to untangle it during commercial breaks with a pair of pinking shears I'd found in the old house. The baby's head felt like it had divided into four and was pressing on every internal organ at the same time. The effort to curl around my belly, with the heavy end of the vacuum propped between my knees, had done me in, and I gave up. So I just vacuumed in five-minute increments and rested between them to let the smell dissipate.

A year before, I would have been able to pry the thread loose. From the age of sixteen, I had vacuumed, washed the sheets, and cleaned the funk from over-the-road truckers off the bathtubs of hundreds of motel rooms. My body could slip between the linen cart and the door while I knocked and called out, "Housekeeping," before pushing the master key into the lock and barging in. I had been tipped with beer and cocaine. I had ridden my motorcycle to work and chewed on the guest mints for lunch.

I was the bass player in my then-boyfriend Kevin's band, but they called me temporary—only a placeholder until they found a guy who could keep up with Kevin's lead guitar and Rich's drums. We all lived together in an apartment next to the train tracks. There were holes in the floor, and the plumbing was connected backward. If you flushed the toilet before you sat down, you could feel heat. I met Tracy that year. I was lying on the living room floor with a bottle of Maalox in my hand, my head propped on the edge of a couch and my feet wedged against a drum set.

Tracy had answered an ad for a rhythm guitar player, but nobody remembered that he was supposed to audition that day, which is why I was startled when he appeared in the living room: twenty-four years old, skinny, shaggy blond hair, thick glasses, bad teeth that he hid behind a closed-mouth smile, shy. I was in love before I could put out my cigarette and stand up.

"Where do you live?" Kevin asked after a few minutes.

"I got a little place outside of Vandalia," Tracy said. "By the prison."

At nineteen I would find myself sober and seven and a half months pregnant, trying to clean up rat droppings and wood chips off the carpet with a paper towel. At the time, it was hard to say whether or not I had made a good trade, but every time I think about the years after that—all that would be, all the mistakes we would make—I think about him standing there in that cigarette smoke amongst the amps and empty beer bottles, trying not to have an asthma attack, hoping he could join us. And every time I'm glad I went with him instead.

In the first months we were together, we impulsively adopted Trekah, a Siberian husky puppy from a pet store in the mall, and brought him home in Tracy's two-seat '87 Fiero, trying out names as we drove. Now, a year later, he was fifty-five pounds of fur and sinew bouncing around the pen we'd built around the well enclosure attached to the old house.

Tracy doted on Trekah. He sent off for sled dog racing boots with little rubber grips on the bottoms for traction that were supposed to prevent snowballs from forming in Trekah's paws and keep his paw pads safe from ice shards. One day, the UPS truck passed our house and stopped in the road just past the farm. I could see the driver looking at the package and then looking at the mailbox as he inched backward to our driveway. He slowly walked the box up the driveway, looking between the destroyed house and the garage, and dropped it when Trekah ran to him and put his paws on the driver's shoulders. I pulled the dog off of him and nudged the box toward the garagehouse. I recognized the packaging. It was the sled harness Tracy had ordered. Over the summer, he had run up and down the road, past the cornfields, with the dog until his asthma stopped him. Then he took scrap metal from work, welded together a dogsled on wheels, and charged the harness to his Discover card. Driving away, the UPS driver didn't wave back when our next-door neighbor, Earl, tossed his hand up.

We still had the Fiero, but we didn't have a name for the baby yet. Tracy was lobbying for Randon Wolfgang, a combo of Randy Rhoads for him and Mozart for me, but Randon and Tracy's last name, Denton, rhymed in a way that made me secretly judge him for advocating for it, and I only aspired to like classical music. My knowledge of Mozart was mostly based on the movie *Amadeus*, and not even so much from that as from the Falco song "Rock Me Amadeus" that came out after that, and that song actually sort of annoyed me. By the end of the summer, we had mostly let the subject of naming the baby drop.

"Don't goooo . . . ," I whined one morning. I said it playfully but meant it. Tracy flopped back onto the bed and lifted both feet into the air. The laces from his steel-toe boots dangled against his work pants, and he wrestled them into tight knots. I tried to entice him to stay in bed, to call in and have a lazy day with me. "I'll make pork chops." That was a cruel carrot. We couldn't afford them until payday.

"I got to," he said. He rested his head and looked up at the ceiling. His thick glasses rested on his nose, and his hair fell straight back off his high forehead. His shirt had burn marks and the name patch was dingy. It smelled, no matter how many times I washed it, like metal shavings and heat. Sometimes he reminded me of my dad.

We repeated this routine nearly every weekday morning, and I knew it was tedious. I knew I was tedious. I knew he would leave every day, and even though he was leaving to bring home a paycheck, I resented it. I missed being able to climb into the low-slung seat of his little Fiero with one pop-up headlight stuck in the up position. I missed starting it in second gear, because first gear stopped working before I met him. I even missed climbing out of that car when the engine smoked to hold the flashlight while he refilled the oil. One in 508 of those cars exploded before the massive recall in 1987, but he coaxed it into service every day. I wanted to get into that car and drive. Maybe nowhere very far, maybe just an hour or so on the highway to the big CATSUP bottle water tower in Collinsville, or maybe to hunt mushrooms on his sister's property—just somewhere.

He sat up and put his hand on my belly. "Take care of the foofer," he said. Since we hadn't decided on a name, we made up a placeholder. He put his face down by his hand. "Take care of the mama," he said. Foofer had become a sort of imaginary being, a presence to which we had assigned a voice. "C'mon buddy," he called to the dog. Trekah ran to the door and looked back before trotting out to the yard. Tracy walked out the door and pulled it closed. I heard the gate on the pen latch, then the car door open, pause, then close. The unmuffled roar of his car crescendoed, waned, and was then overtaken by the KSHE 95 morning show turned up even louder than the engine.

Hey hey mama said the way you move
Gonna make you sweat, gonna make you groove

Led Zeppelin's "Black Dog" faded as he pulled out of the driveway and drove away.

The truth was that it was getting harder and harder to get out of bed in the morning. It felt like my body was a foreign mass of tonnage that I dragged around with me, and sometimes after he left for work at six a.m., I pulled the covers back over my head until ten, maybe even eleven, or until the sound of tiny jaws gnawing at the ceiling became too much to bear and I got up to make noise.

I stared at the window. Dust danced around in the sunlight that made its way inside.

While Tracy welded metal racks and skids thirty-seven miles away, I propped the front door open and listened to Earl cut firewood to sell. Sometimes the sunlight and sound lured me outside so I could drag my swollen self up and down the road with Trekah.

Tracy's sister had given me some maternity clothes, which replaced the surgery scrubs I'd found in the locker room my sophomore year of high school. I'd had to tie the pants and roll the waistband down to get a good enough cinch to wear them for P.E. in lieu of the red shorts and white T-shirt I didn't have. The legs dragged the floor, though, so I tucked them into knee socks and pretended they were baseball pants while I played field hockey with the rest of the class. But now I was heavier than I'd ever been, and the waistband on the scrub pants didn't even fit below my belly anymore, so I resorted to the pink overalls that made me look like a balloon animal. It didn't matter much, since the only person I saw each day was Earl, and he mostly just waved his hand with the missing index finger on his way to his outhouse.

Whenever I got too precious about our living situation, I looked at the toilet and bathtub that Tracy had installed on a sort of stage, two steps up from the concrete so the plumbing would drain through the back wall and into the field, and think he was a damn genius. He had even enclosed it in a proper bathroom, and as gross as it sounds to have your clean shirts and pants hanging on a lead pipe between the water heater and toilet, it worked. The wood stove produced a good, dry heat in the winter. He had made one of those drop ceilings like you see in offices—an aluminum grid that holds white vinyl panels and fluorescent lights. Ours was made of Styrofoam and held two bare lightbulbs where the garage door opener might have once hung. Sometimes I liked to imagine that, above the ceiling, the rafters still held lumber or maybe an old bicycle or sled, waiting for the space to be a garage again. What I'm saying is that it was enough, at least for the moment. Until the rats came.

At first we could only hear faint scraping, which was easy to ignore and assume was a raccoon gnawing on the siding or some little mouse getting into the cabinets, but soon we couldn't ignore it. The sounds of tiny little feet tittered in the dark, and the angry squeaks were too loud to be mice.

I was concerned that the crib Tracy's sister gave us was sitting right under a hole that had been chewed through the Styrofoam panel. The rats scurrying each night made me worry that one of them would fall on the baby, though the prospect of that seemed remote. Still, as my due date crept slowly near, I was desperate to think about something, anything else, which is why I found myself standing in a garage-house armed with a broom.

I poked the ceiling with it a few times, and then tried to maneuver the panel out of its square so I could swap it with another panel somewhere else. Somewhere else proved to be a problem too. I lumbered around with nearly five pounds of baby, plus whatever a placenta weighs, pressing into my pelvis, looking for a good tile to swap out. The muted TV sat on milk crates a few feet away from the wood stove. I just couldn't tolerate Sally Jessy Raphael anymore.

The source of the rats wasn't hard to find. In addition to the destroyed house habitat that sat fifteen feet away from the garage-house, Tracy's cousin Terry had taken over the farm down the road and erected a clubhouse for his motorcycle gang, the Mad Dogs. The feed and crops disappeared and were replaced by bike parts and rottweilers. We were the next best place for food and shelter.

Terry kept the dogs outside and bred the female, Piranha, over and over. She barked and snarled from her pen and foamed at the wire fence when anyone approached.

Tracy and I had walked over to look at her puppies once. Terry kneed Piranha out of his way before pulling one of the puppies up by the scruff of its neck to show it to us and then tossing back into the dirt with its litter mates. Piranha growled from the corner of the pen. A few other dogs roamed around the yard but kept a skeptical distance. So did I.

I turned off the TV and looked around the room. It felt like any step I took would lead me back to this exact spot. My stomach growled, and I wondered if it was me or the baby who felt hungry. I brushed the flaking nonstick coating off the skillet and held the lighter against the burner. Two eggs, over medium, two pieces of brown bread, mayonnaise, a little mustard, a ton of salt, and a shake or two of pepper. I scraped the egg crumbs from the skillet into the trash and took the bag into the bathroom. I dumped the wads of dirty toilet paper onto the top of the kitchen trash and knocked the empty toilet paper roll onto the floor. Even propped on the toilet seat, I couldn't bend over far enough to get it. My fingers hovered a half inch away no matter what angle I tried. I sat on the edge of the tub with the trash bag between my feet. It felt like we were staring at each other waiting for someone to do something about it.

The front door popped open and swung slowly around. The dog was barking in his enclosure. I took two tries and heaved myself up. Now the baby's foot appeared to be lodged against my lung.

I was tired of being pregnant.

My phone rang as I made my way to the front door to push it closed.

"There's no freaking Betty Rubble in my Flintstones vitamins."

While I was contemplating fried eggs and rat droppings, my sister was back in Effingham in Dad's old apartment sorting Flintstones vitamins onto the kitchen table. Jo was seventeen and pregnant with Rich's baby.

"Are you serious?" I pushed the front door closed again. It bounced off the jamb and swung open slowly. I turned around.

"Fred, Wilma, Barney, Pebbles, Bamm-Bamm . . . but no Betty."

"How do you know this?"

"I was counting them to make sure I got all hundred and fifty, because you just never know, and I paid good money . . ." and I knew she did. Illinois public aid took care of the basics, but prenatal vitamins were extra. Flintstones were cheaper. I stretched the phone cord to the couch and held it with one hand while reaching for my plate. I couldn't reach it. I left it there and eyed the hole in the ceiling. Black pebbles of rodent shit fell onto the carpet. *Fuck this,* I thought, and I resolved to be angry about it when Tracy came home from work. I would demand a ceiling repair. He would agree. We would watch a *M*A*S*H* rerun and ignore the ceiling until the day after payday and resolve to think about it again later.

"You're out of your mind," I said.

"I'm going to write a letter."

You know that feeling when you realize you're smiling and it feels foreign? Like your face had to remember a sequence of moves to get you there? Yeah, that.

I figured a good jog up the road would send me into labor, or at least make me feel less guilty for not loving the dog as much as Tracy did. I wondered if there was something intrinsically wrong with me and if I was capable of love the way I was supposed to love. What if I didn't love the baby enough? I mean, why couldn't I think of a name? What if I was supposed to feel more excited about cleaning and organizing the garage-house? What if all of this wasn't absurd? What if this was, in fact, my life— outfitting a dog for the Iditarod in an Illinois summer, packing the laundry for trips to town, sifting through the graveyard of the time before the storm and not recognizing a single thing—just making it up as I go along?

"Hey, buddy, wanna go for a run?" I snapped the leash on Trekah's collar and held on while he pulled me, wheezing and slow, behind him. We paused, and I put my hands on my knees to catch my breath. I caught a glimpse of my pink maternity overalls and high-top shoes left over from high school. The Sharpie graffiti was still visible—OZZY, METALLICA.

"FUCK!" I yelled across the cornfield. We made our way back home. Earl waved. I put Trekah back in his pen and filled his water dish under the well spigot. "Fuck," I whispered. I went back into the garage-house and closed the door. It bounced open again. I slammed it closed.

Fuck.

I turned up the TV and sank into the couch. When I heard barking, I thought Trekah was harassing the mail carrier or scolding Earl for tending his pig. I leaned forward on the couch and strained to hear the dialogue on *Days of Our Lives*. The door popped open, but this time it swung hard on its hinges and slammed into the wall behind it. Piranha moved slowly into the room and stopped, startled to see me. We stared at each other as Trekah barked, safely tucked away in his pen. She sniffed at the air, and I looked slowly away from her and to the poker by the wood stove—my only weapon. Then I looked into the kitchen, where the plate sat on the stove with lacy remnants of eggs and mayonnaise stuck to it.

"Heeeyyy, Piranha. Puppy dog. Good girl." My voice gently shook, disembodied from the rest of my panicked self, which was trying to find a way past her to the door. "Are you hungry?"

She looked back at me and took a step forward.

"What a good girl . . ." I knew I had to launch myself off of the couch without startling her. "I bet you want a snack, don't you?" Trekah ran back and forth along the length of his enclosure outside. I twisted myself off the couch and walked slowly behind it. I hoped that if she jumped, the couch would give me a second's head start. "I've got a few crumbs for you, girlie." I made my way to the stove. Her wide jaw hovered at waist height, just below my belly. I turned to the side, so I could see her and keep the baby out of the way if she attacked me, and fished out a few pieces of egg. I tossed them behind her. "Go get it!" I encouraged her. She stared at me and licked her lips.

"How about a cookie?" I remembered the plastic bag of Rural King dog biscuits we kept for Trekah. I reached behind me to open the cabinet and hoped a rat wouldn't jump out. I broke a bone-shaped biscuit, held it in front of her, and dropped it on the floor. She sniffed at it and ate it.

"Good girl!" I said. "Here's another one . . ." I broke bits of cookie and led her out the door, shut it, and wedged my shoe under it.

"Your fucking cousin's dog just opened the fucking door and fucking came in!" I yelled into the phone. I leaned on the kitchen counter. "Holy shit."

"You mean Piranha?"

"Yes, I mean Piranha." I looked out the window, but she was gone. "Tell Terry to keep her in his yard," I said. "And fix the door!"

I thought about that reflex to turn myself away so the dog wouldn't hurt the baby. Maybe I wasn't as broken as I thought. Even if I couldn't live in my body and didn't yet know why, even if I didn't feel like a mother and didn't yet know who I was or who would love me if I figured it out, I still loved the person resting there under my racing heart.

"It's okay, Mama," he said. "I'll stop by Terry's shop on the way home." His voice already sounded like a memory.

At first we set mousetraps, and when we found the sprung traps empty, with pebbles of shit around them, we went to Rural King and got bigger traps.

"I don't like it," I said. Tracy was reading the directions on the back of the d-CON package. "I mean, I don't want rats, but you know what that poison does to them, right?" I had read the literature. I knew rat poison was a terrible way to go, essentially drowning in your own blood, but we were getting desperate. It seemed like an entire colony had set up residence since Terry moved Piranha and the other dogs onto the farm, and I had already gone to the hospital once with Braxton Hicks contractions. It was only a matter of time.

Tracy opened the tray of pellets and sniffed them. "I'm more worried about Trekah gettin' into it." He rubbed Trekah's ears. "Not for you, buddy."

I was worried about the dog too, but I was even more creeped out by the thought of dozens of rodents stumbling around and dying in the ceiling. The sound of the rats was intolerable, but the silence would feel like a sin. I decided to change the subject.

"The baby book says to take pictures of the baby every week next to the same thing every time so you can see how much he grows." I picked up the giant teddy bear we'd found at Goodwill. "This would be pretty cool."

Tracy peeled open another tray and walked into the bathroom.

"Yeah, that'll be fun," he called through the door.

I put the teddy bear in the crib. Its head flopped against the side. I looked up at the hole in the ceiling tile. "Maybe we can get some film for the camera."

"Just be sure to keep an eye on the dog. Don't let him get into the poison," he said.

"I will," I said. The dog looked at me from his spot in front of the wood stove. "C'mere, buddy." I went into the kitchen and reached into the cabinet for the five-pound plastic bag of dog cookies. I looked back into the dark cabinet and saw an empty plastic bag.

"You're fucking kidding me," I said. I pulled out the empty bag and held it up. The bottom had been chewed open, and all that was left was a dusting of crumbs.

A few hours after Tracy left for work, I had finished another egg sandwich and stood at the kitchen sink, washing my plate. I heard an angry squeak and felt something brush against my foot. I didn't see the rat as much as the movement of the rat, a shadow rushing past me. I screamed and jumped out of the way. Trekah jumped around me and snapped its neck. I pulled the dead rat from his mouth before he could chew it.

"Good boy," I said into his fur. I looked back at the rat. It all seemed impossible. I tied Trekah outside, put the rat on the burn pile, and went inside to cry.

Jo and Rich had decided to name their baby Knighton.

"I don't know. It's some name from Rich's family or something," Jo said. I had driven to Effingham to help her clean out the closet in Dad's apartment, where she and Rich lived. It was only a half hour away from our place, but it felt like more. Way more.

Her belly stretched and sagged over her stirrup pants, and mine was slimmer by only an inch or two. Neither of us had thought about stretch marks when we first got pregnant, and they looked foreign on our bodies. She passed me a black garbage bag. "Keep these. They're Grandma's afghans." I pulled at the knot and saw the folds of brown and orange yarn.

"Knighton's pretty cool for a name. I still don't know what we're gonna name ours," I said. The apartment was the same as it was when Dad moved out to live with our older sister, Terrie. Every piece of furniture remained. Even the big console TV with rabbit ears and the closet full of things like Grandma's afghans and the Barbie-head makeup kit that we'd thrown to the back of Dad's closet when we decided, after a sleepover in our friend Christy's basement, that the Barbie head was possessed by the devil.

"I'm not touching it," Jo said. She poked at the Barbie head with the broom handle.

"Leave it alone," I said. "You'll anger it."

Being in that apartment with her felt like we were still in the basement of the house on Fifth Street when we were in grade school. We used to hang sheets from the floor joists as partitions and pretend we were in apartments. Jo's friend Jennifer would pretend to be her roommate, and I was always the guy next door who came over from time to time to help move a couch or something. My sister has always known who I am.

As we unpacked our old blankets and toys out of the closet and made room for Knighton's car seat, first package of diapers, and maybe a playpen, I kept half expecting Mom to show up and tell us it was time to stop playing house and come upstairs to set the table.

We decided to leave the Barbie head where it was and take a break. Jo's kitchen table was covered with newspapers. Each garage sale in the classifieds was circled and coded according to what kind of baby stuff they were selling, cross-referenced with the distance she'd have to drive her '79 Impala with an eighth of a tank of gas.

"I'm doing all that in the morning," she said. I opened her refrigerator, looked in, and then closed it, a reflex more than a search for food. I planned to drive through KFC on my way home and get two Chicken Littles with extra mayonnaise. I had discovered them after work in the warehouse when I was a few months along, and every time I had eighty-three cents in my pocket and no witnesses, I bought two of them and ate them in the parking lot before I left for home. I quit that job when I got too pregnant to lift boxes on and off the conveyor belt, and I really missed that drive to town in the morning and back home after work, like I had a place to be.

"I plan to get up at the ass crack of dawn," she said. "And if you knew Dawn . . ."

"You'd be offended," I said, finishing one of the many dozens of jokes that had lost all context but were the mortar of the history between us—coded reference points that anchored one year to the next and established a topographical map of our lives so that we never lost our way. Not really.

Put me in any overly serious, tense situation where I'm not sure how to respond, and I guarantee that, in my mind, Jo's long, loud belch is my first answer because it was her answer at some point, and it's nearly always the best first answer.

Jo's due date was six weeks before mine, and she had been the first to tell Dad. She lured him to Hardee's and told him there, and I called Mom. She and Jo hadn't spoken since Jo moved in with Dad and me the year before, and even though we could get up and walk across the parking lot to the office next door where Mom worked, we didn't. Her car sat in a space near the back door every day for three years after I moved in with Dad, and each day until I moved out of Dad's apartment,

I looked for her license plate. Each day I saw it and walked past it without going in, and I'm sure Dad did too. I imagined her walking out to her car every day and looking at the apartment building, doing the same thing.

"Did I tell you about Piranha opening the front door and coming in?" I asked.

"Who's Piranha?"

"You know, the freaking rottweiler from next door." I knew the story would land, and I knew that Jo would find the dog guilty of trespassing and wouldn't mention how at that very moment, the front door of the garage-house was probably open again.

It felt good to be in Jo's kitchen. From Dad's old seat at the table, I could see into the bathroom, where Jo's bath towel was draped over the side of the tub to dry. It was hard to find any evidence of Rich in the apartment. When Jo first got pregnant, she drove around at night looking for him, and usually found him, but since she'd entered her third trimester, the trips to the Orchard Inn and Ichabod's Bar & Grill were more and more humiliating, so she stopped. His voice was on their answering machine, but I couldn't remember the last time I'd actually been in the same room with him.

Jo poured glasses of ice tea, and we sat at the table looking at the classifieds. Salt and pepper shakers and a bottle of 150 Flintstone Vitamins without any Betty Rubbles in it held down the corners of the newspapers. She let out a long, loud belch.

Since the sink incident, I was afraid Trekah would poison himself on a rat, so he spent his days outside in the shade of the old house, and I spent mine in the glow of the TV, which is where I was again when I heard scratching on the door. It popped open and slammed into the wall. Piranha lumbered in and stood in front of me. Mud from her paws streaked down the door and was caked on her elbows. Her teats swung below her belly, and a couple of flies followed her in.

I led her out with a trail of cookies, closed the door, and turned back into the dark room.

Three days in a row.

I was prepared the fourth day. When the door swung open, I had the cookies in my hand.

"Back again?" I asked. She sat down and looked at me. "I can't say I blame you," I said. I tossed a cookie to her. She ate it. I tossed another one closer to me. She crept forward in two resigned, weary steps and lifted her eyes to meet mine.

"The thing is, you need a bath." She sat down in front of me and panted. "And a Tic Tac."

I heaved myself off the couch and got one of the bottles of baby shampoo I had been hoarding from the bathroom. Piranha followed me out the door and lay down between the driveway and Trekah's enclosure while I dragged out the hose.

"We're not gonna have any trouble here, are we?" She flinched when the water hit her paws, but stayed there and let me lather her up. I leaned on the stack of firewood and caught my breath as I rinsed her. Inside, the phone rang. I shut off the hose and answered.

"What'cha doooin'?" Jo asked. I watched Piranha shake herself dry and then roll in the grass.

"You'll never guess."

Each day, Piranha came to my door, pushed it open, and watched *Days of Our Lives* with me, leaving just before Tracy came home. I would watch her walk wearily back to her pen and lie down next to it waiting to be locked in. Then I would walk back into the garage-house, close the door behind me, and lie down to wait until I heard the rumble of the Fiero on the gravel.

The sound of the rats started to quiet, and the baby settled lethargically in the lowest portion of my pelvis in the last weeks of that summer, but everything shifted when Jo had her baby.

The veins on her head bulged with strain, and Jo was not someone who cried, but she had been sobbing. It felt like a thread connected Jo to me, and I could feel her pain and panic in the delivery room, where she lay on a table. I pushed my way past the nurses and caught Jo's eye.

"Let her in," she said. "He can go." She glared at Rich, who sat in a chair at the foot of her bed, yawning. After a brief pause, he got up and stretched as he walked out to the waiting room.

"He keeps saying he's too tired. TOO TIRED." A contraction contorted her face. "Fucker." Rich hadn't come home the night before and had been at work when Jo's water broke. She stuffed a diaper in her pants and drove the Impala to pick him up. "I leaked all over the car," she said. "I don't even care. He can sit in it." She finally focused on me. "What is that outfit?" she asked. I looked down at the pink maternity overalls.

"Shut up," I said.

Jo was in labor for eight and a half hours before her doctor decided to deliver the baby by C-section. When it was time for her to take the baby home a couple of days later, I drove her Impala with a towel on the seat to get her. On the way home from the hospital, we stopped at Aldi for groceries. I lumbered along next to her as she leaned on the cart and staggered behind it. Knighton slept in his carrier as we pushed boxes of macaroni and cheese, lunch meat, and bread into the cart. We both knew Rich wouldn't be there when we got back, and Jo would be taking Knighton home to an empty apartment.

In my mind I was still the guy next door in the pretend apartments. I was the person who drew murals on my high school crush's bedroom wall. I played Cliff Burton bass solos better than any of the other guys. But my body was too pregnant to be that person anymore. I looked down at my own swollen belly, and for the first time it looked like mine. It looked like me. For the very first time in almost nine months, I was in my body. I wasn't watching someone else be a pregnant woman; I was actually pregnant, and soon—very soon—I was going to be a mom. And I was terrified.

As we made our way down the aisles, an old school friend saw us.

"Oh my gosh, a baby!" Vicki smiled down at Knighton. She looked back up at Jo, nearly doubled over, holding the cart and trying not to rupture her stitches, and then at me, wearing a grossly feminine maternity costume that barely fit my very pregnant body. Her smile faded. "Congratulations." It came out as a question. We walked to the checkout.

"Tentenpenguin," Jo said. It was Vicki's old address when we were in school. We sometimes substituted it for her name and couldn't really remember why.

You know when you have to laugh, but it hurts to do it? Yeah, that.

It's hard to say when the contractions started. They were gradual and almost seemed like my imagination. The pain presented itself, disappeared throughout the day, and hinted at what was to come, but you never know what's coming next or who you will be when it does. All you know is what's in front of you. What I knew was the image of Piranha lying in her cage next to her water bowl. The family of rats in the ceiling. The poison that was slowly silencing them. Trekah pacing the yard, the floor, the roads. The Fiero crunching the gravel. A love that would eclipse all of it. I didn't have a name for it. But I soon would.

"Sorry, girl." Piranha looked at me curiously from her place on the couch. "I gotta go."

NUAR ALSADIR

On Boredom

FROM *Granta*

YEARS AGO, when my two daughters and I would come upon an obstacle such as a lamppost while walking down the street, we would play a game that involved calling out opposites as we briefly let go of one another's hands: "Hot and cold!" "Day and night!" One time my older daughter cried, "Love and hate!" Love and hate aren't opposites, I explained, because they are both passionate. The opposite of love would be indifference. She understood immediately. When we encountered the next obstacle, she cried, "Love and indifference!"

Along the same lines, the opposite of boredom is not excitement, but calm. Boredom is a restless state of mind, generally marked by dissatisfaction. Just think of how often you feel uninterested in something without being bored. The monotonous car ride from Chicago through Midwest cornfields to the New England college I attended was never boring to me, but a fertile ground for daydreams. When your imagination is free to roam, you can lose yourself in reverie. But when you're bored, you're unable to fantasize. You can't even think.

"I never quite hear what people say who bore me," observes the writer Édouard Levé. What he gets at here is the psychological goal of boredom—tuning things out, although the person boredom tunes out most successfully is oneself. Boredom is a symptom of an unconscious process—an internal muting, which leaves the conscious mind with both a lack and an itch to re-find what is missing.

From a psychoanalytical perspective, boredom is less a response to something in the external world than a defense against something in the internal world, an impulse or desire that is taboo—often sexual or aggressive in nature—which evokes guilt, anxiety, or fear of punishment. Boredom evades those negative emotions by blocking off thought that might lead to the prohibited impulses or desires that trigger them. "The inhibition of fantasy," writes psychoanalyst Martin Wangh, "often occurs because of an unconscious fear that fantasy might lead to action of libidinal or aggressive nature—an impulse to masturbate or strike out—which in turn would bring about danger or pain."

As children, we learn to use words, then to watch what we say. We move on to control what we think and feel. Thoughts and feelings travel together. One way to get rid of an overwhelming feeling (like anxiety, or guilt) is to repress the thought it is attached to (the desire or impulse that makes us anxious or guilty). That way there is no longer anything to feel bad about. But even after the desire or impulse has disappeared, and the bad feeling with it, the drive toward gratification remains. A bored person is therefore left with a hankering feeling that they want or are bothered by something, but, because their aim has been suppressed, they don't know what it is.

I remember a feeling of immense dread one dark Sunday afternoon in childhood. I turned for help to my mother, who was reading on the couch.

"I feel like there's something wrong," I told her, "but I don't know what it is."

"You should read," she said, lowering her book but not closing it. "Get out of your head."

To my mother, my uneasiness was a symptom of boredom, something that could be dealt with by an activity. But what she ended up teaching me was to reinforce the sort of repression that boredom usually indicates. To respond to my disquiet with distraction.

Childhood is the peak time for boredom because there are so many feelings a child is told not to have. "Life, friends, is boring," John Berryman writes in his famous poem on the topic,

"Dream Song 14," but, "We must not say so." The confession, the poem's speaker recollects his mother telling him, means you lack "Inner Resources." Parents often respond to their children's laments along the same lines: "You're not bored—you're boring." The parent that can't help their child develop Inner Resources will likely defend against the frustration and powerlessness called up in them with boredom of their own (*you're boring*). Perhaps part of what is so irritating to parents about their children's boredom is the amorphous need it expresses—they want help finding something, but they don't know what it is.

Boredom expresses the state of tension between a fear, desire, or impulse that has been repressed and the leftover yearning that remains free-floating in consciousness, looking to attach to something. It is always easier to project that search into the external world than to look internally. But the external search can only fail. "The person who is bored," the psychoanalyst Otto Fenichel writes, "can be therefore compared to one who has forgotten a name and inquiries about it from others."

We often think of forgetting as a bad thing, but for Søren Kierkegaard, "A person's resiliency can actually be measured by his power to forget." The same might be said about a person's ability to repress. Repression is a defense mechanism that disappears thoughts that would be too overwhelming if they were allowed into consciousness. It frees us up to function, to do what is expected, to give others what they want from us. We align with the social order, even if that means having to emotionally shut down.

"The defensive nature of boredom," writes psychoanalyst Charles Brenner, is observed when "a bored patient is *unconsciously* attempting to convince himself that he does not want to gratify the instinctual wishes that frighten him, that, on the contrary, he has no wish to do anything." But this defense, like others, only works for so long. "When we speak of writing something in the book of oblivion," Kierkegaard continues, "we are indeed suggesting that it is forgotten and yet at the same time is preserved." The psychological nature of boredom needs to be understood and worked through in order for it to be relieved.

Boredom that isn't resolved internally frequently causes the bored person to compulsively search outside of themselves for relief. This often leads to overactivity that psychoanalysts term "manic defenses"—scrolling, swiping, substance abuse, constant socializing, actions that clutter out negative emotions that might otherwise have had the space to consciously register.

It's important to note that the psychoanalysts I've quoted here were all writing before the invention of the iPhone, which has become the ultimate tool for managing boredom. I can't tell you how many sessions I've spent listening to someone describe the misery they felt after scrolling on social media for hours—a misery, it always turns out, that was pursued because it was preferrable to some other more miserable thought that was then displaced. An upsetting thought that comes from the external world that is familiar and easy to interpret can defend against a more unmanageable thought by bumping it out of consciousness. But replacing one agitated state with another doesn't bring anyone closer to relief.

At the core of boredom is an urge that is impossible to satisfy because the bored person is always looking in the wrong place. Substitutes in the outside world—either too far removed from the actual desire or too close and thus provoking anxiety—will not only feel not quite right but are likely to call up feelings of dissatisfaction, frustration, even rage. Annoyance, anger, and bad odor are etymological roots of *ennui*, the French loanword. Boredom is a complicated stink of an emotion, one that is far more layered than we presume.

Every Wednesday afternoon, while training to become a psychoanalyst, I would meet with my supervisor in her office tucked into a corner of a prewar apartment-building lobby on Manhattan's Upper West Side. After a bit of conversation that served as a greeting, I'd take out my notebook to discuss the sessions I had conducted that week. Whenever I began to relate the material of one specific patient, I would start yawning. This didn't happen once or twice, but every few seconds. I wasn't sleepy or uninterested. If we talked about something else—even why I was yawning—it would stop.

One day, the patient who induced those yawns walked into my office, sat on the couch, and said, "There's something I've been meaning to tell you." My heart raced. I anticipated a hostile outburst. Instead, the patient relayed neutral information: she had plans to travel so would miss our next session. My physical response allowed me to understand what was happening. For months I had been picking up on strong negative feelings the patient wasn't expressing through words, but were nonetheless present. And some part of me knew it.

My response was an example of "countertransference," an emotional reaction an analyst experiences when associations from the analyst's own past are transferred onto material presented by a patient, in the same way that a patient's associations and expectations from the past can be transferred onto the analyst in "transference." Sometimes countertransference is misplaced—an analyst (like a parent) is, after all, a human being. But at other times, it can serve as a useful tool for picking up on unconscious communication, which involves the body and the intellect. I knew what it felt like to have someone blow up at me. When, at the animal level, I received similar cues from my patient, I anticipated danger.

The patient's rage was being communicated unconsciously, but at that point in my career I didn't know how to work with unconscious communication. That moment of sudden anxiety allowed me to recognize that yawning in supervision had been my unconscious way of bringing the rage—as well as the anxiety it provoked—into our discussion. As soon as we gained insight into what was happening and addressed the feelings beneath the surface—my own and my patient's—the yawning stopped.

Yawning is one of many psychological devices we use to modulate destabilizing feelings, and, like boredom, it's more complex than it seems. A friend of mine noticed her husband yawns before telling a lie. World Cup champion speed skater Apolo Ohno famously yawned before a race. Paratroopers often yawn before jumping; dogs sometimes yawn to avert a fight. Yawning exists on one end of a spectrum of defenses the mind uses against overwhelming emotions. Boredom stands somewhere in the middle, while fainting is at the extreme. At the physiological level, fainting can occur in response to an emotional trigger, such as anxiety, due to vasovagal syncope. Your heart rate slows and your blood vessels widen, making it difficult for enough blood to be delivered to the brain. Excess yawning is a less severe case and can arise from stimulation of the vagus nerve. Whereas yawning functions as an emotional balm, fainting offers an escape hatch to oblivion.

When I was fifteen, I had a job busing tables at a neighborhood restaurant whose owner was prone to hostile outbursts. The dominant emotion among the staff was fear. One evening after I'd been working there for a few weeks, the owner called me into his office, which was off the kitchen beside the walk-in fridge, and exploded at me. I don't remember what I'd done or the content of what he said, only that I was so overwhelmed that as soon as I exited his office and stepped back into the kitchen I fainted, knocking over and falling into a crate of strawberries.

The jam I created by fainting was not the most dramatic of the summer. A few weeks later, someone defecated in their underwear and flushed it down the men's room toilet, causing a clog and overflow. I can't hear the word *shitstorm* without recalling that incident. If I were to make a film about my experience working at that restaurant, the overflowing toilet would symbolize all of the suppressed rage the employees felt in response to the owner's treatment of them erupting into the concrete world.

In the animal kingdom, anal secretions are used for aggressive and defensive purposes, as with skunks. Even in language, we describe an emotional attack as "shitting on" someone. Boredom is also evacuative, but the bored person evacuates inward. They push their impulses into repression—implode rather than explode.

After something has been repressed, Freud tells us, it doesn't just stay in the unconscious, "as when some living thing has been killed and from that time onward is dead"; rather, "the repressed exercises a continuous pressure in the direction of the conscious, so that this pressure must be balanced by an unceasing counter-pressure." Think of holding a beach ball underwater: you can only keep it down for so long before it shoots out in a direction you can't anticipate.

Boredom can be a signal that powerful impulses beneath the surface might explode in an unexpected direction if given an opening. To the extreme, unrelieved boredom can lead to destructive behavior toward the self and others. There are numerous instances of people behaving in harmful ways—engaging in risky behavior, setting fires, committing murder—citing ennui as the cause. "There is perhaps no more reliable indicator of a society's ripeness for a mass movement than the prevalence of unrelieved boredom," cautions philosopher Eric Hoffer.

Boredom itself isn't dangerous, of course, but what lies beneath it may be. The bored have strong desires and impulses that need to be unpacked. You have to get at the root impulse or desire behind boredom—make the unconscious conscious—for genuine relief. Once what's beneath boredom is examined, you can then discover what's beneath that, which is usually hope. After all, you only feel disappointed when you care.

In a recent session, I found myself feeling sleepy. By then a much more seasoned psychoanalyst, I was able to recognize that my drowsiness was not an expression of my interest but a response to an unconscious communication from the patient. I was closing my eyes to some thought or feeling he didn't want me to see. I explained to him what I suspected was happening. "Instead of colluding with the pull I'm feeling to avoid whatever it is you don't want to talk about," I said, "I'm going to ask you to check in with yourself and see if you can identify what feels too huge to allow into consciousness."

He said, "I feel like I'm not living the life I want to live."

A bored person similarly wants more out of the moment, and life, but often in ways that run counter to what is expected of them. Just as with envy, which is easier to work with if you focus on the desire behind it rather than its impulse to destroy—"Tell me what you need to spoil," the psychoanalyst Adam Phillips writes, "and I will tell you what you want"—boredom marks the space where hope is buried. When you are bored, you can't dream, and without dreams, it's hard to care about the future. Taking interest in our boredom, we can uncover what we desire and what we want to change.

GREG JACKSON

Within the Pretense of No Pretense
FROM *The Point*

Wonder

Technology was the wonder of our age. It seemed to promise us power, and we took this power for our own. What kind of power was it? We didn't ask. There was too much to do *on* technology to consider what it permitted in the rest of life. The rest of life in fact fell away, seemed less and less important as a place where technology couldn't help us.

Technology

Technology's magnetism extended invisibly. It did not control us like an overlord cracking a whip, but as the slope of a mountain controls the water falling down it: by bending our actions toward what it made easy at the expense of what remained hard. What technology did not make easy seemed in turn harder and harder.

Power

Power, as it had long been understood, pertained to what you could do to alter reality. First you imagined how reality could be different, then you endeavored to make it so.

The New Power

The new power did not arise from imagining what could be done. What could be done arose from the choice laid out before you. You could choose a product, a politician, or a television program. You could choose a party, a religion or your personal beliefs. There was no need to justify your choice. On the contrary, to be asked to justify your choice implied a sphere of judgment that preceded and limited the choice. Within the logic of the choice this amounted to heresy.

Choices

So many choices. Choices of goods, songs, videos, movies. Choices of podcasts and news sites. Figures to follow, to listen to. "We want to hear what you think." "Tell us what you think." So many opportunities to voice displeasure and approval. So many decisions about where to lavish money and attention.

The sea of choices, the apparent bounty of getting so much, obscured an awkward question: What if you didn't want to *get* but to *give*? What if you wanted to give something other than money or attention, something particular to you? *I want to invent the goods people buy. I'd like to write the songs they love. I want to be listened to.* Impossible requests. You have mistaken the nature of the choice. What you are asking for are not *choices* but *powers*, powers that reflect the long cultivation of skill. To do what you are asking the choice does not suffice. You must make the *right* choice, *hundreds* of right choices in a row. For that you need guidance, judgment. You need a world that tells you some choices are right and wrong, some ideas better and worse.

The Nature of the Choice

The choice resembled a genie granting wishes. But *of a sort.* What sort? The sort a consumer or an audience member would make. Requests to trade places with the genie—to move from consumer to creator, watcher to watched, getter to giver—went unanswered. *I want to have influence in affairs of importance.* Silence. *I want to discharge a special duty that makes me valuable to other people.* Crickets. *I want to matter.* Here at last the genie's lips might curl up in an imperceptible smirk.

Power

Power was freedom *from* the choice, from the terms of the choice as they had been imposed on us. Almost no one had this power, and this made us resentful and weak.

The Opposite of Choice

The opposite of choice was not no-choice. The opposite was responsibility. The purveyors of the choice cast this as obligation. By offering us choice instead of obligation they implied that they had relieved us of a burden. But responsibility was much more than a burden: it was a special duty we could discharge that made us valuable to other people. It was thus the *basis* of our power. Where could we locate power without responsibility? Only in the limited context of being presented with and making a choice. The annihilation of responsibility bound the individual ever more desperately and despairingly to the no-power of making an endless sequence of meaningless choices.

Personal Belief

In the absence of responsibility, personal belief became the locus of identity. In what one liked or approved lived the tiny no-power of raising and diminishing figures and ideas on the tide of attention and votes. So much identity rested in these beliefs that it became terrifying to admit they might be wrong. It was much easier to look for voices that affirmed them than to accept that one's identity might be organized around a mistake.

*

Critics

Critics were people who told you your choice was not a good one, or could be a better one. This made it hard to like the critic since his job was based on *knowing better*. Sometimes the critic didn't know better and was simply concerned with protecting his status as a person who knew better. But at his best the critic protected your power by protecting the division between good and bad, better and worse. Between a real choice and a false choice. Every time the critic said a work of art was bad, this seemed mean. But it wasn't just mean, because in saying a given work was bad he was also saying that within art existed the possibility of good. Taking a stand against inferior work was staking a stand *for* the category as a whole. The critic affirmed that with effort and imagination you could secure a true power: the power to make an authentic choice.

Marvel Movies

The critic made what seemed to him an obvious point. This was that superhero movies were not art. Well, this infuriated people. How mean the critic is! How pretentious and elitist he is to think he *knows better*. But the critic was merely pointing out what people have forever understood: that the strength of our desire, the intensity of our pleasure, is not what determines nourishment or meaning or importance. The measure of nourishment or meaning or importance is what comes *after* a desire has been satisfied. The desire for a drug can be very strong: Does the strength of the desire make it an authentic love? Does it make it nourishing? The people angry at the critic who says an entertainment is not art are not angry at his elitism. They are angry at being reminded that the choice does not offer happiness or power but a brief distraction from our neglect of everything that holds the key to our happiness and power—everything that is hard, long, boring, and not strictly pleasurable. The critic, by reminding us of the work we haven't done, makes us feel small, guilty, and resentful. He reminds us of our distance from power.

Cons

What is the critic's angle, his con? The critic doesn't have one, and this makes him inconvenient. He upholds a criterion of honesty and defends it against self-interest. The critic with a con is called a pundit. Do not confuse a critic for a pundit. Pundits are critics for hire and sell you their thinking to relieve your confusion. They trade you affirmation and reassurance for your attention.

What Is a Critic Really?

A critic is any figure willing to be critical when it is not popular. A critic does not think nice lies are better than hard truths, or that niceness is goodness, or flattery love.

What Does the Critic Do?

A critic needn't write criticism. A critic is any steward of public discourse who sees this duty as more important than popularity or career. The work of a critic is not fact-checking, although there is that, but tending the ropes and anchors that affix representation to reality. It is a gestalt vocation, prone to endless correction and bickering, which looks to see not just that the *facts* are right, but that the *picture* is true. That the significance, the proportionality, is correct.

It matters less that any individual critic gets this right or wrong—there are failed critics, just as there are failed poets and failed professional bowlers—than that a sphere of criticism models certain commitments: to nuanced distinctions and honest reflection; to raising unarticulated feelings and unquestioned desires to the light; to the possibility of upholding other values than self-interest. The critic demonstrates that a person, even a public figure, need not be alienated from her authentic private sensibility. In so doing she keeps this possibility alive for everyone else.

*

Pundits

The pundit is like the critic in a certain respect: he plays one on TV.

Pundits

The pundit is like the critic in this specific respect: he is willing to praise the good when it is liked and condemn the bad when it is disliked. This is as far as it goes. Pundits share the critic's expertise, but the pundit's allegiance is different. The pundit's allegiance is not to honesty but to his career.

Pundits

A pundit derives his power from his audience. The most important thing to a pundit is his platform; take away his platform and he is a preacher without a flock. The audience gradually realized that the no-power of their choice, while it did not permit them to alter reality, did permit them a debased power within the world of representations: they could "cancel" the pundit, as audiences had long canceled TV shows. They could deplatform him. Within the powerless interplay of pundit and audience a bargain was struck: the pundit would get the no-power of telling the audience what it wanted to hear and the audience would get the no-power of deciding whether the pundit kept his job.

Audiences

We can say the following about an audience: it has a powerful but limited range of response (applause, booing). These are *group* responses. They are not qualitatively rich but they are often loud enough to drown out all else. Unlike the solitary reader or viewer, the audience member understands herself as part of a public body, responding publicly. In this the audience claims a power the individual never had. But only if it acts as an audience, which is to say en masse.

Celebrities

Of television George W. S. Trow wrote, "The power behind it resembles the power of no-action, the powerful passive." For a time, movie producers and studio executives had great power. They could decide whether a celebrity could enter or remain in the celebrated space. Their power over an auto mechanic, a park ranger, or a sculptor was not so great. By democratizing the celebrated space, the internet made everybody into a target for elevation or cancelation. This was the passive power of no-action. Your online existence and identity could be sabotaged, destroyed. You could be relieved of virtual citizenship in good standing. If you didn't care to exist online you were safe. The powerful passive would move on. It was a mark of how virtual our lives had become that most people could not risk crossing the powerful passive. Their careers, their lives, depended on it. The powerful passive ruled over life and death.

Pundits

Pundits were one name we gave to celebrities when they appeared in areas of culture that we did not immediately recognize as open to celebrity. One type of pundit was a politician—a new politician who didn't enter politics to make laws but to appear on TV. Increasingly, this was what a politician was.

*

Pretense

The emergence of pretense was a consequence of the shifting nature of pundits and audiences. The pretense was that you were still getting criticism (honesty, knowledge, expertise) when you were instead getting flattery—flattery whose core interest was the pundit's career.

2012

Something changed. Athletes, once viciously competitive and prone to talking trash, became nice. They were complimentary of their opponents, civil toward the media, blithely positive about their own and others' successes. Edginess drained from culture like color from coral. A safe, inoffensive, public "niceness" took over. This was niceness—not goodness or even kindness—a posture, an image, a pretense. It understood that the arena in which one had to triumph was no longer governed by elite opinion or ability but by an audience.

Niceness

Niceness took hold not just in sports but in many walks of life. Critics who had once guarded the borders of culture fiercely became lovers not haters. Maybe they had been too harsh all along, too mean. Maybe popular culture was serious and important. Maybe entertainment was art. Maybe asking something to be elite was elitism. Maybe caring about quality was just something grumpy old people did. A masquerade of seriousness: that is, pretentious—full of pretense.

In fact, the opposite was true: The pretense was the diminished standards, the not caring. The pretense was the niceness. The critic tricked himself into believing being "nice" was being nice to someone else, not just to himself. The critic tricked himself into believing the object of his niceness was the work in question, not his career. He flattered himself that *acting nice* was *being good*. The critic started to become a pundit.

The Unlikable Woman in Fiction

That the narrator of Claire Messud's 2013 novel *The Woman Upstairs* was unlikable bothered people terribly. Wasn't there something wrong with unlikable characters, with expecting us to endure their company? Asked whether she would enjoy spending time with her protagonist, Messud responded, "For heaven's sake, what kind of question is that? Would you want to be friends with Humbert Humbert? Would you want to be friends with Mickey Sabbath?"

The question was more telling than the answer, for there had always been unlikable characters in fiction. What there hadn't been was a significant occasion—an incentive and a platform—to state publicly that *you* found a particular character unlikable. This was a statement not about a book but about how you, as a member of a responding public, wanted to be seen. *You* were likable because on the inside you were not like this character who revealed the muddy puddle of the human soul.

A New Age

So dawned a new age of people performatively congratulating one another on Twitter, of personalities on NPR speaking as though they were reading a children's book to toddlers at the local library, of commentators everywhere venerating the talent and courage of A-list celebrities with questionable talent and courage but vast fan bases you didn't want to cross. In the new age people worshipped success simply in itself, because liking what was liked ensured you were on the side of the powers that determined likability.

Likability

Our new interest in pronouncing on what was and wasn't likable was merely a literalization of the LIKE button on Facebook. *Hit the like button. Smash the like button.* No one could mistake this for a qualitatively rich response. Its binary simplicity—the very thing that made it useful to advertisers as a metric of engagement—mirrored the twofold response of audiences (applause, booing), which likewise drew power from the ease of aggregation its lack of nuance permitted. Like a magnet whose potency and polarity arise from the alignment of its atoms, the audience, by judging simply and en masse, achieved the power to elevate and abase. *Help me have a richer experience of this movie.* No. *Tell me how this work of art engages its tradition and unfolds new ambiguities of human nature.* Please. *Justify, at least, your like or dislike as more than a sense of what you should or shouldn't like in public.* But don't you understand? The reason I am here is to show that I agree, that I am likable because I am willing to like what other people here have agreed to like.

The Professional Smile

Likability was another face of niceness, a smiling face whose owner understood that he was being judged superficially, not as a person who had done something in the world of things. David Foster Wallace called this "the professional smile," the smile "that signifies nothing more than a calculated attempt to advance the smiler's own interests by pretending to like the smilee." He associated it with despair. Its warmth had nothing to do with its recipient, was not warmth.

*

Niceness

Everyone likes niceness. What a nice person! I met her, and I thought because she's so cool and rich and successful and popular that she wouldn't be nice. But she was so nice!

But then: I liked her when she was being nice because I thought it meant she liked me, but I see she's nice to everyone.

But then: I thought we were friends, but because she has to be nice to everyone she doesn't have time for me.

But then: I thought because I appreciated her she might regard me as a peer, but she needs everyone to like her and doesn't distinguish between a peer and an audience member.

But then: If she's nice to everyone, no matter how loathsome, and she's nice to me, am *I* loathsome—is that how she sees me? How would I know?

Niceness

A gradual realization: niceness to everyone does not permit niceness to anyone.

A gradual realization: niceness isn't directed at the object of niceness but at the purveyor of niceness, in particular her career.

A gradual realization: to like everything is to like nothing.

A suspicion: niceness is, in fact, a form of hatred.

Hatred

Trow explained that television has two abilities:

> to do a very complex kind of work, involving electrons, and then to cover the coldness of that with a hateful familiarity. Why hateful? Because it hasn't anything to do with a human being as a human being is strong. It has to do with a human being as a human being is weak and willing to be fooled: the human being's eagerness to perceive as warm something that is cold, for instance; his eagerness to be a part of what one cannot be a part of, to love what cannot be loved.

What attempts to convince you it loves you by pandering to you does you harm. It teaches you that you are so weak that what does not pander to you—does not obscure difficulty, disagreement, and boredom—is to be reviled and punished. To keep you close it teaches you that anything beyond its pandering—anything that does not take your pleasure and comfort, second by second, as its principal consideration—is to be vilified. It insinuates that the very weakness it has cultivated in you is a reflection of the hatefulness of the world beyond.

Coldness

The night had grown so icy, when we looked up from trading sources of authentic warmth for cold things posing as warm, that we could only relieve the chill with lifeless sparks of distant laughter, empty smiles. These were cold things posing as warm—cold because they did not care about us as anything but their audience, their platform, their power—but we asked them to go on amusing and distracting us because we knew the images couldn't love us and that this was the closest we could now come to love.

A Thin Crust

Niceness emerged from the relentlessly public character of modern life—a response to the fear that new communication technologies had made it possible for anyone to tear your reputation to shreds. Niceness was the thin crust atop this hatred. It was toxic in the first place because it was inauthentic and transactional and dominated our relationships to the point that we didn't know whether anyone actually liked us or we actually liked anyone. But it was more profoundly toxic because it rested on a roiling sea of cruelty and resentment that threatened at any moment to swallow the person who dropped her frantic congeniality and showed herself, however briefly, to be *not nice*.

*

Pretense

The pretense was that the niceness was about you. The truth: the niceness was about the nice person's career. The pretense: the niceness was about liking you. The truth: the niceness was a form of hating you. The pretense: there was no pretense.

Within the Pretense of No-Pretense

Our president was a showman, a bully, a carnival barker, a corrupt soul. At heart he was a con man and a cheat. About facts he was relentlessly dishonest. About the pretense, however, he was honest. The legions of pundits who called out and tracked his lies were honest—about facts. About the pretense that pervaded their lives they were not honest. They didn't know how to be. The terms of their lives meant believing there was no pretense. Meant the pretense of no-pretense.

Trump

The best part of Trump was he was willing to show that he liked you by hating the people who weren't you.

Trump

The best part of Trump was he was willing to hate openly in a culture composed of hate—the hatred of niceness—but committed to the pretense that this hate was no-hate, was niceness.

Trump

The worst part of Trump was that the only way out of the hatred of niceness he proposed was hatred of another sort.

Trump

The worst part of Trump was he encouraged people to locate their identity and power in their status as members of an audience. He encouraged them to indulge the dark power of the audience, which was to cancel, pillory, and destroy. This—as the most potent expression of powerlessness, of no-power—was so intoxicating that even Trump's enemies embraced the dark no-power of the cancelation, the deplatforming, the termination.

You're fired!

*

The Power of the Powerless

To the powerless raised on a catechism of their own privilege—to those given choices but not responsibilities—the hunt for this elusive birthright became a bitter quest. They seized on politics for offering a seemingly principled moral language by which to discredit and destroy. That the complaints of the powerless came couched in the language of politics blinded people to the psychological motivations behind the impulse to discredit and destroy, which had nothing to do with politics. They had to do with powerlessness—the apprehension of impotence among audience members as anything *but* audience members—and with resentment at one's relative status and influence compared with the figures empowered by one's attention and applause.

The Impotence of Artists

Artists and writers experienced their impotence with particular acuteness since they had grown up in a postmodern era that attributed singular power to language and discourse. The intensity of political hectoring in the arts increased to the extent that artists felt helpless to change the world. This mistook the nature of language and discourse but even more fundamentally the nature of power, which, although we tend to conceptualize it as coercive, rarely is. Even the state and its police have trouble compelling people against their will without resorting to torture and large authoritarian projects of spying and punishment. The far more common forms of power are not coercive but structural and incentivizing. In the arts they are persuasive and seductive. The power of words—what led Shelley to call poets "the unacknowledged legislators of the world"—derives from their resonance with truths already potentialized within us. The limit of persuasive and seductive power is that it must work in concert with people's moral intuitions and natural wishes; it can guide people to their own enlightened interests—toward themselves—but it cannot remake or reform people according to another's whims. That is brainwashing, hypnosis. The artist or writer who discovers the limits of her work to change the minds of other people in direct, compulsory ways may become frustrated, angry, even vengeful, at a time when moral reformation is seen to be the purpose of all culture.

Generations

To speak of a generation is to speak of the values a group of people were steeped in, their response to these values and the culture they created as products of and rebels against these values. It is to describe the tidal shifts in values across the cycles of birth, aging, and death.

Generations

A generation steeped in the values of sacrifice and modesty found itself able (despite other failings) to venerate difficult but constructive ends. A subsequent generation—raised on TV and the pandering of marketers, living in a culture that had, thanks to Freud and the rise of psychotherapy, learned to understand socialization as a violence inflicted on the individual—came to locate value not in external or transcendent aims but in the wounded self. It took the child's side. Anything that suggested a person should abandon being a child to become an adult elicited resentment. Partly it was true that socialization involved pain and difficulty, but it was never clear how much of this was anything other than the pain and difficulty of growing up. The TV personality, the salesman, and the therapist took the child's side as well. They asked how you *felt*, not what, in the world of things, you had done.

Merit

Merely having responsibilities does not imply discharging them responsibly. It was therefore reasonable, when the meritorious betrayed our trust, to question the regime that had elevated them to positions of power. Perhaps the very notion of merit was debased. But we were wrong to blame merit. The rot set in because the striving of elites had no ultimate end beyond their personal success, their career. Instead of attacking the rot we responded with the resentment of the Marvel movie fan and attacked the elites' excellence—the best part of them—since this was the part that made us feel small, inferior, and weak. In the voice of the salesman we said *of course* it was correct for the elite to covet money, power, and fame. Who wouldn't? We disparaged the healthy value and upheld the sickly one—got virtue and vice backward. At least anyone in celebrity's lottery could *possibly* become rich and famous. The message we couldn't abide was that to succeed you had to work long and hard developing excellence. The message we could abide even less was that success shouldn't come with prerogatives (choices) nearly so much as responsibilities.

Merit

In rewarding the pundit over the critic, the TV expert over the adept, the celebrated person over the accomplished person, we shifted focus from attainment in a world of things to success in a world of representation. Being good at something was less important than appearing good at it was less important than being celebrated (for whatever reason) in public. Success, not excellence, was the mark of merit. Celebrity—being famous for being famous—was the apotheosis of our disbelief in transcendent and ultimate ends.

Reality

To generations steeped in television, nurtured on a public world populated by actors playing not-actors, to discover that what you took to be a TV set—the United States Capitol—was also a real place where people went about real lives that concerned more or less what we had been told they concerned was shocking. It was shocking because—despite the seductive falsehood at the heart of reality TV—it did not seem possible that the world of representation and the world of reality could intersect. When the January 6 rioters stormed the Capitol, part of the allure and lurid fascination was to see the world of reality try to penetrate the world of representation. Instead of representation, they found representatives. Instead of breaching the mystery of television, they merely penetrated the bland thingness of the physical reality upon which television is staged. Watching TV is a form of dreaming, and you cannot be on TV (awake, on a physical set) and watching TV (dreaming) at the same time. You can force your way *onto* TV but not *into* TV, because the world of representation is not a physical place. It is a dreamer's dream. To discover this is to discover that heaven does not exist. It is to lose one's religion.

Religion

Twenty-four-hour cable news was the first medium to propose that you could remain indefinitely in the world of representation, you never had to puncture the dream. It realized that the story was not limited by events as they transpired. Events were always transpiring or threatening to transpire or ready to give up more meanings and portents. The trick was to stitch together an unbroken cadence of feeling that centered on the idea that small things were being resolved within a sphere where nothing would ever resolve. The sense that you were on the verge of a resolution that would never come inflamed an insatiable desire, like addiction, but also inspired a simmering rage at the unresolved, at a hunger stimulated and toyed with but never sated. This format, so central to the TV serial and now cable news, had previously animated apocalyptic and millenarian religion, which suggested that a great reckoning, a second coming, always lurked around the corner. It seemed inevitable, in retrospect, that politics would take on the character of the programming that narrativized it. Like the coming of God or the triumph of order and good over chaos and evil, politics could not end before the ordained denouement. It certainly couldn't peter out into the contingency of history. Not even an election could offer temporary resolution to people hooked on this arc of feeling. The slow meting out of tantalizing clues and the promise of a day of reckoning ever deferred was not just the formula of conspiracy theories like QAnon but of most television news.

2012

The ascendancy of social media and the smartphone, which meant you carried the world of representation on your person at all times, joined with cable news and reality TV to create not so much a new world of representation as a world of representation you never had to leave. It was the never leaving, the never having to leave, that begot everything else.

Within the Context of No-Context

George Trow's 1980 essay described a culture that, thanks largely to television, had lost context and proportionality. The mediating institutions that once bridged national and private life had fallen away, leaving us with only the sphere of 200 million ("the life of television") and "intimate life" (the unit of one, alone). "It was sometimes lonely in the grid of one, alone," Trow wrote. "People reached out toward their home, which was in television." Television was a mystery, he explained, but some of its properties were known. It had a *scale*, which did not vary. "The trivial is raised up to the place where this scale has its home; the powerful is lowered there." Accordingly, distinctions of large and small, near and far, important and trivial collapsed.

From Context to Pretense

Trow understood television's power to enforce scale, but he could not have foreseen the world cable TV and twenty-four-hour cable news would create. (The first cable-news channel, CNN, launched the same year his essay appeared.) He understood that celebrities led a charmed existence as the only figures with both an intimate life and a life in the sphere of 200 million ("Of all Americans, only they are complete," he wrote), but he could not have intuited how great people's desire would grow—as immediate life crumbled before the screen world's unbroken dream—to pass into the world of representation directly. The implicit figure in Trow's essay looked out from loneliness at the shimmering face of culture and tried to answer timeless questions: What is the world beyond my immediate experience like? Where do I fit in it? The key idea was *context*, because it was context that the individual scrutinizing the world and trying to make sense of it needed and context that the culture no longer supplied.

A glance at a newspaper or news show or Twitter suffices to confirm that the collapse of essential distinctions—between large and small, near and far, important and trivial—endures today. But the technological turn from spectatorship to interaction—to commenting, tweeting, influencing, gathering as audiences to respond en masse—has meant a new era of self-presentation in which the key concept isn't *context* but *pretense*. Its central questions are not *What is reality like?* and *Where do I belong in it?* but *What is the world of representation like?* and *How am I, as an object of public scrutiny, to behave?*

*

High School

When I attended high school in the late nineties, I had the sense of participating in an obscure game in which everyone knew the rules but me. To speak of this openly was impossible. To ask what the rules were would have invited mockery. Perhaps there were no rules and I simply found operating without rules terrifying. Or perhaps everyone found this terrifying and we all put on a good show of not caring.

What was clear was that the pretense of not caring—an air of indifference to embarrassment and suffering—was essential to protecting the part of you that was not indifferent. Some people's natural audacity allowed them to get away with things the rest of us would have been ridiculed for, but you could never simply *imitate* them. It was necessary, we somehow understood, to pose and posture without seeming to pose and posture, because then you were a "poseur," and this was one of the worst things you could be.

This meant that authenticity commanded a certain value—a kind of authenticity, which posed without seeming to pose. Some were better than others at striking this posture (this pretense of no-pretense), and the rest of us prayed, I imagine, that life would not continue to require so much posturing later on. Beyond the hermetic confines of high school, we hoped, awaited a world less capable of enforcing the stifling norms and fads that convinced us to hide our true selves in the interest of being accepted.

You can imagine my horror then at discovering in the early 2010s that we had begun reconstructing the social and professional world as a version of high school: a realm of pretense, posturing, and insincerity—insincerity posing as sincerity—all in the hushed, breathless, childish tones of niceness, the voice of NPR. Marshall McLuhan wrote that the "electric" age would eventually collapse the expansive world it knit together into a "global village," possessed of the powers won during earlier ages, now subject to the reactive, integral, mythic logic of the tribal town. Perhaps the implications of his prophecy are brought home more clearly if we describe the culture that arose from our instantaneous networks of communication as a "global high school." The fad of niceness—the hatred implicit in it and in other performances of camouflaged self-interest—always had far more to do with adolescent clique logic than genuine kindness or goodness. We showed up one day and instead of jock bullies, mean girls and judgy slackers, everyone was now excessively, performatively nice. But it was just a new spin on an old game. They weren't being nice because they liked you, but because the pose of niceness had become the coin of the realm.

*

Pretense

Do not be fooled that pretense has no cost. When little lies degrade the bonds between representation and reality, we corrupt the knowledge that guides action. When misconceptions about our nature become fixed ideas, we are helpless to create the human communities we want to live in. The flip side of niceness is trolling. The latter feeds off the former. Trump's appeal always had as much as anything to do with the phoniness and false speech and ridiculously puritanical and unserious idea of human beings espoused by the exponents of niceness, the masters of pretense. A figure like Trump understands that people will often empower a venal cynic if the alternative is a self-righteous child.

Technology

Do not be fooled that technology's trade-offs are obvious. It is technology's nature to make us forget the hidden virtues of the things it overcomes: the temporal, physical processes that cultivate experience, relationships, wisdom. Just as the obligation to exist in a dominant reality dispelled the hallucinatory mists of conspiracy, having to encounter people in physical space placed certain limits on the kabuki of self-presentation. There was no audience to play to, no time to belabor the minutiae of your postures. The truth of who you were leaked out around the edges of pretense and pretend.

Addressing ourselves directly to one another set us up for understanding, for bridging our inevitable differences. But the world of representation, the screen world we now so rarely leave, has taught us to address ourselves to audiences, not individuals. The performer on stage knows it is an act, a charade. But we could not see this clearly, sitting quietly before our laptops and phones. Only in small private moments did we feel the weight of pretense now required of us—if we ever did—and it was very lonely in those moments, in the grid of one, alone. We reached out toward our home in the glowing box, where niceness and hatred, agreement and pretense ruled.

Reality

Do not be fooled that reality is easy to grasp. We use representations to get our arms around what we cannot seize directly, but how can we know our representations reflect the world as it is? Only an immense collective project of inquiry and criticism can keep our stories from becoming conspiracies, from taking on lives of their own. Technology has made this more difficult, just as it promised to make everything easier. People revile the critic, the parent, the teacher because she tells them to step away from the effortless pleasures of the machine to do the hard work of growing, struggling, thinking. Because she says the pain of growing up, of facing up to what you cannot immediately master, must be endured. Endured if you want to grow strong and want responsibilities, not merely choice. Want something you can meaningfully give, not just things you can passively get. But this is simply the only path to having a life and mind outside the Skinner Box of stimuli that condition a person to respond with the words that garner a reward and avoid the words that invite punishment; the only path to preserving the fraught relationship between reality and our means of representing it, which requires humility and toil, lest we become converts to our own mysticism and the credulous apostles of our own invented stories.

LAURA PRESTON

An Age of Hyperabundance

FROM *n+1*

I WAS in a room of men. Every man was over-groomed: checked shirt, cologne behind the ears, deluxe beard or clean-shaven jaw. Their conversations bounced around me in jolly rat-a-tats, but the argot evaded interpretation. All I made out were acronyms and discerning grunts, backslaps, a mannered nonchalance.

I was at the Chattanooga Convention Center for Project Voice, a major gathering for software developers, venture capitalists, and entrepreneurs in conversational AI. The conference, now in its eighth year, was run by Bradley Metrock, an uncommonly tall man with rousing frat-boy energy who is, per his professional bio, a "leading thought leader" in voice tech. "I'm a conservative guy!" he said to me on a Zoom call some weeks prior. "I was like, 'What kind of magazine is this? Seems pretty out there.'"

The magazine in question was this one. Bradley had read my essay "HUMAN_FALLBACK" in *n+1*'s winter 2022 issue in which I described my year impersonating a chatbot for a real estate start-up. A lonely year, a depressing charade; it had made an impression on Bradley. He asked if I'd attend Project Voice as the "honorary contrarian speaker," a title bestowed each year on a public figure, often a journalist, who has expressed objections to conversational AI. As part of my contrarian duties, I was to close out the conference with a thirty-minute speech to an audience of five hundred—a sort of valedictory of grievances, I gathered.

So that what? So that no one could accuse the AI pioneers of ignoring existential threats to culture? To facilitate a brief moment of self-flagellation before everyone hit the bars? I wasn't sure, but I sensed my presence had less to do with balance and more to do with sport. Bradley kept using the word *exciting*. A few years ago, he said, the contrarian speaker stormed onstage, visibly irate. As she railed against the wickedness of the Echo Dot Kids, Amazon's voice assistant for children, a row of Amazon executives walked out. Major sponsors! That, said Bradley, was very exciting.

I wondered if I should be offended by my contrarian designation, which positioned AI as the de facto orthodoxy and framed any argument I could make as the inevitable expression of my antagonistic pathology. The more I thought about it, the more I became convinced I was being set up for failure. Recent discussion of conversational AI has tended to treat the technology as a monolithic force synonymous with ChatGPT, capable of both cultural upheaval and benign comedy. But conversational AI encloses a vast, teeming domain. The term refers to any technology you can talk to the way you would talk to a person, and also includes any software that uses large language models to modify, translate, interpret, or forge written or spoken words. The field is motley and prodigious, with countless companies speculating in their own little corners. There are companies that make telemarketing tools, navigation systems, speech-to-text software for medical offices, psychotherapy chatbots, and essay-writing aids; there are conversational banking apps, avatars that take food orders, and virtual assistants for every industry under the sun; there are companies cloning celebrity voices so that an American actor can, for example, film a commercial in Dutch. The field is so crowded and the hype is so loud that to offset a three-day circus with thirty minutes of counterpoint is to practically coerce the critic into abstractions. Still, I accepted the invitation for the same reason I took the job with the real estate start-up: it was a paid opportunity and seemed like something I could write about.

On the first afternoon of the conference I took a lap around the floor and tried to make sense of what I was seeing. Tech companies had arrived with their sundries: bowls of wrapped candies, ballpoint pens, PopSockets, and other bribes; brochures

An Age of Hyperabundance

fanned on tables; iPads with demos at the ready. The graphics, curiously alike across the displays, were a combination of Y2K screen saver abstractions and the McGraw Hill visual tradition. Many companies had erected tall, vertical banners adorned with hot-air balloons, city skylines at dusk, dark-haired women on call-center headsets, and circular flowcharts with no discernible content. If conversational AI had a heraldic color, that color would be blue—a dusty Egyptian blue, chaste and masculine, more Windows 2000 than Giotto. It's a tedious no-color, the color of abdicating choice, and on the exhibition floor it was ubiquitous in calm, flat abysses backgrounding white text.

The only booth that stood out was at the far end of the exhibition hall. A company had tented its little patch of real estate with an inflatable white cube that looked like a large, quivering marshmallow. Inside the cube was Keith, a soft-spoken man whose earnest features and round physique conveyed a gnome-like benevolence. Beside Keith was a large screen. On the screen was a woman. The woman had dark hair, dark eyes, and purple lips that endeavored a smile. Her shoulders rose and fell, as if to suggest the act of breathing, and though she looked toward me, her gaze was elsewhere.

"This is Chatty," Keith shouted over the roar of the blowers keeping his enclosure erect.

Keith worked for SapientX, a company that makes photorealistic conversational avatars powered by ChatGPT. SapientX had custom-built Chatty for Project Voice. Chatty could answer questions about the conference agenda and show you a map of the exhibition floor, except she couldn't do it just then, said Keith, because they couldn't seem to connect her to the Wi-Fi.

Keith was happy enough to walk me through the visuals. Chatty's face was the collaborative effort of fifty different companies. A company in Toronto did the eyes. "There's like eight guys and all they do is eyes all day," he said.

Chatty's face was a composite of several different races. Her voice was a composite of several different women. Her voice still needed some work, he admitted. "Right now she's kinda mean."

I picked up a brochure that featured a roster of "digital employees," complete with their names, headshots, and "personality scores." I wondered what industries might hire them.

"They're mostly for kiosks," Keith responded with a tone of defeat. "Like at a mall or a museum. Also military training. Stuff like that."

Keith directed my attention to the exterior of the cube. A large banner depicted an older male, prosaically handsome, with a square jaw, a custardy dollop of silver hair, and pale, limpid eyes. This was Chief, said Keith. "He's a navy guy. And he talks like a navy guy. We work in forty different languages. So if you're training someone in Ukraine how to operate an American tool, we have that language built in."

Keith went back inside to rustle me up a T-shirt. He told me that the company was also breaking into health care—nursing homes, to be precise. Keith explained the vision. Your mom is old, and you're constantly reminding her to take her medicine. Why not leave that to an avatar? The avatar can converse with your mom, keep her company, fill up the idle hours of the day. Plus, you can incorporate a retina scanner to check her blood pressure and a motion sensor to make sure she isn't lying dead on the floor.

"Say there's an elderly woman with dementia," he said. "Her avatar will look like she did when she was younger. So she has someone to identify with. Does that make sense?"

I imagined a future geriatric Keith, lying in a nursing home bed, conversing with his younger self. Would such an arrangement appeal to him?

"There's not going to be a choice," he said. "A lot of old people are going to be talking to avatars in ten years, and they won't even know it. When I was touring facilities in San Francisco for people with dementia and stuff, those places are like insane asylums. But some patients still have some cognitive function, and that's who the technology would be for. It's definitely not going to apply to the guys that are comatose."

We stood in silence for a moment, and he faced Chatty, who hovered before us, drifting in her strange, waking trance.

"I wish they could fix the internet," said Keith. "I swear, she gets nasty. She like, looks at me bad."

At the back of the exhibition hall, a daylong program of talks and panels was playing out on a modular stage—the stage on which, in two days' time, I would perform my conference-sanctioned finger-wagging. Like a dutiful student, I had typed out my speech and practiced it against my iPhone's stopwatch. I began to fear this was the wrong approach. The speakers were going at it notes-free and pacing around TED Talk–style.

A woman named Olga was giving a talk about charisma. I listened, hoping to gain some last-minute wisdom for my own remarks. Olga represented a German firm that puts chatbots through some sort of charisma boot camp. According to Olga, here is how a chatbot can show charisma: First, it can remember the customer's name. That is very charismatic. "A charismatic assistant might have a quirky sense of humor, a soothing voice, or a nice and friendly tone," she said. "A charismatic assistant can remind you to take your medicine."

Olga had an important message about charisma. In our pursuit of charismatic AI, we must avoid dark patterns. Dark patterns are manipulative design tactics that steer people toward decisions they wouldn't normally make, and these patterns often resemble charisma. A chatbot using dark patterns might mimic your mannerisms to gain your trust. It might lead you to believe it is a real person. It might have enough data on you to flirt with lethal precision, and then, just after delivering a dopamine hit, ask you to provide a credit card to continue. Better not do any of that, said Olga.

Next up was a man from a company called Journey. I did some light research on my phone. Journey's past projects included Walmart Land, a virtual music festival in the Roblox metaverse meant to "engage the next generation of Walmart fans," and promotional concept videos for NEOM, the $500 billion megacity that is the pet project of Saudi Crown Prince Mohammed bin Salman, which will allegedly include a floating industrial city, a luxury island for the yachting class, and a continuous, one-hundred-mile-long, mirror-clad structure called the Line that will bisect a desert tract the size of Massachusetts, a tract that is the ancestral land of the Huwaitat tribe, of whom some twenty thousand members have already been evicted, among them three activists who, for their noncompliance, have been sentenced to death.

The man from Journey showed us how generative AI could expedite product design. He took us through a branding exercise for a hypothetical breakfast cereal. His ChatGPT-powered tool came up with the packaging: a cardboard obelisk, four times as tall as it was wide, with a picture of what might have been a passion fruit tumbling down a cascade of liquid. If I had to guess what was in such a box, I would guess printer cartridges or chardonnay. The AI had also written some copy: "Are you tired of starting your day with a bland and boring breakfast? Look no further than PureCrunch Naturals." With a few more clicks, the man showed how the right combination of generative AI tools can, like a fungus, spawn infinite assets: long-form articles, video spots, and social media posts, all translated into multiple languages.

"We are moving," he said, "into a hyperabundance decade."

I bought a sweet tea at a downtown lunch spot and reviewed the notes for my talk. Before I arrived at the conference, I had decided to discuss bias in algorithms. The essence of my argument was this: In 2019, shortly after I finished graduate school, I worked for a company that made a real estate chatbot called Brenda. Brenda answered questions about apartment listings and booked prospective tenants for tours. My job was to supervise Brenda's conversations as an "operator," and if she went off script, which she often did, I took over until she regained her bearings.

Over thousands of conversations with strangers, I began to suspect that Brenda's diction—and the very fact of her texting interface—was most palatable to the young, affluent, and white. I feared this had real effects on which people booked tours, and which people were so put off by the experience of speaking to Brenda they looked for housing elsewhere. Was this not redlining by algorithm? The peculiar mental burden of the job was that I was made to live in parallel but opposite realities. On the one hand, our Slack channels were filled with messages from developers claiming righteous intentions. Brenda was making the rental process accessible, democratic, quick as a text. And yet every night I watched how this bot, with her blameless, chirpy affect, was an instrument of isolation, a digital bully that landlords used to create distance between themselves and their tenants.

Though she hadn't crossed my mind for some time, I remembered Ella, a woman who messaged Brenda so often I came to recognize her on my shifts. Ella spoke only Spanish. Brenda did not, and neither did most of the chatbot operators, so we corresponded with Ella by copying and pasting Spanish phrases from a Google Doc we had compiled on our own time. Ella was a tenant at one of Brenda's properties. Ella's messages were urgent and anguished. She spoke of violencia and God. Her situation was unclear. She sent video clips of her walls and ceilings, which came through as still images without sound.

We were fairly certain Ella was trying to report domestic violence in the apartment next door. We told Ella that if she or someone else was in danger she should call 911. Ella did not call 911; it was possible she was afraid to engage the police. We told Ella to call building management, but the management's only phone number rerouted to Brenda, the chatbot who handled rental inquiries.

Ella, I should note, was not the woman's name. She offered us her real name several times, which we manually added to her file. But Brenda, ever keen, kept spotting the feminine singular pronoun *ella*—a more suitable name by Brenda's logic, more like the names she had seen before—and entering it into the name field, obliterating whatever had been there. "¿Como te llamas?" we would ask. "¡Ya te dije!" she would say. The woman's true name was finally lost.

We always pinged our supervisors when Ella's messages came through. At first, our supervisors reacted with twisted excitement, for here was an opportunity for Brenda to flex her empathy—that was what Brenda did best! Ella continued to send vague and frightening reports. Our supervisors grew tired. "In some situations, it's useful to sound like a bot," one said. The last time Ella appeared in my inbox, I scrolled through her message history. Brenda's automated messages had been completely disabled. In their place, I saw a litany of human operators repeating a refrain:

>Soy un agente inmobiliario remoto.
>Soy un agente inmobiliario remoto.
>Soy un agente inmobiliario remoto.

The story of Ella was an example of a chatbot working badly. It was also an example of a chatbot working wonderfully. Not once was a landlord's silence disturbed by this woman and her problems. She was not even a person in the database, but a hysterical pronoun. And how apt, in the end, for her troubles to divert to us, a group of poets and novelists hired specifically for our feelings, who could feel for her endlessly but do nothing else, as we did not know the landlord's name or how to reach him and lived very far away.

As I reentered the conference floor, I was still thinking about the tension between declared outcomes and actual implementations. All around me, the booths posed a collective thesis on the future. This was a future without busywork or buttons, a future of bespoke experiences, a future where the internet was an ambient thing we'd call upon with our voices—not a service we would use but a place where we would live. Beneath this promised future, however, was a shadow future, one that suggested itself at every turn. This was a future of screens in every establishment and no way to get help, a future in which extractive algorithms yielded relentless advertising, a future of a crapified internet, too diluted with sponcon and hallucinated facts to be of any use. In this future, if you wanted to use a product you would have to download an app and pay a monthly fee. It was a future of ultra-sophisticated scams and government surveillance, a future where anyone's face could be spliced into porn. Our arrival in this future would be a gradual surrender, achieved through a slow creep of terms and conditions, and the capitulations had already begun.

And yet no one at the conference seemed worried. This was a room of nerdy, earnest people, people who were good at fixing things and eager to improve the world in whatever ways made sense to them. I couldn't quite figure it out. Was their belief in the goodness of AI so secure that they didn't see the broader threats? Or did they not care how the technology was ultimately used, as long as they came out with the spoils?

I was nervous about the day's closing talk, which was called "Savage Communities and Noble Leadership." This talk would be delivered by Ian Utile, a man of unclear affiliation who was, I could only guess, another leading thought leader of the industry.

Ian strode down the aisle and leaped onstage. He was dressed in black with wraparound sunglasses, black hair greased into a ponytail, a rectilinear beard, and boots so pointy they were practically Arthurian. The look suggested the World Series of Poker, but when he began to speak, Ian's energy transformed into that of a Pentecostal youth minister.

"What I see is a lot of leaders that are either NOBLE . . . or *savage*," he bellowed. "I see a lot of communities that are either SAVAGE . . . or *noble*. How do you balance savagery, confidence, intensity, drive . . . being the IMPETUS! The DRIVING FORCE THAT MAKES THINGS HAPPEN! . . . with? Nobility. Meekness. Kindness. Love. Care. Empathy. And *sympathy*. And congratulations, when I look at this industry I see a lot of nobility. I often wonder, 'Where's the savagery, everybody?' Are your customers savage about you? About your products? Your services? ARE YOUR EMPLOYEES SAVAGE? WILL THEY KNOCK DOWN WALLS TO MAKE THINGS HAPPEN FOR YOU?"

I found Ian's LinkedIn. In fact he did have a history with the Evangelical church. He was the "entrepreneur-in-residence" at Transform Our World, a global ministry led by the Argentinean evangelist Ed Silvoso, and had been a guest on a panel called "How the Church Can Glorify God in the Metaverse."

"When you're a leader, ideally, you are focused on nobility. To lead like a queen, to lead like a king. To build communities on top of your shoulders. Not a pyramid down, but the pyramid upside-down. May we at Project Voice represent savage communities and noble leaders. Bradley, thank you for letting me share that with everybody."

"Collapse of context," I wrote in my notebook. "The ChatGPT-like impulse to write a speech on the noble savage because *noble savage* is something you've heard before, and it sounds badass."

Let's say I got up onstage and did a close reading of Melville or Montaigne. Let's say I told them that each word was a trawl net that heaves up a thrashing, slapping, shimmering school of associations from the deep. Would anyone believe me? Would it matter?

"Hyperabundance—from ecology," I wrote. I was too exhausted from the day to refine my thoughts further. As I drifted off to sleep in my hotel room that night, I thought of white-tailed deer devouring the understory and spotted lanternflies attached to tree trunks in horrible, shingled heaps.

The following morning, the conference dispersed for industry-specific talks. When I arrived at the exhibition hall, a man told me the digital signs weren't working. He took out a pen and drew some arrows on my conference map.

I headed to the health-care room. It was just before nine, and people were looking groggy, but the room was nevertheless full and vibrating with anticipatory energy. A young woman with red hair down to her tailbone approached the lectern.

Her name was Caitlyn, and she represented a company called Canary Speech. Canary Speech had developed a tool that analyzes human speech for "vocal biomarkers." Caitlyn explained that vocal biomarkers are qualities below the level of human hearing that correlate with emotional and physiological conditions. By listening to just thirty seconds of recorded speech, Canary Speech could return a health audit that breaks down the user's mood, energy, anxiety, and degree of depression, and identify pre-Parkinson's traits, as well as early signs of Alzheimer's.

Caitlyn played a video in which she prompted a woman to speak for thirty seconds on any topic. The woman described her morning. She had woken up and fed her child. Her child had played with their dog.

"Canary is analyzing the audio," Caitlyn said. "You have medium anxiety and medium depression. Your energy score is at forty-six. Your power is at seventy-eight. Speed is medium, at forty-eight. Dynamic is twelve."

I could feel a collective intake of breath. A woman raised her hand and asked what would happen to someone's diagnosis if the sound quality were poor.

"That's why we record forty seconds," said Caitlyn. "So we get more audio than we need."

The woman's question poked a hole in the dam, and more questions poured forth. Another woman identified herself as a therapist. "To be told you're mildly depressed will make you depressed," she said.

"How can we be confident this won't fall into the hands of corporations that will figure out how to sell things to depressed people?" asked another woman.

"What about cultural differences?" said someone else.

Caitlyn attempted an answer, but before she could produce anything cogent a male voice boomed from the back of the room.

"WE'RE TALKING ABOUT MICRO-PROSODIC FEATURES BELOW THE LEVEL OF HUMAN PERCEPTION," the voice said. The large and formidable man to whom this voice belonged rolled down the aisle on a mobility scooter. He introduced himself. He was a veteran of the original Alexa build and Canary Speech's cofounder.

"What is the baseline you're comparing it to?" someone asked.

"You compare it to a generic baseline."

"What is generic? Man? Woman? Teenager?"

"These clues are generally universal."

The cofounder yielded the room to Caitlyn. A member of the audience asked if the software might be useful to large enterprises, perhaps to monitor employees.

"Absolutely," said Caitlyn. And in fact, Canary Speech was thrilled to announce a new partnership with Microsoft Teams.

Every talk sent me down a frantic spiral of inquiry. That morning, at breakfast, I couldn't stop reading studies on nursing home robots. (In one, a group of Canadian nurses expressed concerns that robotic equipment could be used as weapons during "behavioural events.") Now that I knew about vocal biomarkers, I felt myself hurtling down a new tube slide of panic. What would the insurance companies do? Would they increase a patient's premium because their voice indicated pre-Parkinson's? What would happen when the company-wide mental health initiative required employee one-on-ones with Canary in the background? Would a sales call debrief include metrics on everyone's mood? In a society that reserves psychiatric care for only its wealthiest members, was there any reason to automate mental health assessments if not for the purpose of mass surveillance? What did it mean to have medium depression? Was I medium depressed?

I was especially alarmed by that turn of phrase: *These traits are generally universal.* Without meaning to, the cofounder had summarized the prevailing logic of AI. The AI industrialists envisioned a future where large language models would replace search engines. Instead of rummaging through a heap of Google hits, we would pose questions and receive answers. Though the answers would be no more than a statistical averaging of existing texts, they would be packaged as authoritative comments and give the impression of thought. All the gnarls of individual style, the eccentricities of argument, the anomalous notions, would be smoothed away, and the resulting summary—mediocre, adequate—would be peddled as absolute knowledge.

If ChatGPT reduced texts into summary, Canary Speech aimed to do the same with individual mentalities. To say that vocal biomarkers were generally universal predictors of mood admitted the existence of outliers that for whatever reason did not matter. So what about those outliers? If your voice test indicated an anxious disorder, but you did not suffer from anxious feelings, whose truth was to be believed? To me, this all had an odious whiff of physiognomy and race science. It was the same logic that compelled white men to fashion their avatar's face as the ghostly average of non-Caucasian women, a de facto stereotype, like some Victorian eugenicist's photography experiment.

In the breakout room for the hospitality industry, a program of presenters took turns spelling out, with fetishistic precision, our communal experiences as conferencegoers. We were pilgrims in a strange city, lying in the austere bedrooms of the Staybridge Suites, in need of food and beverage but daunted by the urban wilderness. "Show me pizza places nearby," a developer said as he pantomimed the ideal food-ordering app. "Now show me ones that deliver." Another man whose entire platform seemed to be lobbying for 24/7 earbud use showed us the perks of having a voice assistant permanently lodged in a bodily orifice. "Where is a good hamburger restaurant in my area?" he said. "Are there any brewpubs within walking distance of the Chattanooga Convention Center?" A dour pair of Germans described the specific burdens of hotel living. For example, you must check in at the front desk. Then, when you get to your room, you must locate the mini-fridge and discover the light switches. The German team was addressing these problems with an in-room, voice-activated AI concierge. You would bypass the front desk and unlock your room with your phone, then a disembodied voice would help you with the lights.

I was an extraterrestrial taking notes on the problems of Earth. Finding pizza in your area was a problem. People being mean to you because you were wearing your AirPods at dinner was a problem. Going on vacation was a problem because the hotels would force you to find the light switches. Elders were a problem. (They never took their medicine.) Loneliness was a problem, but loneliness had a solution, and the solution was conversation. But don't talk with your elders, and not with the front desk, and certainly not with the man on the corner, though he might know where the pizza is. ("Noise-canceling is great, especially if you live urban," said the earbuds guy. "There's a lot of world out there.") Idle chitchat was a snag in daily living. We'd rather slip through the world as silent as a burglar, seen by no one except our devices.

I was excited about the next talk, which was called "Using ChatGPT to Create an Answer Engine for Pets." I pictured my family's terrier—a bedraggled little animal, so endearing and pathetic you wouldn't be surprised to catch him on the train tracks with a bindle on his shoulder—sitting before a computer terminal, counseled by a program that speaks the language of dogs.

I should have known by then to expect disappointment. "Meet VERA," said the compact, magnificently tan CEO of a company called AskVet. A woman materialized on a screen behind him. She spoke, but her mouth didn't move in time with the words. "And if you can believe it, she's not a real person," he said.

VERA was the "world's only veterinary engagement and relationship agent." If your pet fell ill you could chat with VERA, and she would tell you if a vet trip was necessary.

"Let's consider your standard diarrhea exercise," said the CEO. His voice was serene, gentle, trustworthy. And yet below that outer shell of self-possession, I detected a suppressed, slow-burning anger. He seemed aggrieved by what he called pet parents, a fundamentally irrational demographic that was incapable of much besides crowding the vet offices.

A woman in the audience asked if VERA followed up to make sure her diagnosis had been right.

The CEO leaned an elbow on the podium. "I'll tell you a story," he said.

A woman wrote to VERA about her elderly dog, who was having diarrhea.

"Your dog is at the end of his life," said VERA. "I recommend euthanasia."

The woman was beside herself. She told VERA she wasn't ready to say goodbye. Her dog was her only companion.

VERA knew the woman's location. She sent a list of nearby clinics that could get the job done. Still, the woman was unconvinced. Euthanasia was so expensive. She'd never be able to afford it. VERA sent another list, this time of nearby shelters. "If you relinquish your dog to a shelter, they will euthanize him at no cost," she said.

The woman did not respond. But some days later she sent VERA a long and effusive message. She had taken VERA's advice and euthanized her dog. She wanted to thank VERA for the support during the most difficult moment of her life.

The CEO regarded us with satisfaction for his chatbot's work: that, through a series of escalating tactics, it had convinced a woman to end her dog's life, though she hadn't wanted to at all.

"The point of this story is that the woman forgot she was talking to a bot," he said. "The experience was so human."

I needed a break. The day before, a booth on the exhibition floor had been giving away full-size Tony's Chocolonely bars, so I went looking for one of those. As I navigated the rat maze in search of my treat, I came face-to-face with yet another synthetic person. There was something uniquely inept about her appearance. She was diminutive, perhaps two feet tall, with proportions I can only describe as Atenist: broad hips; narrow shoulders; long, willowy legs; and a thigh gap wider than the thighs themselves. Her arms floated beside her, governed by Martian gravity, and again, the proportions were aberrant. The first two-thirds of each arm was an arm, but the remaining third was all fingers. She wore a white doctor's coat. Around her neck was a stethoscope.

A real man came up behind me. He was small, about my height, and in his fifties.

"This is Catherine," he said, "Chatty Cathy."

"Is she a physician?" I asked.

"Yes," said the man, whose name was Norrie. "Quite qualified, I'm told. Talk to her!"

I wasn't sure how wise it was to solicit health advice from a meta-human whose creators hadn't mastered human anatomy, but she was, after all, wearing a stethoscope. Norrie shushed me.

"Don't tell her about your ailments," he said. "That's very personal. Cathy, who are you with today?"

Cathy stared at us silently. Her irises were completely encircled by the whites of her eyes, which gave her a look of permanent startle.

"The Wi-Fi's slow," said Norrie.

"Who are you here with, Cathy?" I repeated, but Norrie diverted my attention to another screen. On this screen was a male avatar, much like Cathy in style and comportment, with broad shoulders and well-developed pectorals.

"My team made him for me," Norrie said with a salacious little grin. "He answers questions about my life."

It took me a moment. "It's you!"

"I asked for a swimmer's build."

I had never been bothered by the singularity of my body; the consensus of this conference, however, was that making your synthetic double was something you should want to do.

"TODAY, I'M HERE AT THE PROJECT VOICE TRADE SHOW WITH MY CODEBABY COLLEAGUES," bellowed Cathy. "WE'RE ALL EXCITED TO DISCUSS THE POTENTIAL BENEFITS OF CONVERSATIONAL AI AND AVATARS IN HEALTH CARE."

I still wanted to ask a medical question.

"Tell her your cholesterol's over three hundred," Norrie said, and I did.

"I'M NOT A DOCTOR," said Cathy. "BUT IF YOUR CHOLESTEROL IS HIGH, IT'S IMPORTANT TO CONSULT WITH A HEALTH-CARE PROFESSIONAL. AS A CODEBABY AVATAR, MY EXPERTISE LIES IN CONVERSATIONAL AI AND ITS APPLICATIONS IN HEALTH-CARE COMMUNICATION."

When Norrie told me his company was developing avatars for elder care, I asked him the same question I had asked Keith: Would he be happy with an avatar in his home who cared for him in his old age?

"Absolutely," he said. "I'm single. I live with two dogs. You can do a lot of good with this technology. You can also do a lot of bad. You can defraud people. It's always the vulnerable who are defrauded. Humans kill each other, let's face it." Norrie let out a deep, sonorous laugh.

After lunch, the industry rooms disbanded and everyone returned to the exhibition hall for talks on the main stage. Bradley moderated a panel on avatars. "If you had to convince me that avatars are here to stay, what would you say?" he asked.

"People will share medical data with an avatar more willingly than with their own family doctor," said the CEO of SapientX, the company with the inflatable tent. "Another reason is the fun factor."

A woman named Reena answered next. Reena's start-up, Wisdocity, aimed to make digital clones of real people in order to preserve their individual skills and knowledge. Reena explained

An Age of Hyperabundance

that her teenage daughter was unhappy with her high school's curriculum, which didn't teach anything of real-world use. Reena suggested we clone business leaders and bring them into the classroom. Students would be enriched by human connection, the mental health crisis among teens would subside, and we wouldn't even have to invent the therapy bots in the first place.

"I think Reena nailed it perfectly," said Norrie, who expanded on the theme of mental health.

"You are alone," he droned. "You don't have any ability to communicate with another human. So you talk to an avatar to have at least some relief from the boredom and loneliness you face."

Everyone at this conference kept invoking loneliness and claiming the antidote was conversation. That didn't track with my own experience. My most desperate moments of loneliness have been in conversation: On a Hinge date, doomed but persisting as a form of protocol. At a publishing party, surrounded by people who look and talk like me, all of us a little drunk but maintaining our nervous, manic professionalism. My moments of connection, by contrast, have been beyond language. Biking along the east edge of Prospect Park on an August night, hearing cicadas chant their reedy iambs, as loud on that stretch of Flatbush as they would be in the countryside, remembering summers of childhood, a house that's gone, and my grandmother's two-handed wave from the threshold.

"It wouldn't be right to have this panel and not talk about ethics, given what y'all are doing," said Bradley. "All y'all's avatars have the ability to bring someone to their knees."

Cathy appeared in my mind like an archangel. Her bat phalanges, her snarl of a smile, her vacant eyes.

"Like, the last thing I want to do is create a racist bot," said a panelist.

"As human beings we experience the fact that we kill other human beings," Norrie said for the second time that day. "We are creating tools that will be misused. We hope there are some barriers in place, but at the end of the day . . . yeah."

"Let's give these folks a round of applause," said Bradley.

*

I still had not seen a demo of SapientX's Chatty, the one inside the inflatable cube. Inside the cube I found Keith as well as the CEO, who had just returned from the stage, and who was sitting on a folding chair in the corner and eating a sandwich. Chatty was no longer on the large screen. Instead, it was Chief, the drill sergeant.

I asked if I could see a demo. "Yes," said the CEO. "Actually no, I just unplugged everything." He asked what brought me to the conference.

"Contrarian speaker," he said. "Is that a company? You're just contrary by nature?"

I explained the general idea.

"So you're a writer!" he said. "One of my ranch hands used to be a writer! She got really beaten up by the industry."

I told Keith I'd try to come back. "Chief's the one designed for military training, right?" I asked.

Keith looked confused.

"We made him for a mall," he said. "A military museum and a mall."

Throughout the conference, a little itch had developed in the back of my brain. It was an ugly, edgy feeling, and I finally recognized what it was. It was the feeling of being scammed. Chief might teach a weapons qualification course, or he might answer FAQs at the veterans' memorial. Chatty Cathy wore a stethoscope because she was a doctor, but she wasn't a doctor—her expertise was in conversational AI and its applications in health-care communication. VERA wasn't a vet—she was a veterinary engagement and relationship agent. When I impersonated Brenda, I was not a leasing agent and had no real estate credentials. I had an MFA in creative writing. My supervisor told me to say I was an offsite leasing specialist, a meaningless title, technical enough for most users to skim over and not question its validity. It all suggested a future of ineptitude, where everyone was a brand instrument disguised as a resource.

I had a little over twelve hours left before my talk. In my hotel room, I set up my iPhone timer and practiced the various turns of my argument. Brenda's conversations were designed by af-

An Age of Hyperabundance

fluent white people, which meant that her rhetorical style was affluent and white.

I wasn't feeling great about this argument. Not because it wasn't true, but because I realized this was exactly the argument people expected me to make. Since I'd been in Chattanooga, there'd been plenty of talk about bias. Lots of companies had called for diverse datasets, for large language models trained on regional vernaculars, for multicultural avatars with whom a wide array of people could identify. But these calls for diversity seemed to represent the far limits of their imagination and stopped short of a more radical truth: that these algorithms—diverse or not—were designed to violate, extract, and exploit. Hito Steyerl describes this problem in the *New Left Review*, citing Racial Faces in the Wild, a dataset aimed at improving facial recognition software that struggled to identify nonwhite people. "Police departments have been waiting and hoping for facial recognition to be optimized for non-Caucasian faces," writes Steyerl. And indeed, a firm called SenseTime was happy to use such a dataset to train surveillance software for the Chinese government, software that was used to monitor members of the Uighur ethnic minority.

If I had delivered this talk exactly as I'd written it, I would provide my audience with just enough critique to pleasantly stimulate their intellects, but nothing I said would be new. If anything, it would make them feel smug—smug that they had drawn similar conclusions without my counsel, smug that they were already, to borrow a word I heard with remarkable frequency, "cognizant" of the issues. I'd noticed during this conference a prevailing idea that as long as you designed a tool with good intentions, you were not responsible for how others misused it. "How do you think of ethics as a concept?" Bradley had asked nearly every panelist on the stage. "We think a lot about ethics," said one panelist. "Ethics are something we want to be aware of," said another. Over and over, I heard people recite variations on this line, like a quaint personal creed, a spell of protection. If the act of thinking about ethics is enough to confer immunity, then to make design choices in the service of diversity is an overachievement worthy of praise. Thus we see companies rolling out synthetic voices for every possible vernacular so that the phone scammers of the future will be blessed with a deluxe toolbox—and if this is not the intention, it will surely be the outcome. If I were to get onstage and ask for diverse datasets, what would I be asking for but a future in which we all have equal opportunity to be defrauded, to be surveilled at work, to be a patient in an Alzheimer's ward with a phantom at our bedside?

I wondered if I had enough time to write a new speech, something truly hostile. Why not go out on a tirade? But to tell a group of people that their invention could destroy the global order was another way of telling them their invention was godlike, supreme, and was exactly what the tech billionaires themselves were saying to bolster their market influence. In any case, I wasn't convinced these technologies were sophisticated enough to hasten societal collapse just yet. Some of them couldn't connect to the internet. What really frightened me was the future of mediocrity they suggested: the inescapable screens, the app-facilitated antisocial behavior, the assumptions advanced as knowledge, and above all the collective delusion formulated in high offices and peddled to common people that all this made for an easier life.

The morning of my speech, I watched ESPN in the lobby of my hotel and ate breakfast potatoes on a Styrofoam plate. There was a man at the table next to mine.

"Excuse me," he said. "Are you with the conference?"

The man was in his late fifties, with silver hair and a nice watch. He asked me what time the program started.

I suspected he knew perfectly well, but I engaged him anyway. He told me he worked in consumer electronics, then asked what industry I was in. I told him that I was the contrarian speaker, but that I didn't particularly relish the title, as it gave everyone permission to dismiss my argument as a by-product of my lame personality. He asked me what my talk would be about, and I gave him a gloss.

"Most people here are going to agree with you."

"I know," I said.

I decided to ask him a question that had been on my mind since the first day.

"Do people feel obligated to invent this stuff?" I said.

Many of the company reps, I noticed, seemed weary, even bored, as if they had no choice but to toil away on these technologies. Their indolent cadences, their rehearsed lines, the way a self-aware, sardonic remark would slip out before they fell back to the techno-optimist script—all this suggested that they viewed their work as nonnegotiable, a cliché of futurity they were required to design.

The man beside me sipped his hotel coffee. We stared at ESPN, lulled into silence by the muted anchors and the headline crawling beneath them: PACKERS TRADE AARON RODGERS TO JETS FOR MULTIPLE PICKS.

"When I was a kid, this news story came on TV," he said. "That guy. Jim Jones. He took those people to Guyana and made them eat poison. My buddies and I were watching that and thinking, *Where did all those stupid people come from?* But you know what? I don't wonder about that anymore."

I asked him what he meant, and he kept his eyes on the television.

"When you're standing in front of that fire, when the drums start thumping, it's the animal brain again," he said. He pounded his chest with his fist. "It'll get you. It'll get you. I promise, you'll start to chant."

The morning audience was sparse. The scattered attendees seemed a little nauseated, zoned out, clutching coffee cups. Last night's mixer at the Chattanooga Pinball Museum had been a great success. First on the agenda was a pitch event. A woman pitched her voice-activated wellness app. "I love these opportunities that take advantage of helping people," said a judge. A man demoed an in-home voice assistant. "Did you take your medications today?" the assistant said. "Oh, no. Medications are important for your health. Please take them."

It was time for me to give my talk. I walked onstage and squinted past the overhead lights. My audience of five hundred was an audience of sixty. I gave my speech exactly as I had conceived it, the speech that by now I felt socially engineered to have arrived at. I was giving the developers my benediction. I, too, had surrendered. As I talked, I could hear people packing up their booths. I got a decent murmur of applause, a singular hoot. Already I could feel my critique mutating into praise.

Bradley took the stage. "We always close the conference with something that will get you thinking," he said. With that, he yielded the podium to the final speaker, whose talk was titled—I read it twice—"Lasting Impact: How the Holocaust Inspired a New Approach to Conversational AI."

The speaker, Sarah, led a project that made digital clones of Holocaust survivors. The clones were life-size, made from composite video clips and sound bites, and could answer questions about their experiences. The idea was that museums could incorporate these clones into their educational programs to combat Holocaust denialism. I wondered about the segment of humanity targeted by this effort—that is, the demographic that would deny the evidence submitted at Nuremberg until a digital apparition set the record straight. Halfway through the talk, Sarah did the classic pivot. "As we evolved our work, we realized that lots of businesses rely on the power of personal presence," she said. She showed us how they cloned a famous Formula 1 driver to represent McLaren at an auto show. Celebrities, athletes, influencers—the possibilities for your brand are endless.

"The concept of conversational AI and the Holocaust demands attention," said Bradley. "I'm glad Sarah talked to us about that. That concludes the program, we wish you safe travels."

"Was it like that movie *M3GAN*?" my Lyft driver asked.

The driver was an ample older woman with a curtain of waist-length hair. She was not from Chattanooga, or even Tennessee, but had driven an hour from her home in Alabama to capitalize on the more fertile rideshare turf.

"I watched that movie four or five times," she said. "I studied it carefully."

We were on the interstate, winding our way along the spine of the Appalachian Mountains, a wide, shimmering basin to our left, a wall of stone to our right. We passed motels, an EZPAWN, car dealerships with their sparkling fleets and neon bunting. We passed truck depots, where 18-wheelers sat in ranks and waited to be filled.

"I think children are addicted to their iPads," she said. "They don't play outside or have a sense of nature."

"I do miss playing outside," I said.

"A few weeks ago, there was a rabbit in my backyard," she said. "Not a brown rabbit, but black and freckled, a gorgeous animal, someone's pet, I don't know. It was happy in the garden. Then one morning I go out to water my beds and my asshole German shepherd had it hanging in its mouth. I called my son hysterical on the phone. My son's in college but he sent his friend. Put it in a grocery bag and hit it with a dumbbell. I can't even tell you the relief I felt when my son said he don't want kids. I am a Christian woman. I've been reading Revelation. I said to him don't you dare give me grandkids. This world is going in a bad direction and I don't want to worry about my grandbabies."

All I saw of her face were her eyes glancing at me in the rearview mirror, then darting back to the road. We pulled up to Departures.

"So how many years we got until this all takes over?" she said.

At the airport bar, I recognized Sarah, the woman who made the Holocaust clones. I suspected she saw me, too. But we had left the conference frame. Out in the puzzling, imprecise world, the rules were ill-defined. We kept to ourselves, sipping our beers in pretend absentmindedness, strangers side by side.

CHRISTIAN LORENTZEN

Literature Without Literature

FROM *Granta*

READERS OF books from the New York publisher Knopf will be familiar with the leaping dog that appears on their spines. In 1915, when Alfred Knopf started the firm, his wife Blanche was "crazy about borzois," and she suggested the animal as the publisher's colophon. Though the logo lingers more than a century on, Blanche's enthusiasm for the breed was brief. "I bought a couple of them later," she told *The New Yorker* writer Geoffrey T. Hellman in 1948, "and grew to despise them. They were cowardly, stupid, disloyal, and full of self-pity, and they kept running away. One died, and I gave the other to a kennel." Hellman relates the story of a weekend in the country when Joseph Hergesheimer, a Knopf bestseller and one of the most critically lauded American novelists of the second and third decades of the twentieth century, came down to breakfast on Sunday morning complaining that the "moans and whimpers of the surviving borzoi" had kept him up all night. "I bet Charles Scribner has no such goddam dog," he said. "The Knopfs exchanged glances," Hellman writes, "and Mrs Knopf went in for Yorkshire terriers."

It's an amusing anecdote and telling in a few ways. The Borzoi logo remains, and is one of the most recognizable symbols in corporate publishing. But its original meaning was erased, at least in the mind of the publisher and his wife, who as vice president, director, and part owner of Knopf, took a strong hand in bringing in new authors. An advertisement from the 1920s reads: "Take home a Borzoi Book and spend a pleasant evening . . . It is obvious by their nature that books can never be uniform in quality of contents. But they must conform to certain well-defined standards of excellence to achieve the imprint of BORZOI . . . Look for the Borzoi label and then buy the book!" Marketing of this kind has long been out of style. The image of the borzoi was immediately vestigial, and so, forty years after Alfred's death, is the name Knopf itself.

Blanche's line about her pets—"They were cowardly, stupid, disloyal, and full of self-pity, and they kept running away"—you can imagine publishers saying it of authors or authors saying it of publishers. I have heard versions from both sides, though mostly from authors. The metaphor of the story, surely not lost on Hellman, is the irritation caused to the talent by the living representatives of management. The talent jokes about leaving for other management. It's a chummy arrangement, an author weekending with his publishers in the country, but they're still all actors in a marketplace.

Then there is the presence of Joseph Hergesheimer. I thought that I'd never heard his name until a couple of years ago when I first read Hellman's profile of Alfred, but he is mentioned a few times by Alfred Kazin in *On Native Grounds.* Like the culture at large, I forgot about Hergesheimer. Kazin groups him among the "Exquisites" championed by H. L. Mencken and George Jean Nathan after the First World War, along with James Branch Cabell, Thomas Beer, and Elinor Wylie. "The vogue of the new decadence was to seem shabby and vain soon enough," Kazin writes, "but it is easy to see now that it had its origin as a protest against the narrowness and poverty of even the most ambitious writing of the day." In place of "the evangelical note that had crept into pre-war modernism" and "grubby provincialism and romanticism"—think of Jack London and Theodore Dreiser— the Exquisites delivered glossy prose styles and glorified wealth as aristocratic amateurs. Kazin writes that Hergesheimer, "the slavish celebrant of the new rich, intoxicated" the public "with endless visions of silver and brocade, introduced them to the very best people, and tittered verbosely on a veritable Cook's tour of colonial America, nineteenth-century Cuba, and the feudal South."

Hergesheimer's third book, *The Three Black Pennys*, was the first original American novel that Knopf, whose initial specialty was bringing out translations of European works of modernism, published, in 1917. Into the 1920s, he was their bestseller, until his fortunes waned with the rest of the Exquisites. During the Depression, encomia to industrialists and contempt for the canaille were less in demand, and the style of the day turned in the direction of Hemingway. (Kazin remarks that Hergesheimer and Wylie inverted Hemingway's aphorism, "Prose is architecture, not interior decoration.") Clifton Fadiman later remarked that Hergesheimer's novels were "deficient in mere brainpower," but in 1962, when asked which American novels he cherished, Samuel Beckett said: "One of the best I ever read was Hergesheimer's *Java Head*." Hergesheimer published his last book of fiction in 1934.

In the autumn of 1948, H. L. Mencken visited Hergesheimer at his home in Stone Harbor, New Jersey, between Atlantic City and Cape May. He found his friend drinking mug after mug of beer, suffering from an eye infection, and full of complaints about Knopf, which had let his books go out of print. "In theory, he has been at work on his autobiography, but in fact he has done nothing," Mencken wrote in his diary. "He has written nothing fit to print in more than ten years. It is a dreadful finish indeed." Hergesheimer died in 1954, and was buried on the South Jersey Shore. A friend of mine who hails from nearby and read a couple of Hergesheimer's novels after coming across his name in one of Mencken's books assures me that there's a plaque by the beach, on a pleasant street with an ice-cream parlor and a mini-golf course, that bears the name of Hergesheimer. Such is the nature of most American literary immortality.

We could say that Knopf abandoned Hergesheimer or that history left him behind, that he failed to change with the times, or that the success, including eight film adaptations, that followed years of toil in obscurity in Pittsburgh, robbed him of the hunger that is crucial to an artist. We could, like Kazin, look at him dialectically, as a casualty in an unforgiving turn in the saga of American literary style. Certainly a glance at a few chapters of *Java Head* leaves the impression of a prose that Hemingway was born to demolish. Kazin's quip about interior decoration holds: the novel opens with an eleven-year-old looking at all the fancy chairs in her family's house. (There is some charm to the passage: it is the girl's birthday and whereas all the different chairs enchanted her the night before—she sees one as a dragon, others as deacons and dwarfs—now as a big girl she sees them just as someplace to sit: omens of her author's fall from grace.) But Hergesheimer's story as we would tell it today is a story of the market.

Among publishers, editors, scholars, critics, and even writers themselves, the stories we tell about literature are more and more stories of the economy of prestige, of one generation's preferences righteously overturning those of its predecessors. Inside the academy, professors attribute great power to the publishing industry and to creative-writing programs. The syllabi of university courses in literature are yielded to student preferences, redefining the objects of literary study as matters of consumer choice rather than recognizable aesthetic criteria. Outside the academy, critics begin to stake their worth on the size and devotion of their audiences. And in the journalistic sphere, two opposing modes have emerged: that of therapeutic literary careerism, on the one hand, as writers make public confessions about their struggles to survive in comfort as authors; and that of accusatory literary consumerism, on the other, as critics express dissatisfaction not with books themselves but with the ways books are marketed, usually to somebody else, somebody they don't like very much, such as a stepparent or a person they kissed a few too many times and would rather forget.

These warped views of literature reflect a shared tendency to explain art with minimal reference to the art itself. Novels are instead considered as commodities and demographic specimens, the products of structures, systems, and historical forces. They become expressions of brands, their authors threadbare entrepreneurs. Fiction recedes behind the chatter it generates and is judged according not to its intrinsic qualities but to the sort of reader whose existence it implies. Authors are turned into role models and style icons, mythologized for their virtues, and crucified for their sins. The numbers, as if they have meaning, are counted. The dream is of literature that can be quantified rather than read.

One critic who has made a stalwart case for reading literature sociologically is the Stanford professor Mark McGurl. Across three books he has charted a descending and demystifying course across the brows, from high to middle to low, and from pre-war modernism to post-war boom to the digital present, from salon to AWP Conference to algorithm. In his first book, *The Novel Art: Elevations of American Fiction after Henry James* (2001), he recast novel writing, on the one hand, as a matter of "product differentiation," appealing to "status-conscious" readers that, on the other hand, resisted the crudities of mass production and offered at least the illusion of aesthetic resistance. His most recent book, *Everything and Less: The Novel in the Age of Amazon* (2021), largely examined mass-market, often self-published genre fiction, from traditional romance and adventure to diaper-inflected fetish porn, with readings that exposed the books' plots as allegories for Amazon itself, fictional erotic partners performing customer service or other exploitative labor for each other, also an allegory for reader-author relations, of course. For all its cleverness, *Everything and Less* faced two disadvantages: the readers of these genre-fiction books don't read literary criticism, and the readers of literary criticism don't care about these books.

In between came McGurl's 2009 study *The Program Era: Post-war Fiction and the Rise of Creative Writing*. It ends with an ode to the "unprecedented" "systematic excellence" of the fiction produced under the regime of university creative-writing programs: all the new graduate students being taught the craft of fiction writing led to "a system-wide rise in the excellence of American literature in the post-war period." A side effect of all this excellence has been an overproduction of creative-writing students from America's more than 350 graduate writing programs, who are statistically more likely to become holders of day jobs than published authors (or writing professors) but also constitute an audience for the ever-burgeoning genre on how to make it (or not) as a writer.

Against "tedious prejudices" such as the "conservative modernism of T. S. Eliot and his ilk" that "has ingrained in us the notion that art never improves," McGurl arrives at his conclusion of excellence by an insouciant method: "to crudely convert historical materialism into a mode of aesthetic judgment, putting literary production in line with other human enterprises, such as technology and sports, where few would deny that systematic investments of capital over time have produced a continual elevation of performance." Crude indeed, in that having only one pair of eyes, each of us tends to read one book at a time and to make particular aesthetic judgments rather than judgments of scale. A golden age of abundance: whether or not art has improved, there is more of it.

McGurl writes that "there is no way for a literary scholar, these days, to engage in strenuous aesthetic appreciation without sounding goofily anachronistic." What he means can be grasped in John Guillory's *Professing Criticism*. Taking the long view, Guillory tells the story of the emergence of literary criticism as a discipline embedded in the university after a long history of competing practices dating back to the eighteenth century and before: philology, belles-lettres, and scholarly literary history. He presents a picture of a discipline that was consolidated on campuses in the middle of the twentieth century on a par with the sciences at the cost of giving up its public role in the shaping of society, a task literary critics had long assumed as an adjunct to their popular expressions of judgment and taste.

Recent decades have seen the discipline enter a crisis on multiple fronts: overproduction of qualified doctoral students for too few jobs, resulting in a semi-autonomous professional sphere of underemployed would-be professors; dwindling enrollment of undergraduates in literary studies; pressure from those students who do enroll to see curricula shaped according to their preferences for diversity and relatability, leading to a shift toward works written after the Second World War and an erosion of attention to the past; and within scholarly production an emphasis on methodology over interpretation, which long ago surpassed judgment as the academic literary critic's main task. Guillory predicts a split in the English major along two tracks: a retrospective program treating works from the age of modernism and before, akin in its historical outlook to the study of the classics; and a track focused on the contemporary, satisfying students' current desires. He has described a situation where the "subfields" of literary study "dominate over the fields" (traditionally historical periods and the broad genres of poetry and fiction), and called for a "recentering of literature" in academic literary study.

It is strange to hear of a subject needing to be restored to the discipline that claims to study it. But it's characteristic of an age when literary discourse is in flight from the literary, in favor of the personal, the political, or, more often, the consumerist and careerist, in favor of thinking about systems instead of individuals, which is to say writers. At the conjuncture of these tendencies is another set of institutions perpetually said to be in crisis—because of the public's failure to read enough books; because of questionable business decisions; because of the threat of new technologies to books themselves; or simply because of the rising costs of paper—that is, the publishing industry.

Petri dish of digital commerce, zone of many a reader's most sentimental memories of shopping, scapegoat for the grievances of unloved and under-compensated authors: the book business has never lacked for eager explainers ready to unspool its secret workings to the public. With latent writers at every level from corner office to cash register, the investigations of an outsider would seem superfluous. But the turn to political economy in the academy and the intellectual press after the financial crisis of 2007–8 created a sense that every sector of society was in need of materialist analysis: surely publishing would not be exempt. Adopting something like the combined sociological and literary approach McGurl and Guillory have applied to creative-writing programs and English departments, Dan Sinykin, a professor at Emory University, arrived last autumn to teach us what it means, as he told an interviewer, for "books to be recognized for what they are: industrial products."

Sinykin's book *Big Fiction: How Conglomeration Changed the Publishing Industry and American Literature* is a thorough and occasionally diverting history of recent trends in book packaging, marketing, and sales. Around 1960, when the consolidation of the independent publishers in New York began through a series of mergers and acquisitions that continue to this day, commercial and literary fiction were sold in mass-market paperback editions that you could purchase at a pharmacy, a gas station, or anywhere with a wire book rack. By the 1970s, blockbuster genre writers like Danielle Steel and Stephen King started to command big advances for hardcover and paperback editions of their prolifically released novels. Publishers adopted a series model for fantasy and science-fiction books that were big sellers at mall chain stores. Literary fiction was sold in trade paperback editions, with less trashy cover designs, to appeal to pretentious readers who liked to get a latte on their trip to Barnes & Noble or Borders. Over the last few decades, independent and nonprofit publishers were founded and staked their identities in opposition to the Big Five, championing marginalized voices, poetry, and, occasionally, difficult (or not obviously marketable) writing.

Students of old-time publicity strategies, obsolete retail models, and fundraising from the government, the Ford Foundation, and miscellaneous charitable entities and persons will find much fascinating material in these pages. There's ample trivia about publishing poobahs whose names you've never heard and will soon enough forget. They wrote catalog copy, filled out profit-and-loss forms, paid out advances, and even at times, if less and less over the years of corporate consolidation, selected books for publication based on their own personal taste. Certain numbers of them invented the transcontinental book tour (Charles Dickens would beg to differ); others set off revolutions in the field of paperback trim size. They were trailblazers of novel marketing categories that found expression on chainstore bookshelves, now largely shuttered. Above all, they ate expensive lunches they didn't pay for themselves.

Sinykin's larger claim about American literature—that conglomeration changed it in a meaningful way—is founded on a category error. Whereas creative-writing programs and the MFA system generally can reasonably be thought of as a site of literary production—places where novels are written and environments that in some ways shape the books written in their confines—the publishing industry is in fact the first stage of literary consumption. Unlike, say, the series of *Star Trek* novels published by Pocket Books in the 1980s and '90s, literary books are not the brainchild of publishing houses. Agents typically represent clients who have already written their manuscripts and editors purchase the rights to publish those manuscripts, a process that involves putting covers on the books, sending advance copies to reviewers, advertising campaigns, and so on (the hypnotic effects of TikTok being the current industry obsession). The work that agents and editors do on literary novels is more akin to tree trimming than tree planting.

Sinykin is aware enough of these realities that he hedges the claims of his theory of "conglomerate authorship" behind a series of trite and familiar ideas: that writers "internalize" the demands of acquiring editors; that the "authorship" we typically attribute to individual writers is but a mask for a process diffused among the "conglomerate superorganism." "Myriad figures introduced or empowered by conglomeration," he writes, "exercise influence on each stage of a book's life, from conception to its acquisition and editing to publicity: subsidiary rights specialists, art directors, marketing managers, sales staff, wholesalers, chain book buyers, philanthropists, government bureaucrats . . . Each working interdependently with the others produces conglomerate authorship." So the idea of "conglomerate authorship" equals the book plus its marketing apparatus. But who could possibly care about the last part of that equation besides someone professionally engaged in the marketing of books?

Sinykin proposes a new method of reading, according to the publisher's colophon:

> To read a book through its colophon is to read it anew. Aesthetics double as strategy. Author and publishing house might be—often are—in tension, a tension that plays out between a book's lines. The game a book plays is significantly different depending on whether its colophon is Bantam's rooster, Doubleday's anchor,

Graywolf's wolves, or W.W. Norton's seagull, for reasons this book unfurls. I linger over books in these pages, reading them through the colophon's portal, in light of the conglomerate era. I show how much we miss when we fall for the romance of individual genius. In novels, the conglomerate era finds its voice.

The cynicism of this notion is impressive, if also disgusting. To reduce aesthetics to the results of sales strategy is to equate the pleasure we take in reading to being duped by a marketing campaign. Falling "for the romance of individual genius," in Sinykin's schema, is akin to thinking there's something special in the soda aisle when you see the Sprite insignia but fail to comprehend that it's just another product of the Coca-Cola Bottling Company.

Big Fiction resembles a systems novel in which the heroes find themselves navigating situations the scope of which they can't comprehend. In Don DeLillo's *Underworld,* Nick Shay and other characters are only flickeringly aware of the way the dynamics of the Cold War and its aftermath shape their lives; a late scene sees Shay—by the 1990s a waste-management executive with an international portfolio—visiting a clinic for survivors of the mutating effects of experimental nuclear blasts set off near their native villages in Kazakhstan and noticing that the victims are wearing surplus T-shirts from a gay and lesbian festival in Hamburg, Germany, "the result of an importing ploy gone wrong," a detail that signals the evacuation of meaning under globalization. In *Big Fiction,* the hero is the reader and the children are novels on the shelf by Jonathan Franzen, Sally Rooney, Scott Turow, Jeff VanderMeer, Marilynne Robinson, and John Waters, all clothed in book jackets with the Farrar, Straus and Giroux colophon: three fish (adopted when the firm acquired Noonday Press in 1960). Are the fish meaningful? Was the goddam dog who kept Hergesheimer up all night cowardly, stupid, disloyal, and full of self-pity?

"If this book has a villain," Sinykin writes—as if a book that purports to be a work of literary criticism should have villains and the villains should turn out to be writers themselves—"it is the romantic author, the individual loosed by liberalism, the pretense to uniqueness, a mirage veiling the systemic intelligences that are responsible for more of what we read than most of us are ready to acknowledge." Those "systemic intelligences" are responsible for what we read only in the sense of manufacturing, distributing, and selling us books. Ultimately, Sinykin insults the reader's intelligence, suggesting a consumer of books in the twenty-first century who lacks awareness of the workings of publicity and marketing, doesn't understand how to read a book review, judges novels by their covers, and can only believe the hype.

As in many works of autobiographical fiction—or autofiction, as we call it these days—there is an episode of personal shame and trauma at the heart of Sinykin's book. He tells the story of his own "aesthetic education" as a reader: Tolkien, Piers Anthony's Xanth books, Fitzgerald, Hemingway, Salinger. His parents were "avid readers," and had shelves full of bestsellers and book-club picks. "That all of these," he writes, in a startling revelation, "from Conroy to Salinger, were white men reveals as much about the homogeneity of the publishing industry as it does my family's gendered and raced purchasing habits." For a time, he broke out of the gender trap, and his favorite book was Ayn Rand's *The Fountainhead*. Then, following a list of recommended reading for the AP English exam, he bought a copy of *Gravity's Rainbow*.

> No one I knew had heard of the book, so it felt like I had made a discovery. (No matter that it was in print and in stock at Barnes & Noble.) It became my talisman . . . Carrying the book made me feel unique, and reading it made me feel smarter than everyone else, but it was more than that. The language was exhilarating, the sensibility hilarious, the politics strange and enchanting. *Gravity's Rainbow* gave me everything I needed to become, years later, an English professor: a talismanic object, with its teal spine and blueprint design, later to be held together with a strip of duct tape; a lesson

in how to distinguish myself from others based on my taste; a fondness for liberatory politics; and a love of challenging prose, lush language.

But the fun could not last:

> It would be many more years before I learned to narrate my aesthetic education not as a triumphant journey of self-discovery but as a slightly embarrassing cliché: my pretension to uniqueness, through Pynchon in particular, was repeated by cocky young white men across the United States. I was a type and played to it. In graduate school I met iterations of myself, again and again.

How awful! It is not a stretch to understand how an individual who prided himself on being smarter than everybody else and then was embarrassed to find that fellow English-department graduate students shared his taste for the bestselling winner of the 1974 National Book Award would go on to distinguish himself from the crowd by writing (or at least putting his name on) a book (authored in truth by the Columbia University Press / Emory University English Department / Modern Language Association superorganism) that reduces aesthetics and their pleasures to market strategies and susceptibilities, that elevates the holders of placeholder jobs in the publishing world to the heights of scholarly scrutiny, and that demonizes and erases writers themselves (or at least the idea of them). It's not hard to see the "game" he's playing: academic careerism.

Along the way, Sinykin's method of reading through the colophon when he lingers on novels, typically for a page or two, leads him to some ridiculous, tedious, irrelevant, and dubious arguments, and others broad to the point of meaninglessness. "Danielle Steel is deeper than you think," he writes, bemoaning the fact that "Toni Morrison generates 3,109 hits on MLA International Bibliography, Danielle Steel six." I read forty pages of a Danielle Steel novel to check his claim, and found she was less deep than I could have imagined, her characters skinny-dipping in a shallow pool (a river, actually) of simplicity, cliché, and soft pornography. Of Morrison, he writes, "*Beloved* capitalized on the new market for horror created by the success of Stephen King," as if the book's true literary forbear were not William Faulkner, as if ghost stories were not as old as time, and as if the novel's more pertinent rivals in the cultural marketplace weren't, per Stanley Crouch, works of Holocaust literature. Sinykin picks up on a remark of Morrison's about writing *Beloved* after quitting her day job at Random House, and so—in his favored mode of reading novels—it becomes an allegory for the conditions of its production. He admits that the claim is "ludicrous" but makes it anyway.

It's also the dullest possible way to read that novel, and the same goes for his readings of E. L. Doctorow's *Ragtime* and David Foster Wallace's *Infinite Jest*, both of which treat the corporatization of American entertainment. That their lessons also apply to publishing isn't exactly a surprise, especially in the case of Doctorow, who like Morrison worked as a book editor in New York. Of Wallace and his crusade against addictive corporate entertainment, he writes: "His dream of saving America from itself was a fantasy that allowed him to complete the project but had little to do with the phenomenon that spurred decades of debates, listicles, and personal essays about the myth of genius, his bandannas and misogyny, and the cultural politics of men recommending books to women." Alas, the achievement of *Infinite Jest* has been felled by a cannonade of listicles.

Sinykin writes that after decades of modest sales, consistent critical admiration, and scant fame—following the death of his long-time editor Albert Erskine—"Cormac McCarthy fell in with an ambitious agent, editor, and publicist and transformed his style from dense prose and aimless plots to more crowd-pleasing literary Westerns." But in fact, at the time McCarthy published *All the Pretty Horses*, he told an interviewer from *The New York Times Magazine* that he had been at work on the Border Trilogy (of which *Horses* is the first volume) for a decade, since before the publication of *Blood Meridian*. His shift in style (not the first in his career, nor the last), the death of his editor, and his move to more effective management were a coincidence, not a case of cause and effect.

Along with Joan Didion, whose final novel *The Last Thing He Wanted* happened to be a thriller, McCarthy and Morrison are, in Sinykin's account, writers of "literary genre fiction," an umbrella term for books by writers with fancy prose styles that partake of forms usually associated with commercial fiction. As usual he sees this as a market strategy, not a purely aesthetic choice (no such thing) by writers who grew up in a culture saturated by film, television, comic books, and pulp fiction, many of them imported from the novel tradition before "literary fiction" was coined as a marketing category. Perennial genres now often sold as literary fiction include the social novel, the domestic novel, the comedy of manners, and so on, but Sinykin doesn't dwell much on these because they predate the era of conglomeration, and their persistence tells us little about it, other than that corporations continue to sell things they can reliably sell.

One of those things is autofiction, a term borrowed from the French that came into vogue among anglophone critics and writers of jacket copy over the past fifteen years, after the rise to prominence of Karl Ove Knausgaard, Sheila Heti, Ben Lerner, and Teju Cole. "Just because autofiction is old, though, does not mean its mode of deployment is unchanged," Sinykin writes. "That it has a new name ought to tip us off. It, for one, is another kind of genre play that makes a bid for a large readership under the current market dispensation." What genre isn't a "genre play"? Were Augustine, Margery Kempe, and James Joyce not making bids for large readerships under their market dispensations, furthering their brands? Sinykin quotes a remark of mine, from an essay in *Bookforum*, that autofiction "restores at least the illusion of autonomy in the hands of an authorial alter ego," but I wasn't talking about the publishing. I was rather drawing a contrast between characters in books of autofiction and those in systems novels. Sinykin's theory of literature is what Guillory would call a "strong theory": it is broad and reductive. When everything a writer does is a market play, nothing written is not a market play. And if everything we read is just a highly evolved marketing campaign, why read at all?

The most perverse of Sinykin's readings is of Percival Everett as an exemplary nonprofit author during the era of conglomeration. Sinykin uses a computational model of analysis he developed with another scholar to analyze the differences between a set of novels published by Random House and a set published by nonprofits. He describes their findings:

> We found that nonprofit novels tend to privilege embodiment, craft, and localism. They give more attention to what it feels like to live in a body, describing perception, sensations. They draw on the language of artistic practice and the world of craft: forms, colors, shapes, surface. They tend toward rural settings. By contrast, Random House novels tend to privilege language of law and power, bureaucracy, and dispositions. They give more attention to the results-driven world of ambition, the linguistic formalism of administration, and the manners and mores of polite correspondence.

Leaving aside the vagueness of these terms and the question of whether the model has an irony filter, I wonder what can be gained by such a method that couldn't be gained by reading the books in question, aside from time saved. Sinykin subjects Everett's novel *Frenzy* to the model and finds that it's "a borderline case, hovering in its language between the poles of conglomerates and nonprofits"—could be Random House, could be Graywolf. After this nonsensical waste of time (the model also thinks *Beloved* must have been published by a nonprofit—"By placing Black women and their embodied experience at the center of her account, she overwhelms the arid institutionalism and racist epistemology of schoolteacher, and thus of conglomeration, leading the model to recognize her novel as nonprofit"—ah yes, the iron logic of a model you made up, performing a task a human can do better than a computer—reading a book—and performing it incorrectly), Sinykin summarizes the novel, a retelling of the myth of Dionysus, and writes: "*Frenzy* is an allegory for the plight of the writer in the conglomerate era. To speak in the city is to be subject to the rationality and instrumentality of capital. To speak in the wilderness is to submit oneself to the embodiment of frenzy." The split between the Apollonian and the Dionysiac is an old one, and no doubt it applies to the divide between corporate and independent publishing. After explaining the business model of nonprofit publishers as in part relying on donors who favor multiculturalism and lists that include writers of color, Sinykin concludes of Everett:

> Close reading Percival Everett reveals a struggle—embedded in his sentences, his characters, his plots—between author and institution. Ironically, Everett, in his essays, interviews, and personal correspondence, fails to recognize that Graywolf and its fellow nonprofits operate according to a parallel racial logic as the conglomerates, one the image of the other in a funhouse mirror. He praises Graywolf as exempt because it publishes him, when, for Graywolf, he serves as a vessel for its mission of liberal multiculturalism, a prized commodity for its niche markets. Although it contradicts his stated motives, Everett's literary project could be read not to condemn markets, but to condemn those markets that propagate inauthentic and constraining racial fantasies; his novels, that is, espouse one more liberal multicultural vision.

Actually, close reading is not necessary because the struggle between artists and institutions is often Everett's explicit subject, as in *Erasure* and *So Much Blue*, to name two of his dozens of books. But poor Everett: all that writing and he turns out to be just another tokenized sellout to the nonprofits. Good thing he took his new book *James* to Doubleday for a decent paycheck.

"This book defers judgment about whether conglomeration was good or bad in an effort to explain what it has meant for US fiction and how we should read it," Sinykin writes. But if what it has meant is that aesthetics are marketing strategies and how we should read fiction is through the colophon on the book's spine, certain judgments are inevitable: that conglomerate publishing, with its reliance on comp titles in its selection of books to bring out, stifles originality by ignoring it until it has a proven track record of profitability (as in the cases of Knausgaard and Roberto Bolaño, whose books were picked up by FSG after they were hits for Archipelago and New Directions); that taste and quality count for less and less if they can't be translated into marketing terms; that even the nonprofit publishers are just checking boxes for their plutocratic donors out for a tax break and for self-perpetuating charitable foundations; that any pleasure we take from contemporary literature is at best an accident and more likely a hoax.

The editor-in-chief of an independent publishing house recently told me that she believes there are about 20,000 serious and consistent readers of literary fiction in America and publishing any novel of quality is a matter of getting that book to them by any means necessary. Another editor at an independent house, a veteran of Penguin Random House, called her current method of acquiring books "throwing shit at the wall" to see what sticks. During the trial that resulted in the government's enjoinment of the merger of PRH and Simon & Schuster, the prosecution argued that the industry proceeds by rationalized methods that can be measured and ought to be regulated while the defense likened the work of acquiring manuscripts to casino gambling. They both had a point. Sinykin is invested in a highly rationalized view of the business because it brings his own efforts closer to the realm of science than to subjective judgment—the longstanding agon of literary study in the academy. But the fact remains that new literature has become a minor and diminishing concern of the publishing industry. If corporate publishers could eliminate the risks inherent in peddling literature at all—by, say, moving to a model whereby they gobbled up the hits produced by independent presses, often called "the minor leagues" at the merger trial—they would do so. The point of the government's enjoinment of the merger was to maintain the competition between the Big Five corporate publishers, which is the only reason authors receive high or even moderate advances. Fewer and fewer of such authors are those we would deem literary; more and more are celebrities.

Corporate publishing is the channel through which literature happens to flow at this moment in history. The legal and political economic imperatives of the moment mean that the rights to backlist titles will tend to accumulate in a few hands to be exploited for as long as the copyright lasts. Most books will go out of print forever, as most deserve to. Those that last will retain trace impurities from the conglomerate system, but the presence of the corporate taint—I mean, the colophon—won't be the reason we continue to read them, nor was it the reason we read them in the first place. Year after year our culture compels people to think of and understand themselves as consumers. This dreary view of life, which advertises itself as critical or at least conscious of commerce, capitalism, and complicity, quickly becomes another form of marketing, and when applied to our reading habits it amounts to a distracting narcissism, looking in the mirror when our eyes should be on the page.

"Books serve our self-image," Sinykin writes. "The books we like say a lot about us, whether we know it or not." He is, like many in his profession, operating under the influence of the French sociologist Pierre Bourdieu, who drew upon and expanded Thorstein Veblen's ideas about conspicuous consumption and "the regime of status" and applied them across classes, especially in the realms of education and culture. I am unqualified to comment on France, but I have always been skeptical when Bourdieu's program is imported wholesale to America. In my experience, most Americans are hostile or indifferent to reading and glad to have gotten done with it in their schooldays if they did it all. They prefer the pleasures of sport, television, and various online distractions. And why not? Those things are fun and mostly painless. In an anti-intellectual country, reading books at all says more than enough about you, and you already know this because the rest of them don't let you forget it.

Bourdieu, Sinykin, and many of those he quotes view reading and writing primarily as social activities, inextricable from our relations with others. Anyone who has read a novel knows this is true and it would be pointless to deny it. One of the reasons we read literature is to experience the author's purchase on society and to see how it corresponds with our own. Literature's perennial advantage over sociology is that it can do this through the means of irony, paradox, and beauty. It is not restricted to the empirical, it is free to invent, it has recourse to fantasies that are truer than real life. It is less enamored with disclosing the obvious. The greater the novelist, the richer the picture of the world depicted within it, but also the more resistant the work becomes to being reduced to sociology. There is a reason why, when Thomas Piketty wants to add flourishes to his map of the economy in nineteenth-century France, he turns to Balzac, and why Lionel Trilling thought there was no better guide to property in Regency England than Jane Austen. But for the novelists themselves this sociological richness is a by-product of their aesthetic ambition, never the main chance.

Though reading is a social activity, the opposite is also true—something novels and their characters are always telling us. Silent solitary reading, removed from religious ritual and the scriptorium, is a recent development in human history. As Guillory points out, in the beginning, reading alone was the subject of moral panic, linked to the sin of masturbation. These suspicions of impurity, corruption, and self-indulgence remain with us today in the menace of book-banning. Like whimpering dogs, philistines will always be with us.

Pleasure is why we read literature, but the pleasures literature delivers are complex and not easily described, defined, or fixed in time and place. As Guillory writes, the pleasures of literature are often only gained at the expense of pains: the initial pain of learning to read, the pain of understanding difficult books, the pain of grasping the literary history from which books emerge, the pain of looking at something we can't yet comprehend though we know we could, the pain of examining the nature of our own pleasure. Perhaps it's these pains that turn our eyes away from the pleasures of literature to the disenchanted explanations of political economy, to the suspicions of paranoid reading, to the preening pondering about what the books we enjoy say about us rather than what they say to us.

Life is lonely, painful, and punishing. On behalf of the freelance book reviewer / London litmag office / Downtown Manhattan scene superorganism that speaks through me, I assert that reading and writing are best done in perfect solitude; that sometimes what you read and what you write should be kept a secret; that when you're by yourself popularity doesn't matter, nor does money, nor does fame, nor does status; that when you are a teenager and you have shut yourself into a room to read Kafka for the first time, your parents and your little sister should stop knocking on the door because you are turning into something else, something they will never understand.

MATTHEW DENTON-EDMUNDSON

How to Love Animals

FROM *The Missouri Review*

WE NEVER planned to get goats. In fact, we'd told ourselves that goats were off limits. My wife, Anna, and I were living in the middle of a two-hundred-acre farm in rural Virginia while she finished up graduate school. The rent was cheap. There was a river with a swimming hole. The defunct chicken coup held hundreds of laying hens back in the 1920s, but was now filled with mildewed furniture and rusty gears from a grist mill that'd been in operation before the Civil War. Driving back from town with a load of groceries one day, I spotted a sign at the local farm supply store: CHICK DAYS.

I brought home a cardboard box full of fuzzy, stumbling, week-old chicks. A few days later Anna brought home ducklings. She'd been cruising the livestock listings on Craigslist. Then came the sheep. A nearby farmer had some pretty spotted ewe lambs he offered to us for a song. He said the name of the breed was Katahdin. We liked the sound of that. You might think that sheep seem like a commitment an order of magnitude greater than chickens. They weren't, though. We released them into the overgrown pasture.

Then a friend offered us a pair of goats. No, we said. Absolutely not. For one thing: I'd once encountered a book, laying open in a coffee shop, titled *Your Goats: A Guide to Raising and Showing*. The first (prophetic) sentence was: "Don't romanticize goat ownership." Another cause for hesitation: our friend wanted no sort of compensation for the animals. "You'll be doing me a favor," she said. We were wary. But she convinced us to come meet them. There was *no* chance we would take them home, we warned her. The pair was a mother and daughter, both mahogany colored with white markings on their faces, one hearty, the other slim as a deer. You can probably guess what happened. We named them Butter and May.

The utilitarian philosopher Peter Singer argued that we owe animals moral consideration because of their capacity to feel pain. Long before the goats, when I was first learning how to love animals, I took this idea to heart. I'm not alone. Singer's work has for decades provided the default line of reasoning for people who care about the rights of nonhuman creatures. But the trials and joys of goat ownership (May and Butter were followed by many more), as well as the ideas of philosopher Elaine Scarry and biologist E. O. Wilson, helped convince me that there is another, better way to love animals. It begins with a thorough understanding of an animal's potential, both as an individual and as a member of a given species, and eventually leads us to embrace closer and more complicated ways of interacting with animals, and finally to entangling our lives with their lives.

From infancy, I refused to eat meat. This confounded my parents, who had always been omnivores. At first—the way my mom tells it—the stuff simply disagreed with my stomach. She'd try to feed me a sliver of chicken, and I'd spit it out. Gradually, though, the aversion turned into something more complicated. I came to understand that many of the things my parents regularly ate had once been animals. Thus began a child-sized crusade. I never missed an opportunity to tell adults that they were wrong to eat animals. I recall a dinner party during which I caused my parents no little embarrassment by announcing that the food on the table had only recently been alive. To their credit, though, I was never punished and never forced to eat meat. On the contrary: one afternoon, my father picked me up from middle school with a present in the front seat—a copy of Peter Singer's *Animal Liberation*. The book became my bible.

Animal Liberation makes a thoroughly reasoned case against the abysmal treatment of livestock and laboratory animals. Singer's central argument is that we should stop dwelling on the differences between ourselves and other creatures. For him, attributes like intelligence and communicative abilities have nothing to do with the moral question of our relationship with animals. Instead of drawing these arbitrary distinctions, he says, we should focus on a unifying similarity: the capacity to feel pain. Singer wants us to remember our own vested interest in avoiding sensations of pain and extend that consideration to members of other species. "All the arguments to prove man's superiority cannot shatter this hard fact," he writes. "In suffering the animals are our equals."

I wielded these arguments pompously in my middle-school classroom, where I was (with some justice) ridiculed by other kids and on several occasions by a muscular gym teacher named Mr. Brag. I once repeated to my peewee football coach one of Singer's more controversial arguments: in a few short decades, he writes, when the next generation or the next looks back on the suffering we inflict on animals in labs and on feedlots, they may view that behavior in much the same way that we now view slavery—as despicable and inexcusable, an expression of extreme cruelty and selfishness. My coach wasn't a brute, far from it, but the point didn't go over so well. A hefty number of pushups were assigned.

Despite these less-than-satisfactory outcomes, Singer's arguments were powerful for me at the time, and they remain so to this day. But there was one thing that bothered me tremendously about *Animal Liberation*—a throwaway line halfway through the introduction, in which Singer admits that he doesn't have any pets and doesn't care much for people who do. He says that keeping a pet doesn't have anything to do with believing in the rights and the welfare of animals. In fact, he suggests, the two things are maybe even antithetical.

With an absolute conviction that may be the exclusive domain of middle-school boys, I knew this was wrong. I couldn't say why exactly, but I felt sure that being around animals and caring about animals had *everything* to do with one another. I loved my pets: an iguana named Terry, Meowy the (half-feral) Maine Coon, and Pipkin, a squat and ugly (but, to my mind, darling) mutt. If it weren't for those creatures, I don't know if I'd ever have given *Animal Liberation* a second look.

Many hardcore animal rights advocates are against the breeding and keeping of pets. They believe that animals are born with the same inherent rights as human beings, including the right not to be treated as property. Therefore, they say, breeding animals that are maladapted to the wild, animals that can only survive in human custody, is unethical. They hold that we should care as best we can for those domesticated animals that are already alive, and do everything within our power to prevent the birth of even one more of these animals. Singer never goes quite this far. And yet, one can see how his arguments point this direction: in order to avoid the possibility of causing animals pain, maybe it's simply best for humans to distance ourselves from them altogether. In a recent essay, Singer quotes the writer Karen Dawn, calling pets, "slaves to [human] love."

As a child, I instinctively rejected Singer's disavowal of pet ownership. And I still believe that the position outlined above is wrongheaded (in a moment I'll try to explain why). But we'd probably do well to admit that many pets—even ones showered with love—don't always seem especially happy. A recent survey in the UK suggested that about seventy-five percent of domesticated dogs suffer moderate to severe depression. Another study found that one in four dogs, and almost as many cats, experience separation anxiety on a daily basis (usually when their owners head off to work in the morning), and that this anxiety leads to some of the most common behavioral problems. These problems, in turn, are the most common causes of pet abandonment.

How many people do you know who own a slightly neurotic dog? Sure, perhaps the animal experienced a trauma early in its life. The owners might be undertaking the difficult and admirable task of restoring the animal's faith in humanity. But many dogs I've known (dogs whose owners are genuinely fine people) don't seem so much traumatized as they do mildly discontented. The majority of dog owners say that if their dogs could talk, they would ask them to answer one question before all others: *Are you happy?* Despite everything we do to try to make our companions happy—the cuddles and high-dollar chow and the walks in the foothills—many of us are at least a bit anxious that maybe, for all that, they might not be.

Are pets slaves to our love? It seems to me that there's an uncomfortable element of truth to the thought. But maybe a better way to put it is to say that our love is sometimes misplaced. We *want* to love our pets the right way, we're just not always sure exactly how to go about doing it.

I've been as guilty as anybody of this charge—probably more so.

For a while, the goats were a joy. The popular idea that goats are smelly and eat trash is unfounded slander. Healthy does (female goats) smell pretty good, and they're immensely picky eaters (this may be the origin of the word *capricious*, which comes from the Latin *capra*, meaning goat). In the mornings, before heading off to work, we milked Butter and May into a pail. Sometimes we brought out our mugs of coffee out and added a few squirts of froth right from the udder. When Butter kicked over the milk bucket with a precise jab of her back hoof, we didn't sweat it too much. There'd be more tomorrow. We made chevre and spread it over tomatoes plucked from the vine. We invited our friends over to pet and admire the animals. We started buying an expensive brand of fermented alfalfa hay that comes in a plastic bag. We ordered, from a boutique company in Ireland, nice-sounding bells for the animals' collars. Pictures of the goats figured daily on an Instagram account.

Then, one morning, I came out to the barn and found that the goats were not where they usually waited to be fed and milked. Standing in the doorway, with the chickens still clucking to be let out, I spotted a tan shape lying in the grass. I'll spare you the description of the bodies I found there—two sheep and one goat scattered across the pasture. Whatever had killed them hadn't been much interested in the meat. It had wanted the animals' milk and gotten to it by the most expeditious and brutal method. May had been my favorite, the younger and more emotional of the two goats. I'd learned to distinguish her bleat from across the property by its distinct plaintive double note. Now here she was, splayed and bloody.

By noon there were several neighbors helping us look for Butter, who was nowhere to be found. One or two were cattlemen, longtime farmers who'd seen more than a few calves lost to coyotes. They were a bit perplexed by the way the animals had been killed. Coyotes usually eat at least part of their kill. And they're not known as milk lovers. After hours searching the property, we at last found Butter hidden in a thicket a quarter of a mile away, alive and by all appearances unscathed. We took her back to the barn, fed her, and closed her inside. The book in that coffee shop had warned me: don't romanticize goat ownership. But I had, and the animals had paid the price.

The culprit of the killings returned later that night. I caught him in the beam of my flashlight sniffing around the outside the stall where Butter was now staying. A large adolescent black bear. I'd later learn that it's uncommon for bears to attack livestock. But it happens sometimes when young males are pushed out of their territory by hunters. In Craig County, Virginia, late summer is when hunters run their dogs through the National Forest, tracking bears for practice before the start of the real season in November. Running dogs is legal but extremely disruptive to the bears, who get "treed" by the dogs (that is, chased until they climb to the top of a tree) over and over until they're forced out of the wilderness into more populated areas. These stressed, hungry bears are much more likely to attack livestock.

I bought an airhorn and tried to scare the intruder away. He came back night after night. Butter, meanwhile, was depressed and frightened. She stopped kicking the milk pail. She ate very little. Before May's death, she used to turn her head to look me right in the eye when I spoke to her. Now, I might as well have been a ghost.

A few months before the bear made his unwelcome visit, I'd heard an interview on NPR's *Science Friday* with someone called the Ant Man. At the start of the interview, Ira Flatow asked this question: "What should we do about those dang ants in our kitchen?" The Ant Man's response: Watch your step and consider feeding them a dab of whipped cream.

The Ant Man turned out to be E. O. Wilson, a prominent biologist and a prolific and eccentric writer. I had to confess, I'd wiped an ant or fifty off my counter with a wet sponge (the traps have always freaked me out a bit). Still, I was sufficiently intrigued by the interview to order one of his books. The oddness of the title attracted my attention: *Biophilia*. The book—alongside the joys and tribulations of goat ownership—would soon begin to change the way I went about loving animals.

Already, I'd gradually become dissatisfied with Singer's model: the idea that the shared capacity for suffering sets the moral ground for the best treatment of our fellow creatures. For one thing, I'd discovered that many people don't find his argument as powerful as I had as a child. It's true that vegetarian menus have become more common than ever before. And it's true that in many parts of the world, animal welfare laws have improved significantly. But we still raise millions of pigs snout-to-tail in feed lots and test industrial chemicals in the eyes of hundreds of thousands of rats and rabbits. It would be difficult to argue that anything like the revolution Singer predicted in *Animal Liberation* has come to fruition.

I'd also seen that many of us have complex responses to other beings' suffering. Working fourteen-hour shifts at a slaughterhouse in rural Texas (researching a book I hoped to write), I found that most of the employees there did not reject the idea that the animals they killed on a daily basis could feel pain. On the contrary, they were quite willing to admit that ducks and chickens are at least *almost* our equals in suffering. The abattoirs' justifications for their line of work ran in other directions: Pain is a necessary part of life, they said. Or simply: we all gotta eat. I was troubled by these conversations. They didn't quite square with Singer's idea that by acknowledging a shared capacity for suffering we stand to change the way we think about animals.

It wasn't until after the bear attack, though, that I was sure I needed a new approach. I knew that Butter was grieving for May, that she was experiencing significant emotional pain. She ate less enthusiastically. She spent more time than ever in the corner of her stall. When I squatted down and tried to look her in the eye, she looked past me, as if for something that wasn't there. My heart went out to her—of course it went out to her. And, yet, as days turned into weeks, I also felt further away from her than I ever had before. The qualities that had made Butter herself (her sassiness on the milk stand, her waddling swagger as she led the other animals out into the pasture, and a hundred other peculiarities) had vanished. Despite my sympathy for her suffering, and my sincere hope that she'd soon recover, I no longer felt I knew her all that well. The connection we'd once shared had been deeply altered by the bear attack. Shame of shames, I began to dread going out to the barn to tend to her.

At the time, I felt more than a little guilty about my ambivalence. But, in retrospect, I don't think my feelings were all that unusual. The philosopher Elaine Scarry argues in her book *The Body in Pain* that our response to other *people's* pain is complex. "For the person whose pain it is," she writes, "it is 'effortlessly' grasped (that is, even with the most heroic effort it cannot *not* be grasped); while for the person outside the sufferer's body, what is 'effortless' is *not* grasping it." This dynamic, she argues, works to create a sense of alienation between those in pain and those witnessing (or inflicting) the pain.

Scarry goes on to say that pain not only distances sufferers from those around them, it also distances sufferers from themselves. That is, when people are in severe pain, they become less like themselves. Our preferences and peculiarities, habits of speech and gesture, even our most deeply held beliefs are likely to be forgotten in the face of suffering. Scarry doesn't have much to say about animals, but I felt that, at least to some degree, I was seeing this dynamic at work in my relationship with our surviving goat. Butter was less than herself, and despite my best intentions, I'd grown less attached to her.

For a long time, I'd held onto Singer as a guiding force in my life. Now, I felt I'd been at least partly mistaken to do so. His philosophy might help us redesign animal welfare laws to spare livestock needless suffering, and already is in some nations, to good effect. But I'd been wrong to try to use him as a means of *connecting* more deeply with animals. By focusing too much on animal suffering, we risk coming up against the limits of human sympathy. If there's going to be any kind of revolution in our relationship with other species—not just domesticated animals, but wild ones, too—it will instead, I've come to believe, arise from excitement about who they are, what they can do, and what they have to teach us.

Butter did stop grieving, and much sooner than I had feared. Other goat farmers in the area gave us a key piece of information. They said there was only one way to lift her spirits—she needed a herd. It turns out that people who know goats consider it an act of cruelty to keep just one as a pet. Two is barely acceptable. Six is much better. And so, we adopted a squat, sickly goat named Chaga; a strong, stubborn doe we called Basket (after Gertrude Stein's many poodles, all Baskets), and an Alpine goat, Eggs. We borrowed a friend's buck—Cato the Strong—and bred the three healthy does. It wasn't long before we were the owners of sixteen goats.

We also got a dog, a breed of livestock guardian called a Great Pyrenees. We called her Mayday after the fallen goat (and with the hope that she'd sound the alarm against marauding bears). It was fascinating to watch the goats and the dog figure each other out. Butter sniffed the dog's head and then, for the first time in weeks, looked up at me, with her strange, oblong pupils. Studies have found that when presented with a puzzle box, containing a treat, that they're unable to open, goats are the only animal besides domesticated dogs that will turn to a human being and look them in the eye. Researchers speculate that they're requesting help getting the box open. Presented with the pup, Butter seemed to be doing something similar—asking me, *What the hell is this?*

One of E. O. Wilson's enduring fascinations was the way different kinds of creatures work to figure one another out. *Biophilia*, his most provocative book, is based in his deep conviction that human beings (and other creatures, too) are hardwired for curiosity about other forms of life.

The biophilia instinct, he argues, is a gainful adaptation in keeping with Darwin. He describes the process of specialization of species, whereby competing organisms evolve strategies to foil aggressors and invite collaborators. During this slow-motion melee, each species comes to occupy a certain ecological niche, which shifts ever so slightly over time in response to the advancing tactics of aggressors and the fluctuating needs of allies. Wilson says that because humans evolved within a rich array of species diversity, we developed instincts for gauging and testing the perimeters of our place within the ecosystem. Biophilia proved advantageous because it allowed our progenitors to maintain their position in an ever-changing, unpredictable environment. In other words, an accurate knowledge of the other organisms in one's vicinity is a competitive edge. We *need* to keep tabs on competitors and reaffirm our bonds with partners. And for this reason, the instinct to understand and interact with plants and animals and fungi is not a romantic whim but a deeply seeded element of human psychology.

You might be wondering: what does any of this have to do with how we might go about loving animals?

Wilson says that the more we learn about any species (especially those we come into contact with regularly) the more we'll scratch the evolutionary itch that is biophilia. The better we understand, the more *meaningfully* sympathetic we'll become to other forms of life. He studied animals, especially ants, at their *best*, witnessing them displaying complexities of behavior beyond anything he'd imagined. Far from demystifying his object of study, Wilson found that with each discovery his love for ants only increased.

It's a deceptively simple conclusion: the first step in loving animals is to understand them as thoroughly as possible.

Even with the bear gone, owning goats was no cakewalk. Eggs the Alpine got a rare spinal parasite called Meningeal worm, more ominously known as brainworm, which lives inside the poop of whitetail deer and crawls out onto damp grass blades in the early fall. She almost completely lost the use of her rear legs, and needed thrice daily injections of ivermectin and over 40 cc daily (i.e., a *lot*) of a rather expensive dewormer called fenbendazole. Despite a poor prognosis, Eggs eventually made a full recovery. While she was convalescing, Butter escaped the pasture and ate down our neighbor's marijuana plants. (Did she blast off? You'll have to ask her.) Mayday, normally very easy to work with, proved impossible to transport to the vet for her annual shots: she drooled puddles and barked and cowered.

What does it mean to "understand" an animal à la Wilson? As Anna and I tried to become better goatherds, I'd begun asking myself this question. There are, of course, many practical things one learns about any animal when interacting with them on a daily basis. For example, goats, like many domesticated animals, are creatures of habit, who become distressed if milking happens even a few minutes later than the norm or when a snowstorm keeps them in the barn for the day. Another example: goats have a sixth sense for when you've got a copper bolus or a syringe of dewormer hidden in your pocket, and then good luck catching them.

This practical level of understanding becomes quite useful when it's combined with a basic knowledge of the animal's biology. Apparently, goats can smell almost as well as dogs. (Sealing that dewormer syringe into a plastic baggie helps hide it.) And we'd already helped Butter simply because we'd been reminded of a key fact about goats: they're herd animals. Soon after May's death, I managed to get ahold of the bible of farm animal information through an interlibrary loan—*Mason's World Encyclopedia of Livestock Breeds and Breeding*, which consists of two thick volumes.

From *Mason's* we learned that the progenitor of the domesticated goat, the bezoar (*Capra aegagrus*), were browsers and not (as sheep are) grazers. They prefer to consume the foliage of shrubs and small trees rather than grass. Geneticists believe that goats' curiosity and intelligence may come partly from the fact that, living in varied mountain ecosystems, they had to sample small amounts of many different kinds of plants on a daily basis and then remember which ones were safe. In this sense, their varied diets are an element not just of their bodily health, but also a means of exercising and expressing their intellectual capabilities. Anna and I fenced in a large area overgrown with Virginia creeper, autumn olive, black haw, and honeysuckle. The goats never touched orchard grass again. They seemed happier, and we were happier too, watching them explore and sample.

These facts, and dozens of others, were useful for the day-to-day of goat ownership. They helped us create a space for the animals in which they could come closer to fulfilling their potential as animals, where they could be more *themselves*. As I studied up on goats and observed them on a daily basis, I found that my affection for them only increased. The experience helped convince me that human beings, witnessing *any* animal at their best, can only form a deeper appreciation for that species.

There was still something missing, though. Understanding, in Wilson's mode, felt like an important part of affection. A deeper knowledge of my animals gave me the tools to make them happier, and to make myself happier in the process. But the biophilia theory didn't completely explain the way I felt about my ruminants. It wasn't quite a model for *love*.

Reading *Mason's Encyclopedia*, I was struck by something besides all the wonderfully useful information. The book documents the extent to which human life and culture was, for thousands of years, deeply *intertwined* with the lives and (dare I say) culture of animals. "Goats are able to produce all that humans could need," Valerie Porter begins her eighty-page entry on goats. "Meat, milk, hair, pelts, leather, dung for fertilizer and fuel, muscle power as small draught or pack animals, units of exchange and symbols of wealth, subjects for ceremonial sacrifice, and mythological characters."

In one sentence, Porter manages to create a kind of condensed history of humanity, from the pursuit of dependable sustenance and warmth to the advent of money, religion, and the impulse to create art. And *all* of that was tangled up in the existence of *Capra aegagrus*. I reflected on the deep satisfaction I felt around my goats, and wondered if it had something to do with reclaiming a corner of this ancient and essential relationship.

Anna and I began to immerse ourselves in what we called, half-jokingly, "the animal life." We stopped romanticizing goat ownership and started trying to do it right. We hung up the old milk pail and got a milking machine. There'd been something undeniably old-timey and romantic about the pail. But the machine mimicked the rhythmic sucking of a baby goat (as opposed to the pinching and squeezing of hand milking), and the goats seemed to greatly prefer it. Our schedules revolved around the animals, milking in the morning and evening, separating the kids into their own stall at night, administering copper boluses to reduce barber pole worm, assembling concoctions of slippery elm bark and raspberry leaf for the pregnant does.

We learned to identify the signs of an ailing animal—first by looking for pale inner eyelids or a slight split in the shape of the fur lining the end of the tail, and then almost intuitively, by anticipating problems based on the smallest behavioral changes. Come weekends, we'd often follow the goats on their daily rounds through the overgrown pastures, and up through the cedar forest to the edge of their twenty-acre enclosure. They made the same loop each day, with minor variations, Mayday following along at a respectful distance, keeping us all safe.

Dogs, goats, and humans have shaped one another's behavior and development for thousands of years. Some geneticists have started arguing the case for "co-evolution," the idea that as wolves began to adapt to life with humans, humans learned new hunting skills and social cooperation strategies from wolves. Goats, too, effected, if not human evolution, then the development of a new mode of existence for humans. We claim to have tamed goats. And yet their ways of life (less nomadic than that of Mesolithic humans, more settled and habitual, and yes, more ruminative) in many respects became the new dominant mode of *our* lives during the Neolithic Revolution, as we began living side-by-side with them, often sharing the same dwellings, feeding them and protecting them from predators. The ancient history of humans is so complexly intertwined with that of domesticated animals that it's impossible to tell one story without telling the other.

But sometime around the sixth century BCE, certain groups of people began prying themselves away from the animal life. The walls of growing city states kept animals away from ruling class homes, government structures, and temples, except during times of sacrifice. Artists began focusing on human facial structure, more rarely blending our form with animal characteristics. Philosophers worked to establish the essential differences between man and beast. This was the age of Apollo, whose human figure was sharply defined, who lived high above the chaotic, clamorous earth with its uncivilized, unrefined creatures. Apollo was a model of humanity, self-made, proud of his equanimity, strength, and intellect. He celebrated the so-called civilized arts. It was during this era that the kernel of Peter Singer's thesis was first articulated. In the third century BCE, Theophrastus wrote that men and animals "do not differ, above all in sensation."

Today, we tend to interact with animals in the Apollonian mode. We take pride in our dogs' obedience, we eliminate their sex drive, we "housebreak" them, we dock their tails, we breed them for hypoallergenic fur, we extol their reason and intelligence. We do everything in our power to adapt them to life in human civilization. In the last few decades, we've begun treating them more and more like our own children. The result is that, in many superficial ways, they've become more and more human. But never have humans been less doglike.

Loving animals (*really* loving them), I think, means first understanding them more thoroughly, and then working to shed a few of our Apollonian habits, recapturing bits and pieces of the animal life. That is, a more complex, *entangled* relationship with animals, one in which we allow them to alter us almost as much as we alter them.

Of course, not everyone can (or wants to) adopt a ragtag herd of goats. So how might the majority of us go about carving out a corner of the animal life?

One answer is that many of us are already taking the first step, deepening our understanding of animals (especially wild animals) in Wilson's mode. The popularity of shows like *Chimp Empire*, which follows a conflict between two groups of chimps in the Ngogo Rainforest, suggests that we're interested in an unromanticized view of the lives and struggles of our closest animal relative. And a number of recent bestselling books have given in-depth looks at the hitherto-unheralded abilities of animals: David M. Peña-Guzmán's book on animal dreaming comes to mind, as does Jennifer Ackerman's *What an Owl Knows*, which includes a fascinating section about the way certain sounds activate the visual cortex of owls, dilating their pupils for more effective hunting. It seems clear that many of us are itching to more deeply understand—and thus more deeply value—all kinds of wild animals. As habitat destruction and climate change loom, this impulse is more important than ever.

It seems to me, though, that there's still much to be gained by tying our lives more closely and complexly to the lives of animals, especially our domesticated animals. If we believe the studies, many of our pets are probably depressed. Dogs were selectively bred for hundreds (and sometimes thousands) of years to be active and useful. Now they sit around all day waiting for us to get home from work (a recent video study showed that whining, barking, pacing, and sleeping were the most common activities for dogs left home by themselves). We admire how well dogs adopt our ways of thinking and behaving, but rarely are *we* trying to engage their skillsets, or learn much of anything from *them*. Dogs are our best friends. Are we theirs?

But wonderful models for entanglement are everywhere—people allowing animals to help shape their lives and imaginations. Backyard chickens are maybe the most ubiquitous example. One could spend years browsing all the online information about coop designs, hawk protection, and procedures for relieving an impacted crop (one involves iodine and a razor blade, ask me how I know). Even the most polished chicken keepers find themselves adapting to the habits and needs of their animals.

Better yet: one of my wife's coworkers adopts injured Chihuahuas and abandoned parrots from around the country. The parrots live in an enormous enclosure that dominates the inside of their home. The dogs wander in and out in a ragtag pack, receiving intermittent medical attention for their many ailments. It's difficult to say whose house it is more, the peoples' or the animals'.

Another instance of human-animal entanglement can be found in the work of a few contemporary artists, who are reaching back to pre-Apollonian times for inspiration, blending animal and human forms. Wangechi Mutu's "A Fantastic Journey" in the Brooklyn Museum comes to mind: a goatish human figure with jellyfish feet ascends a mountain, driven upward by ambiguous shapes resembling headless adolescent geese.

An old teacher of mine, Richard Dillard, captured his own corner of the animal life when, after observing a blond-nosed groundhog on his property, he allowed his yard to return to meadow so that she could enjoy an improved habitat (of course, this outraged his neighbors to no end). When Dillard found out that the foundation of his house was falling apart, he went to heroic lengths to ensure that Blondie's burrow would be protected during the construction to shore up the structure.

There's a man-mule team in Boise, Idaho, that travels the foothills trail system selling coffee to hikers, bikers, equestrians, and dog-walkers. Richard (the mule) seems to enjoy the work and attention. Matty, Richard's human partner, said in an interview that when he first found Richard on Craigslist he had little idea how to train or keep a mule, but that Richard eventually shaped *him* into the kind of person a mule needs, even as he trained Richard to the ins-and-outs of the "Café Mulé" vending life. Despite the remote locations of the coffee stand, there are always dozens (and sometimes hundreds) of people in line to get a drink. They're drawn, I believe, partly by interest in the powerful bond between man and mule.

Anna and I lived with the goats and dog (as well as our sheep, ducks, chickens, rabbits, and geese) for just over five years. Our lives revolved around the animals', and the animals' around ours. Then, abruptly, that way of life came to an end. Our landlord gave us notice. He planned to convert our house into a complex of Airbnb apartments, believing (probably rightly) that people from Charlottesville and DC would pay good money to spend a few days at a place with—as the listing later described it—"rustic atmosphere." A friend agreed to take the animals to her farm, where they continued to thrive. Anna and I considered remaining in the area, but it's difficult to find steady work in rural Virginia, and cheap land like we'd had in those years isn't easy to come by either. Anna was offered a great job in Boise. We made the difficult decision to accept. It turns out that real estate in Boise has gotten so expensive that it's difficult to find a house with enough space for even backyard chickens, much less a herd of goats.

One of the most convincing arguments for the power of the "animal life" is the awful feeling of leaving the creatures that have defined your daily routine for so long. After more than a year away from our animals, that feeling has receded a bit, but not gone away. I suspect it never will. I miss the steady *chuga-chuga* of the milking machine and the smell of clean goats (a bit like olive oil and dry grass) and the impatient cooing of chickens waiting to be let out of the coop. I even miss the unpleasant parts: shoving balls of medicine down past unwilling tongues, stringing up fence wire, dragging Mayday to the vet.

These days, I'm thinking about a new way to entangle myself with animals. I know it won't be easy—it would probably demand a bold leap away from my life's new trajectory. I suspect that human-animal entanglement almost always runs counter to the middle-class ideas of success. It tends to be chaotic, unpredictable, inconvenient. With my first child born recently, I'm feeling the pull of comfort and security. But I also haven't forgotten the deep satisfaction of early autumn in Virginia, when the botflies are gone for the year and the trees start to turn and the goats get lazy and chew their cuds in spots of cool midday sun.

WILLIAM DERESIEWICZ

Respect, or the Missing Relation
FROM *Liberties*

I CONTEMPLATE a bird. In fact it is a photo of a bird, many times larger than life, hanging on the wall of a café. I've never had a chance to scrutinize a bird so carefully before. After I finish admiring its beauty, I turn my attention to its claws, which are pointed and hard, its beak, which is open in a cry, its eyes, which are empty of pity or warmth. I think: this creature is intensely alien to me. It is not a cute little bird, a sweet little bird, look at the pretty little bird. It is not a bird in a children's book. And it comes to me that I have never understood an animal this way before. That whether in a zoo, on a farm, in my yard—still more with a photo or video clip of the kind that are forever being passed around online—my response to animals has always been to anthropomorphize them, to project my subjectivity onto them, to slobber over them with my emotions, with my needs. To place them in relation to myself. And it comes to me as well that to refrain from doing so, to let the bird, the goat, the possum be exactly what it is, in itself and for itself, without reference to me, to accept it in its otherness, would be to treat it with profound respect.

I am talking with a former professor of mine. She is telling me that she believes that part of our job as teachers of undergraduates is to help our students, as she puts it, "instrumentalize" the things they learn from us—instrumentalize them, she means, for the sake of social change. I'm skeptical. What do academics know about instrumentalizing anything? More to the point, what business do we have telling students what they ought to do with what we teach them? "Fine," I say at last (this is some years ago), "as long as you would be okay with one of your students instrumentalizing what they learn from you to try to overturn *Roe v. Wade.*" She is stunned. The possibility has clearly never crossed her mind—the possibility, that is, that students might have goals that conflict with hers. That they possess an otherness that we as educators must respect.

A few years later, I come across an essay by this same professor in *The Chronicle of Higher Education*, the principal organ of news and opinion about the academy. Titled "In Praise of the Academic Cliché," it champions buzzwords such as "performativity," "intersectionality," and "heteronormativity" as agents of transformative social potential, especially once "they quietly wriggle through discourse, swimming from theory to classrooms" and thence, beyond the college walls, to essays, podcasts, Twitter, "mainstream journalism and popular entertainment." The student's function in the process is to carry them, the way that a deer might carry a tick. "Not all of our students will be original thinkers," she writes, "nor should they all be. A world of original thinkers, all thinking wholly inimitable thoughts, could never get anything done. For that, we need unoriginal thinkers, hordes of them, cloning ideas by the score and broadcasting them to every corner of our virtual world. What better device for idea-cloning than the cliché?" Instead of teaching undergraduates to avoid clichés, as generations of instructors have done, "we should instead strive to send our students forth—and ourselves too—armed with clichés for political change."

My professor had progressed from wanting to teach her students to instrumentalize ideas to wanting to instrumentalize her students: to recruit, enlist, train, mobilize, and deploy them—"armed," in "hordes"—for the purpose (her purpose) of "getting things done." Or rather, she had shown me that the second impulse was implicit in the first. Forget teaching people to think; forget uniqueness, individuality, the soul. The ideas are cloned, and so are the students. Nor is she alone in her desire, as anyone familiar with contemporary academia will know. Quite the opposite, in fact. Some years ago, to take one data point, I spent a couple of weeks at a moderately selective Catholic university: not an elite institution, not one you would think of as a redoubt of progressive ideology. Across the board, across the disciplines, the dean informed me, younger faculty believe their job to be indoctrination. Which means they think their mission is to serve the cause, not the students. The students are tools.

This is the antithesis of what I am calling respect, be it for a creature or a student: the recognition of another as other and the willingness to let them be such. Call this antithesis projection, intolerance, the will to power, it is surely a persistent part of being human, and it is also surely getting worse. Academics are not the only professionals who have decided that their mission is to save the world and that their clients must be proselytized and propagandized, their personhood be damned, in order to do so. So have teachers, librarians, and social workers. So, perhaps worst of all, have counselors and psychotherapists, who practice the one line of work in which it is even more important than in education to treat one's charges as individuals, people with their own particular histories, qualities, needs. All around us we are witnessing the loss of this thing that I'm calling respect.

The problem is bipartisan. The left speaks constantly of "difference," but it cannot abide it. This is, again, an old phenomenon freshly intensified. "Deviation" from the party line was a cardinal sin in twentieth-century communism. Leftist groups, accordingly, were notoriously fissiparous, splintering into ever-smaller factions of doctrinally pristine believers. As class politics became self-expressive lifestyleism, the purism seamlessly transferred. A friend from redneck small-town southwest Georgia lived for many years on a commune in central Virginia largely populated by Northeast liberals. They were, she told me, the most intolerant people she'd ever met: accepting and open to all, as long as you were exactly like them. (Those acquainted with other progressive bastions—Berkeley, Cambridge, Brooklyn, et al.—will know what she was talking about.) "Do your own thing," went the countercultural slogan, with the tacit addendum, "as long as I approve of it." You could wear beads or berets or dashikis (or later, mohawks or dreadlocks or flannel), but never khakis or a suit, let alone a cross. And now that politics and self-expression have become coterminous (the personal is political, the political is personal), it is all Stalinism all the time. To be my "ally" means that you agree with me, not on a specific issue, as it once would have done, but on all of them, unquestioningly. There's no more ordering à la carte; you have to swallow the entire menu.

But the right is no better these days, having likewise largely extirpated its liberal commitments in the name of an epochal moral crusade. Epistemic modesty, à la Edmund Burke, is gone, as is libertarian toleration. Red America, as David French and others have reported, is as heavily policed as Blue. MAGA admits no dissent; its idol is a jealous god; Never-Trumpers are "human scum." Progressive social power is answered by state censorship, Kendi and Butler by DeSantis and Abbott. Christian nationalism, including in its juridical manifestation as "common good constitutionalism," promises to make us do what's best for us, whether we like it or not. In his *Dobbs* concurrence, Clarence Thomas started to prepare the ground for the repeal of rights to contraception, gay marriage, and gay sex, and thus to their legislative suppression. The Libertarian Party, as Cato's Andy Craig remarked not long ago, having "experienced a hostile takeover by far-right culture warriors" has embraced "a program of openly bigoted authoritarianism." In this it is aligned with conservatism's Orbanists and Putinists, their retreat from democratic pluralism to a fantasy of church and *volk*.

This is politics, but beneath it, it is narcissism. Or rather, politics has become a mode of narcissism, which can be defined as the need to make the whole world over in one's image, to fill it with the self. For its hypertrophy, which has gone beyond the darkest dreams of Christopher Lasch, there are many things to thank, but above all is the internet. We now have the ability not only to create our own reality, but to live uninterruptedly within it. The phrase "my truth" originated as an assertion of the validity of subjective experience, of feelings as real and important. Now it signifies the triumph of subjectivity, its abolition of the objective, the external, the empirical. "The Bible was written by Africans," I overheard a fellow author confide at a booksellers convention. "I know some people disagree," she added, having clocked the nearby Semite, "but that's my truth." Her right-wing counterparts include the individuals who, dying of COVID, continued to insist that the pandemic was a hoax.

Narcissism governs the contemporary stance toward art as well. Instead of going to it in the fearful hope that art will trouble us out of ourselves—confront us with genuine difference, and therefore make us different—we insist that it affirm us. Women will aver that they prefer to read books by female authors; sometimes that that's the only kind they read. Pedagogical authorities concur that children should be given stories about people who "look like them," that anything else is an injury. When a work remains refractory to our desire for validation—often because it belongs to the past, that foreign country—we rewrite it. Shakespeare is "queered," Austen is revealed to be a radical feminist, and so forth. Once again, this is an oldish story—it dates to the rights revolutions and the reading practices they spawned—that has in our century become immensely worse. For with its two-way social traffic, the internet has given rise to the phenomenon of fandom, with its enormous powers of insistence. Not just fans—"fandom," like "kingdom." Now the audience is able not only to project its desires onto its idols (devotees of Elvis or the Beatles could do that as well), but to make those figures answerable to its projections. Now artists and audience mirror each other, the ego duplicated in an infinite regression.

I have struggled with these things myself (and not just with regard to birds): with intolerance, with projection, with the impulse to convert. When I started teaching in my late twenties, still in my militant-atheist phase, I had a student, fresh from Catholic school, named John Luke. I really gave that kid a time—not quite explicitly, which was maybe worse, because I never said anything that he could argue with directly. It was all insinuation, a subtle sort of intellectual bullying. I remember bringing in some Nietzsche once (this was freshman composition; other graduate instructors—we were a bunch of smug little bastards—were sneaking in swatches of Marx or Foucault). This will give my students something challenging to chew on, I thought, and if I can win one away from the pale Galilean, then so much the better. I feel a kind of psychic nausea when I think of this today. One definition of evil, I later discovered, understands it as the effort to impose one's will on others.

Slowly, however, I managed to learn. Many years later, I had another avowedly Catholic student. One day, in office hours, she mentioned that she belonged to a campus organization called CLAY, or Choose Life at Yale. I inwardly recoiled. Holy crap, I thought, she's one of them. (I also thought, good name.) But I managed to keep my mouth shut. She's got a right to her belief, I reflected, and what's more, I respect her for standing up for it under what are surely challenging conditions. (It was she whom I was thinking of, in fact, when I reminded my professor that there might be people in her classes who want to overturn *Roe v. Wade*.) I had gotten to know a lot of students over the years, and I cherished those connections, but there was something special about this one—something cleaner or purer, and precisely because of our differences. It is pleasant to have disciples, but it can also be corrupting. The moment I accepted her for who she was, she got a little realer—became more of an actual person, not an idea of myself echoed back to me—and so, I think, did I. I was over here; she was over there. I didn't like her for being like me, and she didn't like me for being like her. We eventually grew to be friends, and some twenty years later we still are.

Friends. I have an old one, someone who has perpetually disappointed the expectations that people have had of her. We met in a Zionist youth movement, but she later stepped away from any form of Jewish practice or affiliation. She went to a leading professional school, but she abjured the prestigious career paths that her classmates pursued. Raised in an affluent suburban environment, she went off to live in a working-class rural community. "The worst thing you can do to your friends," she once remarked, "is not be the person they want you to be." I thought of that when I was having dinner with another friend, another former student, a young man who was taking his time about getting his life on track, in a way I was getting impatient about. He had just broken up with his girlfriend, he told me. Again? I thought. "I'm sorry to hear that," I said, though he didn't seem sorry at all. And then I caught myself. "That was a stupid thing to say," I said. "Why should I care if you have a girlfriend?" Why indeed? Who was I to be "impatient"? I was too identified with him. I needed to let him be who he was going to be, whatever he was going to be.

If this is difficult to do with friends, it is virtually impossible to do with children. Virtually, but not completely. A parent was telling me that she couldn't wait for her teenage daughter to go off to college so that she, the parent, could finally get some distance from her. I thought, for years I've been advising young adults that they need to separate from their parents. It hadn't even crossed my mind that parents ought to try to separate from their children, because I hadn't imagined that such a thing was possible. Later, I read this in Louise Glück, a writer who knew about separateness:

> I'll never understand
> the claim of a mother
> on a child's soul.
>
> So many times
> I made that mistake
> in love, taking
> some wild sound to be
> the soul exposing itself . . .
>
> The soul is silent.
> If it speaks at all
> it speaks in dreams.

A child's being is their own. Mothers and fathers, it's not about you.

Respect, as I am calling it, shows up in the political realm as tolerance. I used to hate that concept, back in my days as an angry young Jew. Who are you, I thought, to merely *tolerate* me? Am I supposed to be grateful for that? But our politics of mutual negation has made me wiser. Tolerance, compared to what we have, would be tremendous, would be a terrific achievement. Tolerance, in a democracy, signifies the recognition that the people whom you hate the most—Nazis, let us say, to put it in the starkest terms—have a right to share the political community with you: to speak, vote, advocate, educate, organize, assemble, just like you do. That they are your equals as citizens—I would add, as human beings. Being a Nazi is a civil right; being a Nazi is a human right. To grasp that is to understand the stony way of tolerance.

My own instruction in this virtue came courtesy of Dave

Chapelle. It was one of his Jew jokes, about the Jews controlling Hollywood or some such. My first thought was, fuck this guy. My second was, I'm never going to watch a thing he does again. My third was, idiot, this is what tolerance *means*, spiritually if not literally: not having to approve of everything another person does, and not disengaging from them even when they anger you, even when they offend you. Being okay with not being okay. What you are tolerating, ultimately, is your own discomfort.

It's hard. It's definitely hard. And it goes the other way as well. I am white, middle-aged, middle-class. When I encounter someone from the other side of one of those divides, my self-consciousness kicks in. It isn't guilt; it's a feeling of inauthenticity, like I can suddenly see through my act (I'm so white, so stiff, so deeply uncool) because I imagine that they can. My instinct is to pander, to assimilate myself to them: to fall in with their way of speaking, standing, holding themselves, with their point of view. (Anyone who's watched a grown-up try to talk to a bunch of teenagers will understand what I mean.) But in time I've learned to check that impulse. When faced with difference now, I don't reject it and I don't surrender to it. (Keep your back straight, I sometimes literally tell myself.) I've also learned that people will respect you more (in the familiar sense) if you just be yourself. And it's the only way, of course, to build a genuine relationship.

So what am I saying here? What exactly is this "respect" that I've been mulling over ever since I saw that picture of a bird? To help me consider the matter a little more rigorously, I turned to Martin Buber, with his famous I-Thou and I-It. Where does respect fall in relation to that distinction? I-It is instrumental: you use the thing, the creature, the person, for your own ends. I-Thou is relational, being to being. "I contemplate a tree," Buber writes. "I become bound up in relation to it. The tree is now no longer *It*. I have been seized by the power of exclusiveness." In the moment of I-Thou, in other words, the Thou is all there is. I apprehend it in its wholeness, its unity, its being. "The tree is no impression," no bundle of separate sensations, nor is my relation with some kind of indwelling spirit. "I encounter no soul or dryad of the tree, but the tree itself."

There is much to admire in *I and Thou*, but also much, I find, to question. Buber tells us that to meet the Thou—which finally means the divine—to enter into what he calls a genuine relation, one needs a "full acceptance of the present," of reality ("The Word of revelation is I am that I am. . . . That which is is, and nothing more"). One needs to practice not a "seeking" but a "waiting." Very good. What Buber is describing is a mystical experience, the suspension of time and space and ego, such as we learn about also in other traditions. It is rare; it cannot be achieved by will alone; it is a gift of grace. But it doesn't, for that very reason, help us much in ordinary life. And the only alternative, he says, is I-It. All is relation ("There is no *I* taken in itself"), and there are only two relations.

This will not do. Conversations with friends, acts of love and care, the connection of teacher to student—all these are instrumental? No. There must be something in between his two extremes. We do not need to "Thou" the other in order to refrain from instrumentalizing them. The essence of respect, in fact, is non-identification. It is a refusal of projection. For that, I think, is what the I-Thou ultimately is. It is a strangely non-relational relation. He's vibing with the tree, as the kids would say, but is the tree vibing with him? It's just a tree, after all. He may *feel* a reciprocity (the tree "has to do with me"), but a feeling does not tell you anything except that you are having a feeling.

Buber gives the game away when he turns from trees to human beings. "Even if the man to whom I say *Thou* is not aware of it," he writes, "yet relation may exist." But to call this a relation is to strain the term beyond its breaking point. It seems, instead, a private experience, however exalted, one in which the other person functions as a kind of spiritual trampoline. As for creatures, wild animals, Buber has the hardest time with them of all, perhaps because, unlike a tree, they visibly respond to us. Contemplate an animal, be it a backyard bird or a deer in a forest, meet its eyes, and what you are likely to register is not "relation" but a sense of threat, as in, *what is this ape and why is it staring at me?*

For Buber, I-Thou is the ground of morality. Its essence is love, the "responsibility of an *I* for a *Thou*." But if we need to love the other in order to treat them correctly, then we're all in a great deal of trouble. We should not have to empathize or sympathize or understand or "leap the chasm of otherness" or "be in relation." We only have—but this is not an easy thing—to see the other in itself and for itself. I think of an acquaintance who lives in western Massachusetts and has spent some time in California. He much prefers the Yankees, he has told me, as dour and unfriendly as they often are, because when push comes to shove, you can count on them. They don't have to like you to help you. The Californians appall him, precisely because their morality is based on feeling, on spurts of universal love. No love today? No help, no recognition, no concern—go soak your head.

No doubt this is partly a matter of temperament—Buber is terribly moist—but I am for a dry morality. I am for detachment, even alienation, as a hedge against over-identification. I am for letting the other be other (including the universe, which some ventriloquize as the divine). You can love the other, but you can equally leave them alone. Buber speaks of community, the form that "relation" assumes in collective life, but this is not to be confused with actual communities. The latter means that everyone is in each other's grill, whereas my ideal is the city, where people mind their business unless otherwise requested. Many years ago, I spent some months on a kibbutz. "People here," a resident told me, "will let you into their living room, but they won't let you into their bedroom." He wasn't talking about polyamory; he was talking about the fact that close quarters can militate against intimacy, because they force you to defend your boundaries. But cities, with their ethic of noninterference, can make not only for strong individuals, but also, in my experience, for strong attachments. No distance, no crossing. No separation, no connection. If I am over here and you are over there, then at least we can say that we know where we are.

I had been trying to come up with an alternative to Thou and It, a third term for a third dyad: I-That? I-Them? Then I realized the real problem is that pesky "I," with its knack of getting in the way. We can't be rid of it, and so we must constrain it. I think of the concept of *tzimtzum*—the act, in Kabbalah, whereby an infinite God creates the world by contracting himself to make room for it. The ego also tends to fill immensity. Self-contraction is a decent rule of conduct, and a useful prayer would be *Lord, help me to make myself small.*

Contributors' Notes

KHALIL ABUSHAREKH was born in Al-Shati refugee camp in Gaza City, Palestine. In 2008, he moved to Houston, Texas, where he has lived ever since. He came to the US to learn English and to write, telling the stories he witnessed growing up in Gaza. He was selected for the Tin House 2025 Winter Workshop for Fiction and received a Kone Foundation grant (Finland) to write his debut novel, *The Beach Camp*, as part of the Gaza Trilogy. "Zeppole (aka Awama)" was nominated for a Pushcart Prize.

MOSAB ABU TOHA is a Palestinian poet, short-story writer, and essayist from Gaza. His first collection of poetry, *Things You May Find Hidden in My Ear*, was a finalist for the National Book Critics Circle Award for Poetry and won the Palestine Book Award, the American Book Award, and the Derek Walcott Prize for Poetry. Abu Toha is also the founder of the Edward Said Library in Gaza, which he hopes to rebuild. He recently won an Overseas Press Club Award for his Letter from Gaza column for *The New Yorker*. His new book, *Forest of Noise*, has been named a Notable Book of the Year by *The New York Times* and is a *New Yorker* Essential Read.

HANNAH KEZIAH AGUSTIN is from Manila, Philippines. Her work appears in *Prairie Schooner, Michigan Quarterly Review, Guernica,* and elsewhere. She is pursuing an MFA in literary reportage at New York University.

NUAR ALSADIR'S most recent book, *Animal Joy: A Book of Laughter and Resuscitation*, was a *Time* magazine must-read of 2022 and a *Publishers Weekly*

Best Book of 2022. She is also the author of two poetry collections: *Fourth Person Singular*, a finalist for the National Book Critics Circle Award and the Forward Prize for Best Collection, and *More Shadow Than Bird*. She is a fellow of the New York Institute for the Humanities and a member of the curatorial board of the Racial Imaginary Institute. She works as a psychoanalyst in private practice and teaches in New York University's MFA program in creative writing. The essay "On Boredom" will be included in a forthcoming book. The working title is *Boredom*.

SARAH AZIZA is a Palestinian American writer, artist, and translator with roots in 'Ibdis and Deir al-Balah, Gaza. Her work has appeared in *The New Yorker*, *The Baffler*, *Harper's Magazine*, *Mizna*, *Lux*, *The Guardian*, and *The Nation*, among others. She has received grants, residencies, and fellowships from Fulbright, the Pulitzer Center on Crisis Reporting, Tin House Workshop, and the Asian American Writers' Workshop, among others. Her first book, *The Hollow Half*, is a hybrid work of memoir, lyricism, and oral history exploring the intertwined legacies of diaspora, colonialism, and the American dream. She will see a free Palestine in her lifetime.

EULA BISS is the author of four books: *Having and Being Had*, *On Immunity*, *Notes from No Man's Land*, and *The Balloonists*. Her work has been translated into a dozen languages and has been recognized by a National Book Critics Circle Award, a Guggenheim Fellowship, a New America Fellowship, and a 21st Century Award from the Chicago Public Library. She is currently at work on a collection of essays about how private property has shaped our world.

MATTHEW DENTON-EDMUNDSON is a writer who divides his time between Idaho and rural Virginia.

WILLIAM DERESIEWICZ is the author of five books, including *Excellent Sheep*, *The Death of the Artist*, and *The End of Solitude: Selected Essays on Culture and Society*. His work, which has been translated into nineteen languages and included in over forty anthologies, has appeared in *Persuasion*, *Salmagundi*, *The Atlantic*, and many other publications. He is on the editorial board of *The Metropolitan Review* and the advisory board of the Matthew Strother Center for the Examined Life, a retreat and study program in upstate New York.

Contributors' Notes

CAROLYN FORCHÉ'S fifth collection, *In the Lateness of the World*, was a finalist for the Pulitzer Prize. Her memoir *What You Have Heard Is True* was a finalist for the National Book Award and winner of the Juan E. Méndez Book Award for Human Rights in Latin America. In 2023 she co-edited, with Ilya Kaminsky, *In the Hour of War: Poetry from Ukraine*. A recipient of the Windham-Campbell Prize, she is chancellor of the Academy of American Poets and a member of the American Academy of Arts and Sciences and the Royal Society of Literature. She is Distinguished University Professor at Georgetown University.

DR. ALEXIS PAULINE GUMBS, author of *Survival Is a Promise: The Eternal Life of Audre Lorde*, is a queer Black feminist love evangelist and an aspirational cousin to all life. *Publishers Weekly* calls her writing "groundbreaking." She is also the author of four earlier books, aka portable textual ceremonies, including *Undrowned*, which won the 2022 Whiting Award in Nonfiction. A recipient of the Windham-Campbell Prize in Poetry, a National Endowment for the Arts Creative Writing Fellowship, and a National Humanities Center Fellowship, Dr. Gumbs lives and loves in Durham, North Carolina. Visit her at www.alexispauline.com.

SUMMER HAMMOND grew up in rural Iowa and Missouri, one of Jehovah's Witnesses. She earned her MFA from the University of North Carolina-Wilmington. Her writing appears in *New Letters*, *Moon City Review*, and *Tahoma Review*, among others. She won the 2023 New Letters Conger Beasley Jr. Award for Nonfiction. Summer is currently at work on a memoir, supported by the Granta Writers' Workshop. Her debut novel, *The Impossible Why*, is forthcoming in 2026.

GREG JACKSON is the author of the novel *The Dimensions of a Cave*, named a Best Book of 2023 by *The New Yorker*, and the story collection *Prodigals*, for which he received the National Book Foundation's 5 Under 35 Award and the Bard Fiction Prize. His stories and essays have appeared in *The New Yorker*, *Harper's Magazine*, *Granta*, *Virginia Quarterly Review*, *Tin House*, *Conjunctions*, and *The Point*, among other publications, and have been previously collected in *The Best American Essays* and *The Best American Short Stories*. In 2017 *Granta* selected him for their list of Best Young American Novelists.

LINDA KINSTLER is a Junior Fellow at the Harvard Society of Fellows and the author of *Come to This Court and Cry: How the Holocaust Ends*, which won a 2023 Whiting Award in Nonfiction and was short-listed for the Wingate Prize for Jewish literature. Her writing appears in *The New York Times Magazine*, the *London Review of Books*, *The Atlantic*, and elsewhere.

CHRISTIAN LORENTZEN writes for the *London Review of Books*, *Harper's Magazine*, *Bookforum*, *Granta*, and other publications.

Born in Macao, LAURA GLEN LOUIS grew up in Oakland and shares an alma mater with the Pointer Sisters, Huey Newton, and Clint Eastwood. An essay on this period appears in her forthcoming collection, along with meditations on music, memory, murder, and hallucinations. Her story collection, *Talking in the Dark*, includes work anthologized in *The Best American Short Stories*.

LAURA PRESTON'S writing has appeared in *n+1*, *The New Yorker*, and *The Believer*. She is working on a book about artificial intelligence. She lives in New York.

ANGIE ROMINES is a writer, teacher, and Dolly Parton enthusiast living in Columbus, Ohio, with her husband, two sons, and an emotionally needy rescue pup named Pockets. Her work has appeared in *The Kenyon Review*, *New England Review*, *Literary Hub*, *The Rumpus*, *The Columbia Review*, and elsewhere. She is working simultaneously on a historical romance novel set on the prairie and an essay collection that explores the dark narratives of Kentucky women in her family tree and is not open to feedback about whether or not splitting her writing focus is a wise decision.

NAMWALI SERPELL was born in Lusaka and lives in New York. She received a Windham-Campbell Prize for Fiction, the Caine Prize for African Writing, and a Rona Jaffe Foundation Writers' Award. Her debut novel, *The Old Drift*, won the Anisfield-Wolf Book Award, the Arthur C. Clarke Award for Science Fiction, and the Art Seidenbaum Award for First Fiction; it was named one of the 100 Notable Books of 2019 by *The New York Times*. Her second novel, *The Furrows: An Elegy*, is a finalist for the National Book Critics Circle Award for Fiction and one of *The New York Times*'s 10 Best Books of 2022. Her book of essays, *Stranger Faces*, was a finalist for a National Book Critics Circle Award for Criticism. Her book of criticism, *On Morrison*, is forthcoming. She is a professor of English at Harvard.

CHRISTINA SHARPE is a writer, professor, and Canada Research Chair in Black Studies in the Humanities at York University in Toronto. She is the author of three books, most recently *Ordinary Notes* (2023), winner of the Hilary Weston Writers' Trust Prize in Nonfiction and the Hodler Prize and finalist for the National Book Award in Nonfiction, the National Book Critics Circle Award in Nonfiction, the James Tait Black Prize in Biography, and the *Los Angeles Times*'s Current Interest Book Prize. She is the recipient of a Molson Prize, a Windham-Campbell Prize in Nonfiction, and a Guggenheim Fellowship.

JAREK STEELE writes creative nonfiction and poetry with themes of family, queerness, gender, nature, and politics. His work has appeared in HuffPost, *Fourth Genre*, *Electric Literature*, AWP's *Writer's Chronicle*, the *Colorado Review*, and elsewhere. He lives in St. Louis with his wife, Barbara, where he teaches writing.

JOHN JEREMIAH SULLIVAN was born in Louisville, Kentucky, in 1974, and has lived in Wilmington, North Carolina, for the past twenty-one years. His work has been published in a wide variety of American magazines and journals, including *The New York Times Magazine* (where he is a contributing writer), *The New Yorker*, *Harper's Magazine*, *The Paris Review*, *The Yale Review*, and the *Oxford American*. He has been the recipient of several awards, including the Whiting Award, the Windham-Campbell Prize, a Guggenheim, two National Magazine Awards, a Pushcart Prize, and a fellowship at the New York Public Library's Cullman Center for Scholars and Writers. His last book, a 2011 collection of essays and articles, titled *Pulphead*, was recently named one of the Best 100 Books of the 21st Century in a poll conducted by *The New York Times Book Review*. His next book is titled *The Prime Minister of Paradise* and involves an eighteenth-century utopian philosopher who lived among the Indigenous Cherokees in present-day East Tennessee.

Notable Essays and Literary Nonfiction of 2024

SELECTED BY KIM DANA KUPPERMAN

Farah Abdessamad
    Blood Antiquities, Arab Tears, *Ploughshares*, 50.1, Spring 2024

Sufiya Abdur-Rahman
    Consider the Sunrise, *Passengers Journal*, 5.4, 2024

T. Abeyta
    Tributary, *Prairie Schooner*, 97.4, Winter 2023 [published in 2024]

Joelle M. Abi-Rached
    The View from Besieged Beirut, *Boston Review*, October 2, 2024

Marilyn Abildskov
    The Body Asks Its Questions, *Sonora Review*, September 20, 2024

Philipe AbiYouness
    Geographies, *Brink*, 7, Spring 2024

Ciara Alfaro
    Kind of Monster, *Southeast Review*, 42.2, 2024

Jenny Apostol
    The Desire We Were Becoming, *The Kenyon Review*, XLVI.1, Winter 2024

Natalie Appleton
    our brothers started dying, *Room*, 47.2, 2024

Amir Ahmadi Arian
    In Search of Zabihollah Mansouri, *The Yale Review*, 112.4, Winter 2024

Megan J. Arlett
    The Female Nude, *Pleiades*, 44.2, Fall 2024

Gabeba Baderoon
    Adjacency, or, Words for Pain, *New England Review*, 45.4, Winter 2024

Anna Badkhen
    Another Way to Begin, *World Literature Today*, July/August 2024

Peter Balaam
    Burying a Fox, *Alaska Quarterly Review*, 40.3–4, Summer/Fall 2024

Richard Bausch
    A Memory, and Sorrow (An Interval for Bobby), *River Teeth*, 26.1, Fall 2024

Gorman Beauchamp
    Art and Moralities, *Salmagundi Magazine*, 224–25, Fall 2024–Winter 2025

Kate Beck
    Damming the Sentimental, *Saranac Review*, 20, December 2024

Elvis Bego
    Mother's Hands: On Grief in 33 Beginnings, *Agni*, 100, 2024

David A. Bell
    In My Mother's Archive, *The New York Review of Books* (online), February 20, 2024

Claire A. Berman
    A Love Story All the Same, *Bellevue Literary Review*, 47, Fall/Winter 2024
Emily Bernard
    My Name Is Emily, *The American Scholar*, 93.2, Spring 2024
Andrew Bernstein
    Picking Up the Pieces, *Bicycling*, Summer 2024
Sven Birkerts
    Thirty-Seven Theses on Time and Memory, *The Common*, 27, Spring 2024
Edna Bonhomme
    "Who Shall Let This World Be Beautiful?," *Virginia Quarterly Review*, 100.1, Spring 2024
Wendy Brenner
    Don't Bleed on the Artwork: Notes from the Afterlife, *Oxford American*, Spring 2024
Patrick Breslin
    Ukraine: A Love Story, *Irish Pages*, 12.1, 2024
Sam Brighton
    Windows Open, *Exposition Review*, IX, 2024
Victor Brombert
    Sofa Sessions with Babushka: In the Weimar Years, *The Hudson Review*, LXXVII.1, Spring 2024
Jason Brown
    A Chest of Drawers, *The Florida Review*, 47.2, Spring 2024
Katy Butler
    Abortion and the First Precept, *Tricycle* (online), November 10, 2024
Matthew Byrne
    Life Sentences, *Washington Square Review*, 51, Spring 2024
Miriam Camitta
    Sanctuary, *Image*, 122, Fall 2024
Charis Caputo
    Against Language, *Liber*, 2.4, Winter 2024
Nona Caspers
    Canby the Goat, *The Southern Review*, 60.4, Autumn 2024
Beth Castrodale
    My Injured Brain, *Ars Medica*, 18.1, 2024
Daniel Chacón
    The Writers' Block, *Another Chicago Magazine*, January 25, 2024
Casey Chaffin
    Nowhere to Hide, *Oregon Humanities*, Summer 2024
Brooke Champagne
    Piernas Bonitas, *Fourth Genre*, 26.2, Fall 2024
Shirley Chan
    Her Story | My Story | History, *The Iowa Review*, 54.2, Fall 2024
Ruella Che
    Nihao in Afrotopia, *Epiphany*, Fall/Winter 2024
Jennifer S. Cheng
    A Catalog of Falling Things, *The Iowa Review*, 53.3, Winter 2023/24
Aleksandr Chernousov
    Speaking in Tongues, *Oregon Humanities*, Spring 2024
Phil Christman
    Adventures Close to Home, *The Hedgehog Review*, Summer 2024
Jill Christman
    Spinning Webs in Space, *The Rumpus*, October 8, 2024
Aldyn Chwelos
    The Pathfinder, *The Malahat Review*, Spring 2024
Paul Collins
    Why Can't My Son Vote?, *The Believer*, 146, Summer 2024
Burl N. Corbett
    The Prisoner of Building 54, *Minutes Before Six*, October 27, 2024
Paul Crenshaw
    Prescribed, *North American Review*, 309.2, Summer 2024
Hal Crowther
    The Measure of All Things?, *Narrative*, January 2024
Caleb Daniloff
    Running with Hank, *Runner's World*, Fall 2024
Susan Muaddi Darraj
    Taken From You, This Joy, *The Massachusetts Review*, 65.4, Winter 2024
Starr Davis
    Pawn, *Craft*, January 17, 2024

Heather Davis
  On Touching Coral, *Transition: The Magazine of Africa and the Diaspora*, 135, 2024
Lydia Davis
  Absolute Darkness, *The Yale Review*, 112.2, Summer 2024
Alison Hawthorne Deming
  The Eye of Water, *Prairie Schooner*, 97.4, Winter 2023 [published in 2024]
Sarah Deming
  Street Fights, *The Threepenny Review*, 176, Winter 2024
Bathsheba Demuth
  Where the Language Changes, *Granta*, 167, Spring 2024
Laurie Ann Doyle
  Intruder, *Fourth Genre*, 26.2, Fall 2024
Mark Doyle
  The Consolations of Waterloo Sunsets, *Potomac Review*, 75, Fall 2024
D. L. Duda
  Tapeworms, *The Threepenny Review*, 178, 2024
Ellie Duke
  Religious None, *The Surfer's Journal*, 33.5, October/November 2024
Jannie Edwards
  The Desiring Soul: The Liver and the Writing Life, *The Examined Life*, 12, 2024
Rachel Eisendrath
  A Portrait on the Wall, *The New York Review of Books* (online), July 14, 2024
Wiam El-Tamami
  Stranger Kin, *The Sun*, 577, January 2024
Abdelrahman ElGendy
  Al-Thakla—Arabic as the Original Mourner, *The Markaz Review*, March 3, 2024
  On Execution, *Mizna*, March 13, 2024
Rosetta S. Elkin
  Narratives at the Margins of Extinction, *Arnoldia*, 81.2, Summer 2024
Merve Emre
  Love as Aesthetic Education, *Raritan*, XLIII.3, Winter 2024
Alexander T. Englert
  We'll Meet Again, *Aeon*, January 2, 2024
Shala Erlich
  Lost and Unlost, *Southern Humanities Review*, 57.1, Spring 2024
Eve Esfandiari-Denny
  Nearly White Girl Girling on Behalf of Sonic Fluency, *Granta*, 166, Winter 2024
Claire L. Evans
  Living in a Lucid Dream, *Noema Magazine*, July 1, 2024
Olivia Fantini
  She Writes You Letters, *New Letters*, 90.1–2, Winter/Spring 2024
Lauren Fath
  Cherries, *CutBank*, 101, 2024
Deb Fenwick
  Escape Route, *In Short*, 1.1, Spring 2024
Gustavo Pérez Firmat
  Questions of Home, *The Southern Review*, 60.4, Autumn 2024
Alyson Foster
  The Life and Timescapes of Joseph Priestley, *Humanities*, 45.2, Spring 2024
David Fowler
  The Noblest of Things, *The Threepenny Review*, 179, Fall 2024
John Freeman
  Olive Trees, Midwinter, *Alaska Quarterly Review*, 40.3–4, Summer/Fall 2024
Abby Frucht
  Otter and Flotsam. Glove, Gill, and Goose Feather. Tonic and Air., *Lake Effect*, 28, Spring 2024
Elisa Gabbert
  Fear as a Game, *The Believer*, 146, Summer 2024
Forrest Gander
  Desert Visions, *The New York Review of Books* (online), September 4, 2024
John Ganz
  The Dead Admonish, *Harper's Magazine*, July 2024

Ross Gay
  Gooseberry Mary and the Un-Green Beans, *Orion*, Autumn 2024
Ellyn Gaydos
  On Stones, *Harper's Magazine*, August 2024
Tanya Gold
  My Auschwitz Vacation, *Harper's Magazine*, September 2024
Glen David Gold
  Someone with a Faster and a Keener Eye, Just Over the Horizon, *Zyzzyva*, 127, 2024
Albert Goldbarth
  Danaë, *Willow Springs*, 94, Spring 2024
Xochitl Gonzalez
  My Mother the Revolutionary, *The Atlantic*, September 2024
Emily Fox Gordon
  Tramping with Virginia, *The American Scholar*, 93.2, Spring 2024
Naomi Gordon-Loebl
  Lost Uncle, *The Florida Review*, 48.1, Fall 2024
Sarah Gorham
  Three Papers, *North American Review*, 309.1, Spring 2024
Torrin A. Greathouse
  The Crooked Child, *Copper Nickel*, 39, Fall 2024
Jaime Grechika
  Wings and Earth, *Iron Horse Literary Review*, 26.1, February 2024
Jazmine Becerra Green
  Old Soles and New Shoes, *Hypertext Review*, Fall/Winter 2024
Rachel Greenley
  Here in Umatilla, *New England Review*, 45.3, 2024
Jacky Grey
  Things of My Mother's, *The Sewanee Review*, CXXXIII.2, Spring 2024
Helena Guerin
  When You Ghost Your Midwife, *Another Chicago Magazine*, May 16, 2024
Caitlin Gunthorp
  Conversations in Colic Season, *The Pinch*, 44.1, Spring 2024
Anika Gupta
  Love, Disease, *Prairie Schooner*, 97.2, Summer 2023 [published in 2024]

Beth Gutcheon
  Bright Medusas, *The Hudson Review*, LXXVI, Winter 2024
jade guthrie
  Hanged/drawn/quartered, *or* imagining my great-grandmothers' hands on a Sunday morning, in four parts, *Phoebe*, 53.2, 2024
Christine Hale
  His Body, *The Cincinnati Review*, 21.1, Spring 2024
  Inside Outside In-Between, *Southern Humanities Review*, 57.3, 2024
Mark Harris
  The Body Keeps the Score, *T: The New York Times Style Magazine*, August 18, 2024
Holly Haworth
  Woman in the Woods, *The Bitter Southerner*, 8, June 2024
Christopher Hawthorne
  For Whom the Monuments Rise, *Alta*, 29, 2024
Nathan Heller
  The Battle for Attention, *The New Yorker*, May 6, 2024
L. I. Henley
  Dispatches from the Ridge, *The Southern Review*, 60.2, Spring 2024
Michael Hersch
  The Harrowing and the Beautiful, *Nautilus*, 577, July/August 2024
Judith Hertog
  Journey to Tibet, *Tricycle*, XXXIV.1, Fall 2024
Jennifer Hildebrandt
  Stability, *The Masters Review*, January 22, 2024
Jen Hirt
  Survivor Tree U106, *Witness*, 37.1, Spring 2024
Amy Hoffman
  Israel & Me, *Solstice*, Summer 2024
Garrett Hongo
  Franklin Odo: Flâneur of Asian American History, *The Georgia Review*, 78.2, Summer 2024
Elizabeth Hoover
  Our Waste and Our Potential, *Southeast Review*, 42.1, 2024

Pam Houston
> A Is for Aardwolf: A Sub-Saharan Prose Abecedarian, *Alaska Quarterly Review*, 40.3–4, Summer/Fall 2024

Nancy Huggett
> I am a good mother. I am a bad mother. I am no mother at all., *The Fiddlehead*, 301, Autumn 2024

Patrick Hunt
> The Backpack, *New Letters*, 90.3–4, Summer/Fall 2024

Korey Hurni
> My Brother's Keeper, *The Massachusetts Review*, Spring 2024

Vedran Husić
> Empathy in Three Movements, *The Cincinnati Review* (online), November 15, 2024

Gary Indiana
> Five O'Clock Somewhere, *Granta*, 166, Winter 2024

Nafisa A. Iqbal
> Those Who Came Before, *Fourth Genre*, 26.1, Spring 2024

Leslie Jamison
> A New Life, *The New Yorker*, January 22, 2024

Annabel Jankovic
> Ghost Story, *Apple Valley Review*, 19.2, Fall 2024

Mitchell Morgan Johnson
> On Delivery, *n+1*, 47, Spring 2024

Louis B. Jones
> Power Failure, *The Threepenny Review*, 176, Winter 2024

Kat Joplin
> How to Be a Super-Duper Hospital Patient in Japan, *The Examined Life*, 12, 2024

Somi Jun
> Half-lives of empathy, *Phoebe*, 53.2, 2024

Julia Juster
> Rendered, *Conjunctions* (online), July 24, 2024

Fowzia Karimi
> A Cosmic Alignment, *Texas Highways*, July/August 2024

noam keim
> A Disappearance, *The Kenyon Review*, XLVI.3, Summer 2024

Garret Keizer
> Maintenance Man, *Salmagundi Magazine*, 222–23, Spring/Summer 2024

Steven G. Kellman
> If You See the Translator, Don't Shoot, *Michigan Quarterly Review*, 63.4, Fall 2024

Sophie Kemp
> New Tyrannies, *Los Angeles Review of Books*, November 14, 2024

Charles Kenney
> In Search of Herzog's Chicago, *Chicago Quarterly Review*, 40, Fall 2024

Jesse Lee Kercheval
> Minerva, *Ploughshares*, 49.4, Winter 2023/24

Sarah Khatry
> Experiments in Light, *Virginia Quarterly Review*, 100.3, Fall 2024

Sam Klug
> Who's Afraid of Frantz Fanon?, *Boston Review* (online), March 27, 2024

Laura Knott
> 43 or 44 Notes for an Essay on Skill and Ignorance, *The Georgia Review*, 78.3, Fall 2024

Rita Koganzon
> The Coddling of the American Undergraduate, *The Hedgehog Review*, 26.1, Spring 2024

Daniel Kolitz, Geoffrey Mak, Danielle Carr, Leon Dische Becker, Amber A'Lee Frost, P. E. Moskowitz, Joshua Tempelhof, Elena Comay del Junco, Kendall Waldman
> Club Med: Dispatches from the Adderall Epidemic, *Broadcast*, March 31, 2024

Ted Kooser
> Whistling Past the Graveyard, *New Letters*, 90.3–4, Summer/Fall 2024

Heather Lanier
> The Body of Apologies, *River Teeth*, 26.1, Fall 2024

Elissa Lash
> Twelve, *Craft*, June 14, 2024

Anna Lee-Popham
> These Malignant Years, *Brick*, 112, Winter 2024

Raven Leilani
: Death of the Party, *n+1*, 48, Fall 2024

Andrew Leonard
: Dark Cloud, *Sierra*, Fall 2024

Dana Levin
: Lessons of the Line: Charles Simic and Me, *The Yale Review*, 112.1, Spring 2024

Brandon Lewis
: A Certain Heft of Stone, *New Letters*, 90.1–2, Winter/Spring 2024

Yiyun Li
: The Seventy Percent, *Harper's Magazine*, November 2024

Ann Linder
: Regrets of a Snake Wrangler, *Alaska Quarterly Review*, 40.3–4, Summer/Fall 2024

Nicole Graev Lipson
: Macho Baby, *The Sun*, 577, January 2024

Vic Liu
: Hell Is Real and It Is Beige, *Inquest*, May 7, 2024

Mel Livatino
: That September Light, *Notre Dame Magazine*, 53.2, Summer 2024

Phillip Lopate
: "Thus I Lived With Words," *The New York Review of Books*, April 4, 2024

Chanlee Luu
: In Martinsville (2021), *Phoebe*, May 15, 2024

Lily Lynch
: Go West, *The Baffler*, 75, September 2024

Thomas Lynch
: The Open-Armed, Beckoning Embrace, *Image*, 120, Spring 2024

Marina Magloire
: Moving Towards Life, *Los Angeles Review of Books*, August 7, 2024

Kristine Langley Mahler
: A Girl Who Watched, *Multiplicity Magazine*, 5, 2024

Evan Malmgren
: The Fever Called Living, *Harper's Magazine*, October 2024

Sayantika Mandal
: Mother Tongue, *December*, 35.1, Spring/Summer 2024

Celeste Marcus
: After Rape: A Guide for the Tormented, *Liberties*, 4.2, Winter 2024

Rob Marks
: Wholly Bloody, Holy Land?, *North American Review*, 309.2, Summer 2024

Sage Marshall
: Powder Daze, *Catamaran*, 12.2, Spring 2024

Hugh Martin
: Shooting a Dog, *The American Scholar*, 93.1, Winter 2024

J. D. Mathes
: On the Origin of Time: A Meditation, *Ploughshares*, 49.4, Winter 2023/24

Wilson McBee
: Trouble the Sky, *Southwest Review*, 109.2, Summer 2024

Siobhan McKenna
: Officium, *Bellevue Literary Review*, 46, Spring/Summer 2024

Erin McReynolds
: And These Too Are Defensive Wounds, *The Sun*, 585, September 2024

David Meischen
: "*I Am*, I Said," *The Common*, 27, Spring 2024

Askold Melnyczuk
: War Stays for Dinner, *Irish Pages*, 12.1, 2024

Ryan Van Meter
: An essay about coyotes, *The Iowa Review*, 53.3, Winter 2023/24

Jacob Mikanowski
: Teeth, *The Point*, 33, Fall 2024

Ben Miller
: Pillville Diary, *New England Review*, 45.2, 2024

Brenda Miller and Julie Marie Wade
: Sea of Troubles, *Fourth Genre*, 26.1, Spring 2024

Surya Milner
: Protolith, *Colorado Review*, 51.1, Spring 2024

Sarah Minor
: On Waiting, *The Kenyon Review*, XLVI.1, Winter 2024

Kyle Minor
    Junk Temples, *New England Review*, 45.1, 2024
Judith Claire Mitchell
    Ephemerals, *New England Review*, 45.3, 2024
Keya Mitra
    Almost Born, *The Missouri Review*, 47.4, Winter 2024
Nadine Monem
    Close to the Slaughterhouse, *Black Warrior Review*, 50.2, Spring/Summer 2024
Carley Moore
    Fill in the Blank: Addiction, Family, Trauma, and How (Not) to Write About It, *Majuscule*, August 2024
Dinty W. Moore
    There Was a Time in My Life When I Knew, *Short Reads*, November 13, 2024
Wesley Morris
    How to Mourn a Black Icarus and His Fall, *The New York Times*, April 12, 2024
Jay Morse
    Triumph, *Door Is a Jar*, 30, Spring 2024
Gabriel Mundo
    Margarita Night, *Black Warrior Review*, 51.1, Fall/Winter 2024
Ruby Hansen Murray
    Kansas Tries to Say Goodbye, *CutBank*, 101, 2024
Jane Myer
    bleeding, *sneaker wave*, September 15, 2024
Kathryn Neurnberger
    Onslaughts, *The Iowa Review*, 54.1, Spring 2024
Lilly U. Nguyen
    The Possibilities of a Line, *Colorado Review*, 51.2, Summer 2024
Maggie Nye
    June 1, 2020: A Photo Essay, *Southern Humanities Review*, 57.2, 2024
Jeff Oloizia
    All the Lonely People, *Madison*, January 2024
Qais Akbar Omar
    I Hate WhatsApp, *Agni*, 99, 2024
Stuart Lane Osborne
    Unfinished, *West Trade Review*, 15, Spring 2024
Chante Owens
    Wedding Colors, *The Sun*, 585, September 2024
Cynthia Ozick
    Like Peeling Off a Glove, *Liberties*, 4.3, Spring 2024
Karla Pahel
    The Trapeze Dress, *Image*, 122, Fall 2024
Nii Ayikwei Parkes
    Mauve Is a Song Worth Singing, *Prairie Schooner*, 97.3, Fall 2023 [published in 2024]
Ed Pavlić
    Heaven Knows, *Evergreen Review*, Fall/Winter 2024
Alexandria Peary
    Sleeping with Knickknacks, *Arts & Letters*, 47, 2024
Ian Penman
    Lady Day of the Alhambra: Billie Holiday's Changeable Shade, *Harper's Magazine*, March 2024
Lindsey Pharr
    Unfinished Foxes, *Southeast Review*, 42.2, 2024
William Pierce
    The Page and Beyond, *Agni*, 100, 2024
Adrian S. Potter
    How to Write a Political Poem During These Unprecedented Times, *Solstice*, Spring 2024
Mona Susan Power
    Bloodthread, *The Georgia Review*, 78.4, Winter 2024
Lia Purpura
    Anthropomorphism Today, *The Harvard Review*, 62, 2024
Donald Quist
    Be Not Afraid: Notes on Jackass Forever, *The Hopkins Review*, 17.2, Spring 2024
Aaron Rabinowitz
    Invitations, *Jabberwock Review*, 44.2, Winter/Spring 2024

Emily Raboteau
  Gutbucket, *Orion*, Spring 2024
Tauheed Rahim II
  Dear Queen, *Oxford American*, Summer 2024
Santiago Ramos
  "Paraguayans Don't Read," *Plough Quarterly*, 41, Autumn 2024
Brooke Randel
  The History of the Holocaust Survivor, *Split Lip Magazine*, December 15, 2024
Nancy Reisman
  Death Lessons, *Five Points*, 23.1, 2024
Glen Retief
  Ghost Fish, *Michigan Quarterly Review*, 63.2, Spring 2024
David Rieff
  Just War, *Irish Pages*, 12.1, 2024
Chloe Garcia Roberts
  Fire Eater: A Translator's Theology, *Conjunctions* (online), October 2, 2024
Gabriel Rogers
  68091: or, Every Death a Different Death, *Boulevard*, 38.3–4, 114–15, Winter 2024
Jay Rogoff
  Race, Taste, and Fred Astaire, *Salmagundi Magazine*, 224–25, Fall 2024–Winter 2025
Alex Ross
  What Is Noise?, *The New Yorker*, April 22 and 29, 2024
Carlo Rotella
  A Tempo, *Virginia Quarterly Review*, 100.3, Fall 2024
Sumana Roy
  Guests of Honor, *Orion*, Spring 2024
Diana Ruzova
  The Sauna, *Brevity*, 76, May 2024
Scott Russell Sanders
  Mending the Riven Planet, *Notre Dame Magazine*, 52.4, Winter 2023/24
Nina King Sannes
  Redneck Folk Medicine, *Colorado Review*, 51.3, Fall/Winter 2024
Ali Saperstein
  Darkness Erased, *River Teeth*, 25.2, Spring 2024

Lucy Schiller
  Harmas, *Off Assignment*, November 12, 2024
Kathryn Schulz
  Each Mortal Thing, *The New Yorker*, November 4, 2024
Augustine Sedgewick
  Thoreau's Pencils, *The American Scholar*, 93.4, Autumn 2024
Jennifer Senior
  The Art of Survival, *The Atlantic*, June 2024
Todd Sformo
  Personality of Probability: Probability of Personality, *Catamaran*, 12.4, Fall 2024
Jeff Sharlet
  I Am Watching You Disappear, *Switchyard*, 2.1, Summer 2024
Adam Shatz
  The Father of Anti-Colonialism, *Stranger's Guide*, 21, 2024
Marguerite Sheffer
  Wire Nanosecond, *The Massachusetts Review*, 65.3, Fall 2024
Susan Hand Shetterly
  Long Way Home, *Down East*, April 2024
Romus Simpson
  The Ocean Knew, *Black Warrior Review*, 50.2, Spring/Summer 2024
Shalini Singh
  Iowa = Gujarat (?), *Hayden's Ferry Review*, 74, Spring/Summer 2024
Hasanthika Sirisena
  Jamais Vu, *Copper Nickel*, 38, Spring 2024
Yuri Slezkine
  Lifetimes of the Soviet Union, *Granta*, 166, Winter 2024
Clint Smith
  Is Forgiveness Possible?, *The Atlantic*, November 2024
Kylie Smith
  The Moth Effect, *Colorado Review*, 51.1, Spring 2024
Nell Smith
  Fragments of Bone, Fragments of Light, *Southern Humanities Review*, 57.3, 2024

Gerard Smyth
   From River Gulls & City Horses: A Dublin Memoir, *New Hibernia Review*, 28.1, Spring 2024
Gina Alexandra Srmabekian
   Empty Fields, *Ninth Letter*, Fall/Winter 2023–24
Mairead Small Staid
   M. & I, *New England Review*, 45.1, 2024
Maureen Stanton
   The Birds, *The Missouri Review*, 47.1, Spring 2024
Teri Stein
   Penumbra, *The Sun*, 586, October 2024
Emily Stoddard
   Flight Risk, *The Kenyon Review*, XLVI.1, Winter 2024
Sarah Anne Strickley
   Scar Face, *Lake Effect*, 28, Spring 2024
Caroline Sutton
   White Ash, *North American Review*, 309.1, Spring 2024
Anca L. Szilágyi
   "Apply a Little Sugar with a Feather": A Cultural & Personal History of Marzipan, *The Fiddlehead*, 301, Autumn 2024
Fargo Nissim Tbakhi
   What It Means to Speak with the Dead, *Jewish Currents*, Summer 2024
Wei Tchou
   Little Seed, *Virginia Quarterly Review*, 100.1, Spring 2024
Nandi Theunissen
   Everything Is Out of Water, *The Point*, 33, Fall 2024
Wright Thompson
   Mapping Mississippi's Violent Past, *The Atlantic*, October 2024
Tayi Tibble
   Te Moana-nui-a-Kiwa: Ocean Memory, *Alta*, 27, 2024
Sallie Tisdale
   Completely Hazardous Experiments, *Harper's Magazine*, December 2024
Pauls Toutonghi
   There Was and There Was Not, *Harper's Magazine*, July 2024
Alex Tretbar
   Chain of Memory, *The Threepenny Review*, 179, Fall 2024
Arlene Tribbia
   Rate My Professor: Allen Ginsberg, *Your Impossible Voice*, 31, Fall 2024
M. H. Tse
   Hello from the Children of the Planet Earth, *Alaska Quarterly Review*, 40.3–4, Summer/Fall 2024
Emira Tufo
   The Wisdom of Onions, *The Iowa Review*, 54.2, Fall 2024
Priscilla Turner
   The Bookman Vanishes, *Chicago Quarterly Review*, 40, Fall 2024
Debbie Urbanski
   I Am Writing This to You Not Because I Want to Understand You But Because I Want to Understand What Love Is, *Diagram*, October 2024
Gaby Del Valle
   Live Free or DEI, *The Baffler*, 75, September 2024
Katrina Vandenberg
   The Water Lilies, *Orion*, Autumn 2024
Cecilia Villarruel
   The Pianist, *Under the Gum Tree*, 53, Fall 2024
John Vurro
   Guardians, *The Sun*, 582, June 2024
Julie Marie Wade
   The Plague of Frogs, *Salamander*, 57, Fall/Winter 2023–24
Beth Walker
   My Arm Is Steady, My Hand Does Not Shake, *Under the Sun*, May 15, 2024
Rosanna Warren
   My Mother's Oysters, *Harper's Magazine*, August 2024
McKenzie Watson-Fore
   The Chicken Harvest, *Psaltery and Lyre*, May 27, 2024

Sana Wazwaz
  How to Say "Survival" in Latin, *Hayden's Ferry Review*, 75, Fall/Winter 2024
Philip Weinstein
  Free, *The American Scholar*, 93.4, Autumn 2024
Whitney Weiss
  P-Town, *The Sewanee Review*, CXXXII.3, Summer 2024
Emilio Williams
  Queering le Septième, *Slag Glass City*, 10, November 2024
S. L. Wisenberg
  Against "It Is What It Is," *New City*, August 2024
Emily Withnall
  Creating Art in a Burning World: Reckoning with New Mexico's Largest Wildfire, *After the Art*, 26, December 2024
Baron Wormser
  The Loss of Literature, *Vox Populi*, December 8, 2024
Jenna "J" Wortham
  The Afterlives of Audre Lorde, *The New York Times Magazine*, August 25, 2024
Emily Wortman-Wunder
  Geography of Forgetting, *Colorado Review*, 51.3, Fall/Winter 2024
James N. Wray Jr.
  Voices, *Raritan*, XLIV.1, Summer 2024
Beina Xu
  Bonus Child, *The Offing*, February 15, 2024
Arielle Zibrak
  One Need Not Be a Chamber, *The Missouri Review* (online), November 8, 2024
Diane Zinna
  Astonish, *Brevity*, 76, May 2024

Errata: *The Best American Essays 2024*

Copyright, p. v: Yiyun Li is listed as Yiyun Yi
Essay: "The Ones We Sent Away," p. 134: the word "seventeen" should be "seventy"
Essay: "Memory's Cellar," p. 245: "Ottoman-era" is incorrectly hyphenated
Notable Essays and Literary Nonfiction of 2023—corrected names:
  p. 353: George Cotkin (not Corlan)
  p. 356: Hanna Saltzman (not Hannah)
  p. 356: Shaan Sachdev (not Shawn)

Explore the rest of the series

bestamericanseries.com